I07958 33

IMAGES
of America

GRAND TRAVERSE LIGHTHOUSE

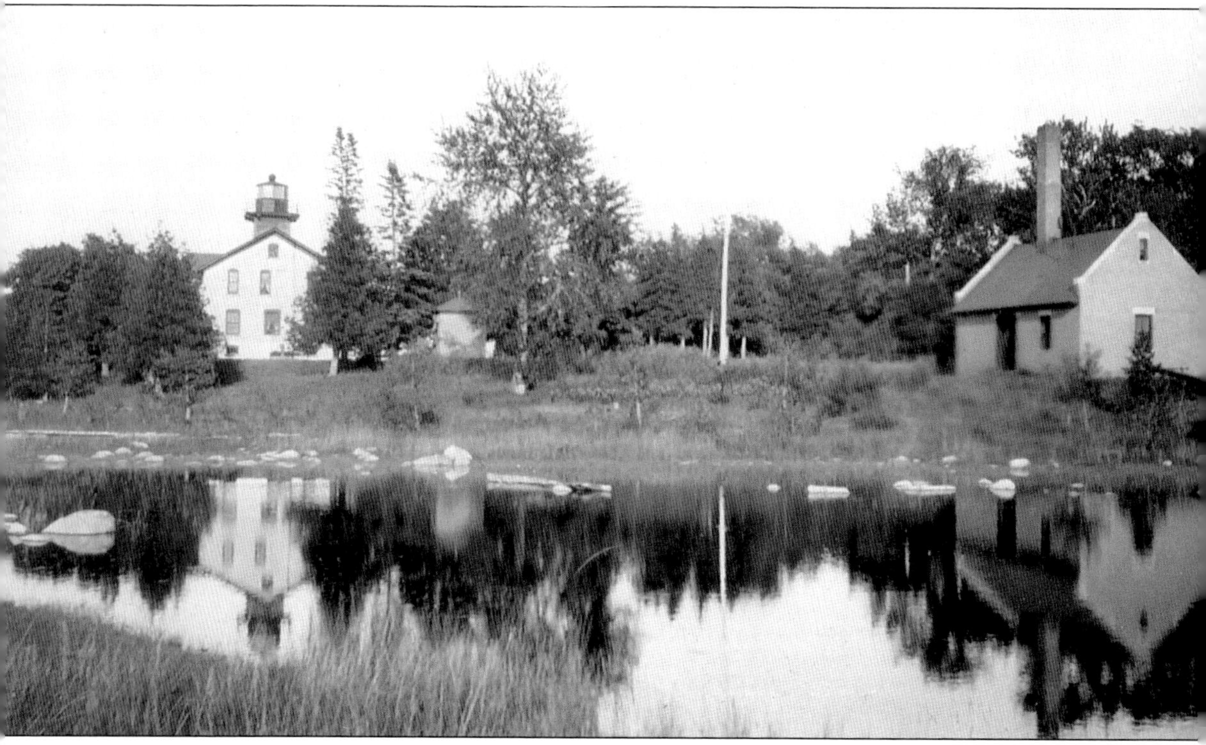

The Grand Traverse Light Station, located 35 miles north of Traverse City at the mouth of Grand Traverse Bay, was an important aid to navigation for more than 150 years. Throughout its history, 66 lighthouse keepers and coastguardsman and their families have called it home. It is pictured around 1927. (Courtesy Robert Koch.)

On the cover: Please see page 44. (Courtesy U.S. Coast Guard Historian's Office.)

IMAGES
of America

GRAND TRAVERSE LIGHTHOUSE

Grand Traverse Lighthouse Museum

ARCADIA
PUBLISHING

ISBN 978-0-7385-5223-1

Published by Arcadia Publishing
Charleston, South Carolina

Printed in the United States of America

Library of Congress Control Number: 2007942458

For all general information, please contact Arcadia Publishing:
Telephone 843-853-2070
Fax 843-853-0044
E-mail sales@arcadiapublishing.com
For customer service and orders:
Toll-Free 1-888-313-2665

Visit us on the Internet at www.arcadiapublishing.com

This book is dedicated to the lighthouse keepers and U.S. Coast Guard personnel who tended the light from 1852 to 1972. It is also dedicated to the volunteers and staff who gave their time, talents, and energy to the restoration and preservation of the Grand Traverse Light Station.

Contents

ACKNOWLEDGMENTS

Since the Grand Traverse Lighthouse Museum was founded in 1984, hundreds of volunteers have contributed thousands of hours to preserve and restore the Grand Traverse Lighthouse in cooperation with other concerned agencies for the enjoyment of the public and to enhance knowledge and understanding of the area's cultural and natural heritage. It is important to thank all of those volunteers individually because without their hard work and passion for this lighthouse, this book would not have been possible. The Grand Traverse Lighthouse Museum's research library and archives offers a wide variety of photographs, historic materials, and artifacts that tell the stories of the keepers and coastguardsman and their families. The staff members and volunteers who maintain these collections are to be commended for their many hours cataloguing and accessioning every single item.

There are many people who have paved the way for this book through research, writing, oral history interviews, and generous donations of archival material and artifacts. Specifically, the Grand Traverse Lighthouse Museum would like to thank Barbara and John Adams, Daniel Baressi, Ruth Brown, Marie Cain Baumberger, David Briggs, Gil Connell, Suzette Cooley-Sanborn, Bobbie Dame Ditzler, Cindy Gaudette, John Elias, Ira Flagstad family, Sally J. Frye, William Green family, Terry Herring, Philip and Beverly Kellogg, Pauline McClure, Doug McCormick, Elbert McKinney, Ann Martin, David and Irene Nelson, Sterling Nickerson, Bette McCormick Olli, Guy Patterson family, Martha L. Roberts, Mary Russell, Ruth Oleson, Alice Thomas Stoppelberg, Ken Stormer, Margaret and Albin Tarsa, Virginia Thomas, John Tombolillo, John D. Tregembo, William Wilson family, and Grace Wisneski.

Introduction

Why Lighthouses? The waterways of the world have served as man's most important mode of transportation, connecting continents and countries alike and tying the economic systems of the world together. When the first recorded lighthouse on the North American continent was constructed in 1716 at Little Brewster Island outside of Boston, the idea of a beacon to guide ships around treacherous passes and into safe ports was far from fresh. The ancient Egyptians and Romans had already built what many claim to be the first lighthouse at Alexandria, Egypt, centuries before.

George Washington believed lighthouses were so important that the ninth act of the newly established Congress in 1789 created the U.S. Lighthouse Establishment to build and maintain lighthouses along the East Coast. The opening of the Erie Canal in 1825 made the international trade of the East Coast accessible to the Midwest. The vast sources of raw materials in the Midwest led to an explosion of maritime activity. Soon ships filled with coal, iron ore, timber, limestone, copper, fruit, and grain were traveling back and forth across the Great Lakes.

Dangers of weather, islands, and coastline came hand in hand with this newly discovered waterway. The shores of the Great Lakes became littered with shipwrecks and once again the call for navigational aids went out. The first lighthouses built on Lake Michigan in 1832 were at Chicago and St. Joseph, Michigan. By 1837, 16 lighthouses illuminated the entrances to port cities along the lake.

While the village of Northport may seem quiet today, in the mid-1800s it was one of the bustling shipping hubs supplying cordwood to steamships traveling from Milwaukee, Chicago, and other ports across Lake Michigan. Northport's location at the tip of the Leelanau Peninsula made it an important refueling station for the steamers. It was also a safe port for fishermen, farmers, and others who relied on the shipping industry, thus uniting it to the overall economy of an expanding nation. By 1860, Northport was one of the main ports between Chicago and Buffalo, New York.

Northport was located on the inside of one of the most dangerous passageways on Lake Michigan, the feared Manitou Passage. The combination of unanticipated storms and shallow shoals made traveling through the passage extremely treacherous. Due to the increase in shipping activity and dangers of the passage, a light was needed to mark the entrance to Grand Traverse Bay. This light was to serve as the safe gateway to port cities such as Northport, Suttons Bay, Traverse City, and Elk Rapids. After two shipwrecks in Cathead Bay five miles to the southwest of the tip of the peninsula and one at the west end of the tip, the necessity of a lighthouse on the Leelanau Peninsula was realized in 1850.

One

A New Light on Lake Michigan 1852–1858

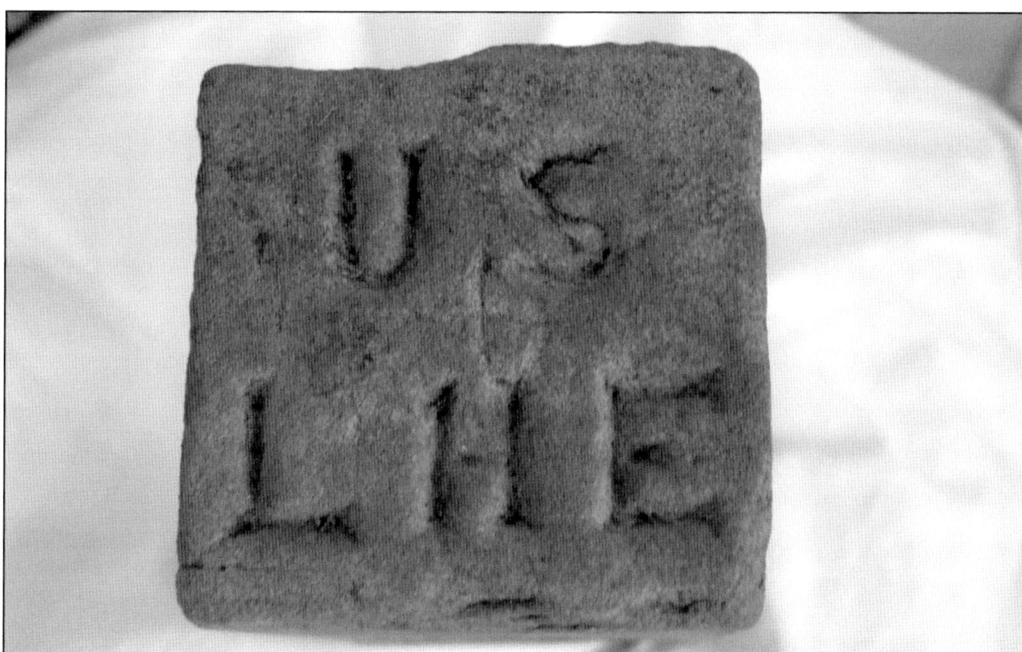

This is a U.S. Lighthouse Establishment (USLHE) property marker. This marker was originally located on the northeast corner of the lighthouse reservation that marked the entrance to Grand Traverse Bay (Grand Traverse Light Station). The USLHE was administered under Stephen Pleasonton, the fifth auditor of the treasury, from 1820 to 1852.

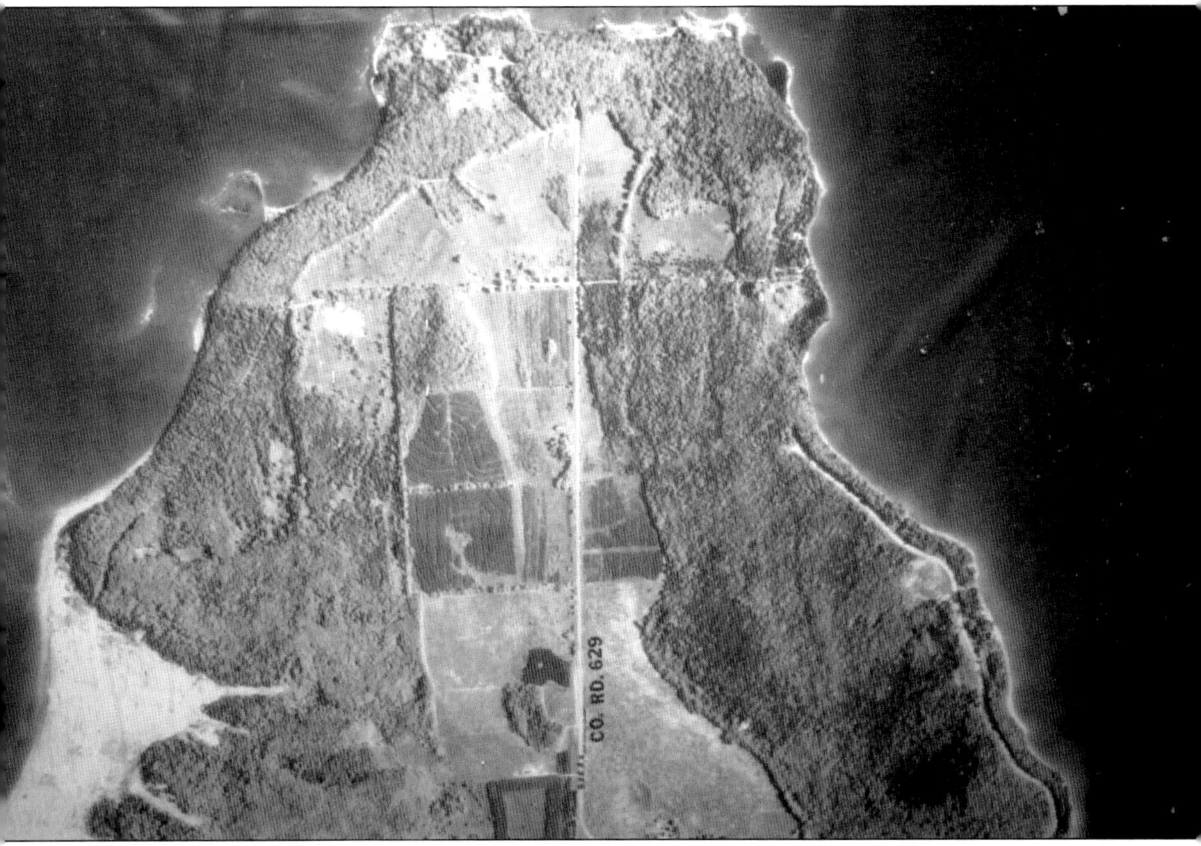

On June 30, 1851, Pres. Millard Fillmore signed an executive order reserving land and $4,000 for the construction of a lighthouse lying at the northwest cape of Grand Traverse Bay and the northern entrance to the Manitou Passage. This area consisted of 45.01 acres, entirely made up of thick-growth birch, pine, beech, maple, and balsam. A combination of the increase in shipping across Lake Michigan and the importance of Northport, a safe haven for ships on their way to Buffalo, New York, and other eastern ports, made a lighthouse necessary on the end of the peninsula to mark the entrance to the bay. (Courtesy National Archives and Records Administration.)

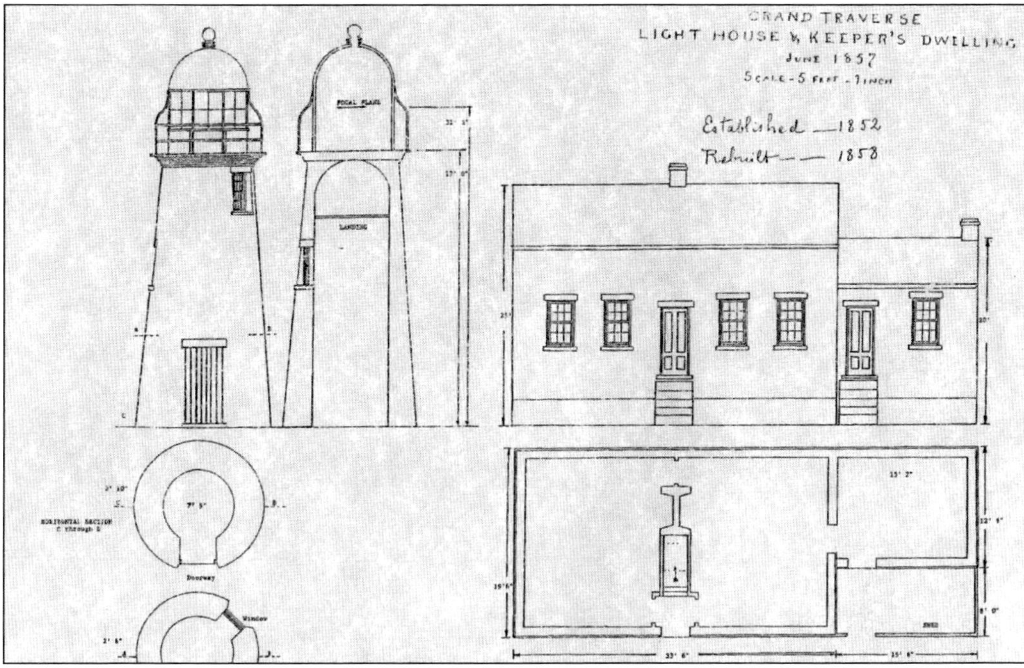

Construction on the new light began in late 1851. There was no easy access via land, so materials were shipped by schooner to the building site. From the schooner, supplies were loaded on rafts then poled ashore by pushing rocks aside to make the transport easier. This process created an underwater "roadway" which can still be found today. The keeper was housed in a two-room building with an attached kitchen and shed. The separate, conical light tower stood 30 feet tall. (Courtesy Grand Traverse Lighthouse Museum Collection.)

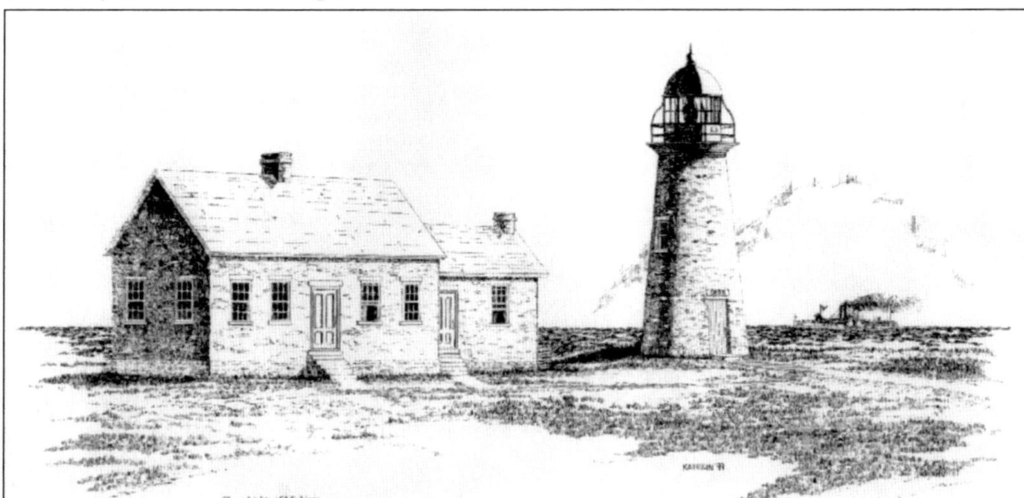

In September 1852, the Grand Traverse Lighthouse cast its first beam of light, powered by six oil lamps with 14-inch silver-colored reflectors, when David Moon accepted the position as the first light keeper. Shortly thereafter, in April 1853, Philo Beers and his family took up residence, replacing Moon. (Courtesy Rich Katuzin.)

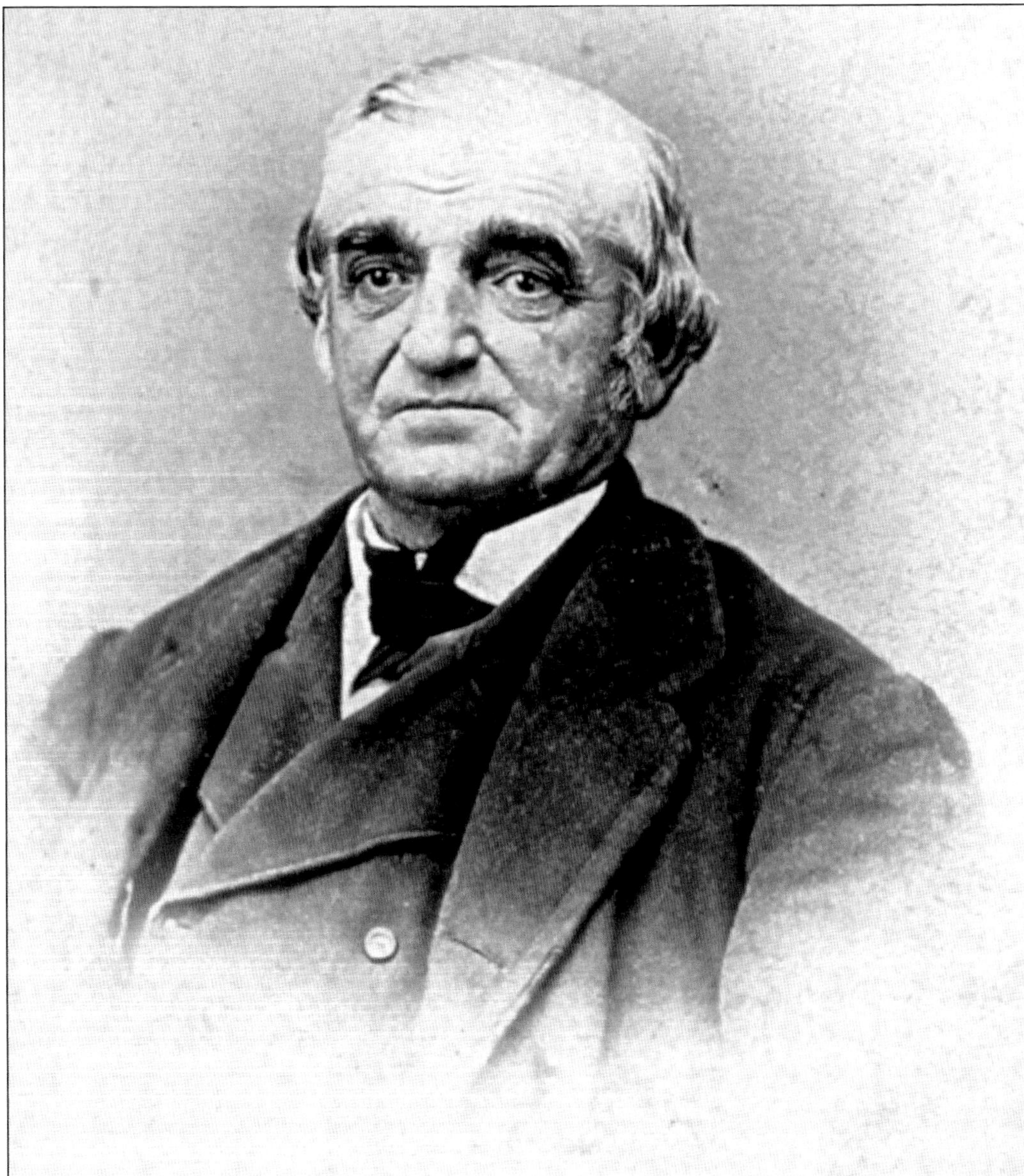

Philo Beers faithfully kept the light burning and even defended the light and his station supplies on May 30 and August 2, 1855, from night marauders sailing in from an island to the north. Beers held his post as keeper until 1857, when Gilman Chase took over and maintained the light until its decommissioning in 1858. While Beers served as keeper of the light, his family was there with him. Beers was a widower and his children were boarded in Northport where they attended school during the week. On the weekends, they ventured out to the tip of the peninsula to visit their father and help him with his duties. After supervising the construction of the current lighthouse in 1858, Beers purchased the southeast corner lot of Nagonaba and Shabwasung Streets in Northport. He and his son Henry constructed a home around 1869, which still stands today. By 1867, Beers moved to Charlevoix. There over the next 15 years, he served as postmaster and probate judge and was a member of the Masons until his death in 1872. (Courtesy Grand Traverse Lighthouse Museum Collection.)

This photograph from about 1911 represents four generations of Beers women. The elderly woman sitting in the chair is Julia Charter Beers. During Philo's tenure as light keeper, she was employed as his housekeeper. She met Philo's son Henry, who followed his father's footsteps and became a keeper at the Grand Traverse Lighthouse in 1859. Henry and Julia married in 1861 and had five children. From left to right are (first row) Alice Louise Thomas (age 21 months) and Julia (age 74); (second row) Edna Thomas (age 27) and Alice Charter (age 54). (Courtesy Grand Traverse Lighthouse Museum Collection.)

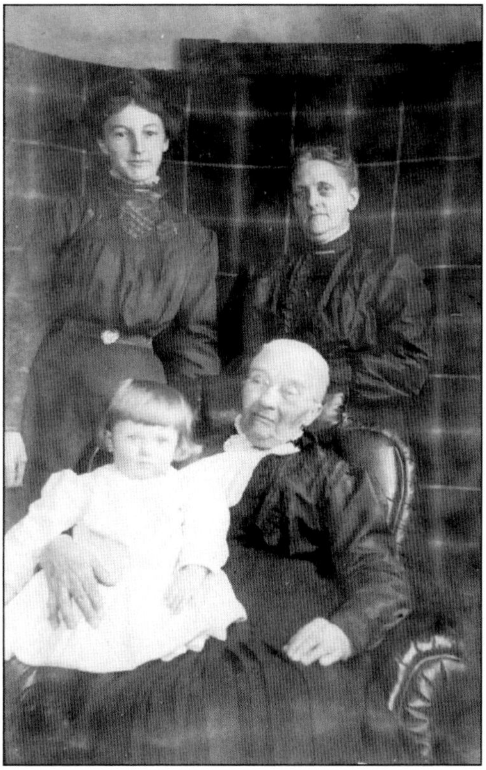

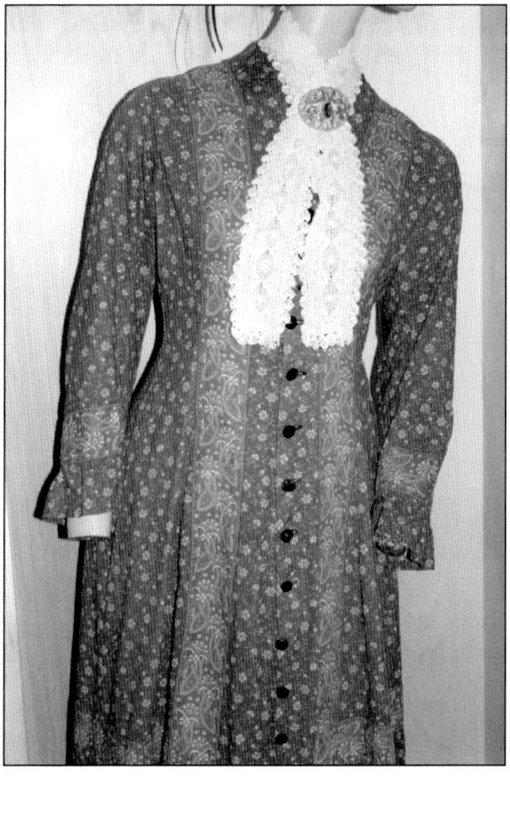

This dress was made by Julia for her daughter Alice Charter on her wedding day in August 1869. It was passed down through the three generations until it finally was given to Alice Louise, who married a Stoppelberg. She donated the dress to the Grand Traverse Lighthouse Museum for display in 2000. She passed away in September 2007 at the age of 95. (Courtesy Grand Traverse Lighthouse Museum Collection.)

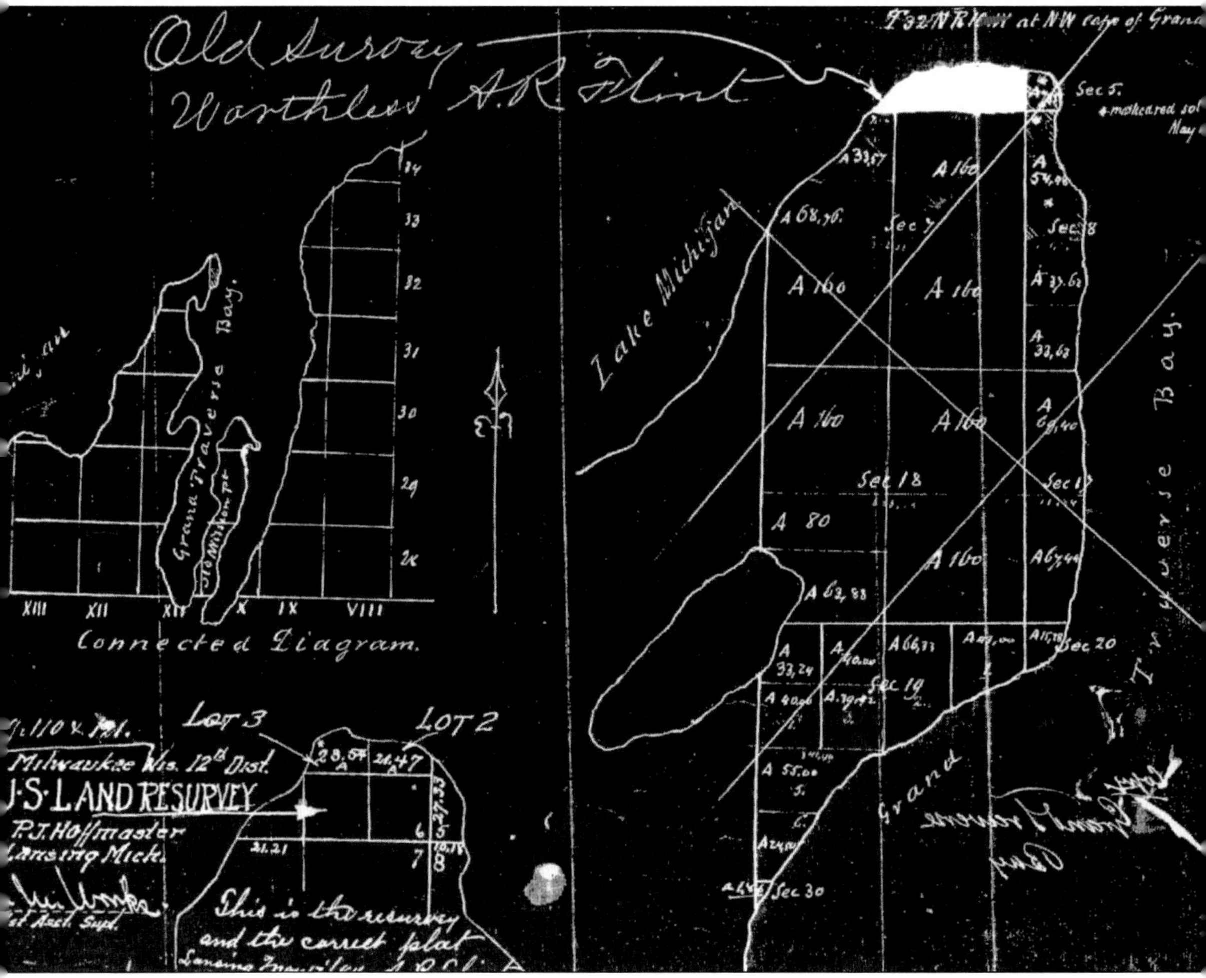

After only six years of service, the original Grand Traverse Lighthouse was found to be poorly designed and positioned. Located to the east of the current structure, the light was visible only to shipping traffic heading east and west. North and south traffic could not see the light until it had almost entirely rounded the point of the peninsula. While its service was brief, the original lighthouse at the mouth of the Grand Traverse Bay and Manitou Passage marked the beginning of the lighthouse's duty on Grand Traverse Bay. The new structure was much improved in design and location and cast its beam until 1972. The original light and tower were dismantled, and the materials were recycled into several houses in Northport. The keeper's dwelling was disassembled in pieces, put on a barge, and taken to Northport. In 1869, Philo Beers and his son reconstructed the home and added a second story. (Courtesy Grand Traverse Lighthouse Museum Collection.)

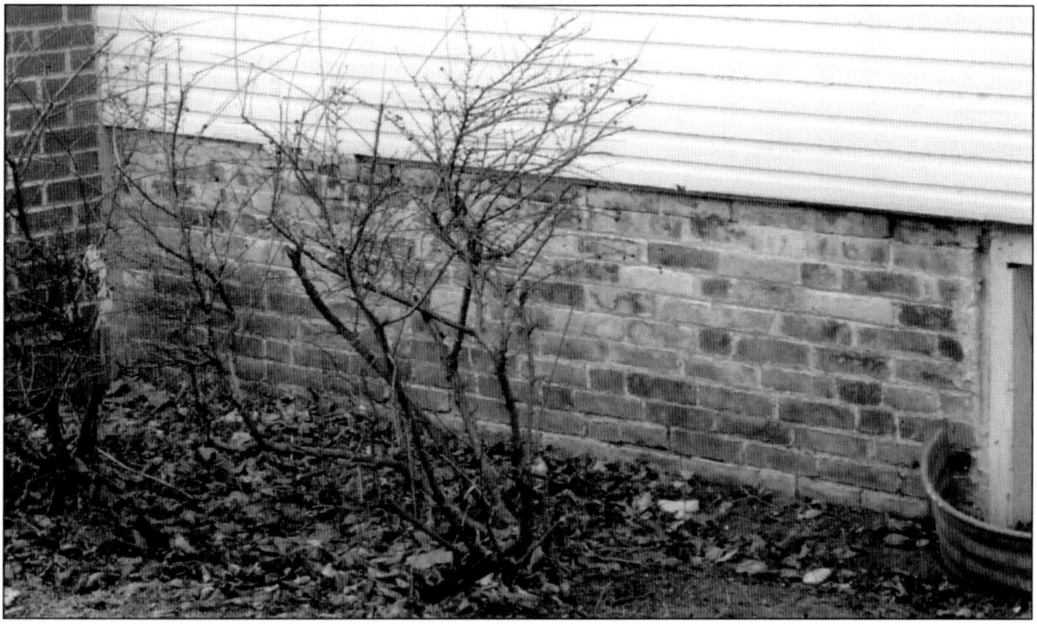

The Beers house is still standing today. In addition to the original pieces of the keeper's dwelling, the foundation was constructed of Milwaukee Cream City bricks. These bricks were used to construct both Grand Traverse Lighthouses. Milwaukee Cream City bricks were used throughout Lake Michigan's towns on both sides of the lake. (Courtesy Grand Traverse Lighthouse Museum Collection.)

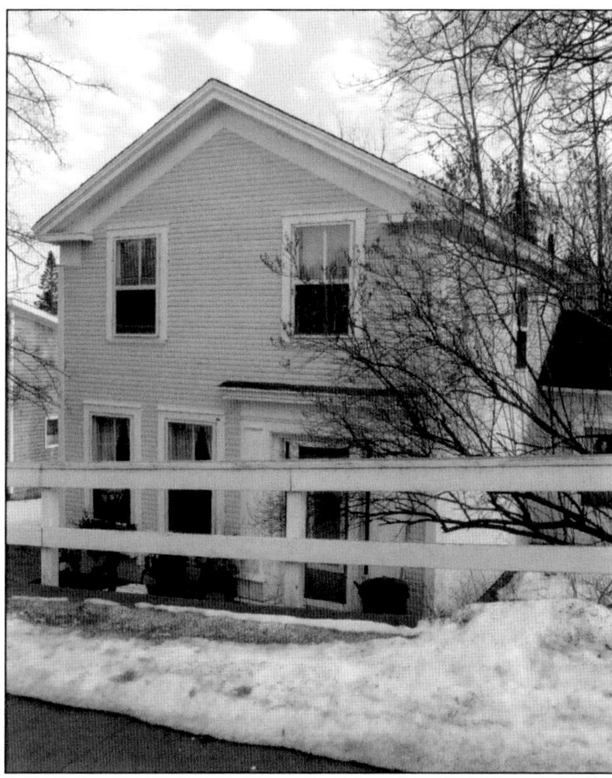

For a number of years, after Beers left this house and moved to Charlevoix, his son Henry J. and wife, Julia, resided here. Henry J. and his daughter Carrie died in 1872. The house remained in the Beers family until 1918, when Alice, another daughter, sold it to Delbert and Ida Russell. Today it is owned by lighthouse museum member Phil Kellogg. (Courtesy Grand Traverse Lighthouse Museum Collection.)

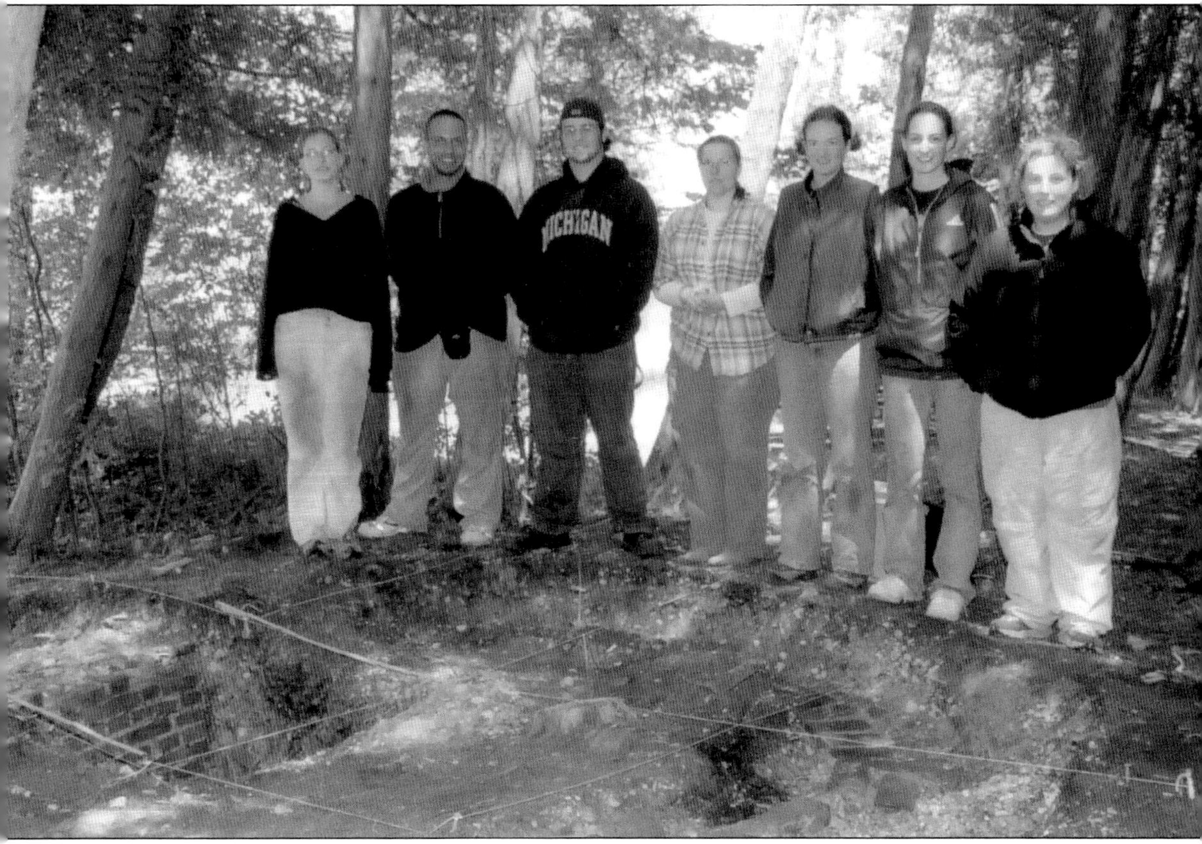

For a week in 2004, graduate students from the University of Michigan excavated the original light station's site. The foundation of the keeper's dwelling was identified and the four corners were marked. An eight-foot-diameter hole to the northwest of the dwelling was identified as either the remains of the original well or an outhouse. To the northeast of the dwelling the bottom three feet of the 30-foot light tower was completely intact, including the floor, and buried just below the surface of the rocks and topsoil. Upon the floor, students discovered fish bones left from years passed. When assembled, there were 18 complete Great Lakes Whitefish skeletons. Other discovered items included shards of glass, pottery fragments, a metal latch, and many partial pieces of brick. Some of these artifacts are on exhibit in the current lighthouse museum. Today the tower's excavation site remains covered and protected from the elements until further preservation efforts can be implemented. (Courtesy Grand Traverse Lighthouse Museum Collection.)

Two

A Second Light 1858–1900

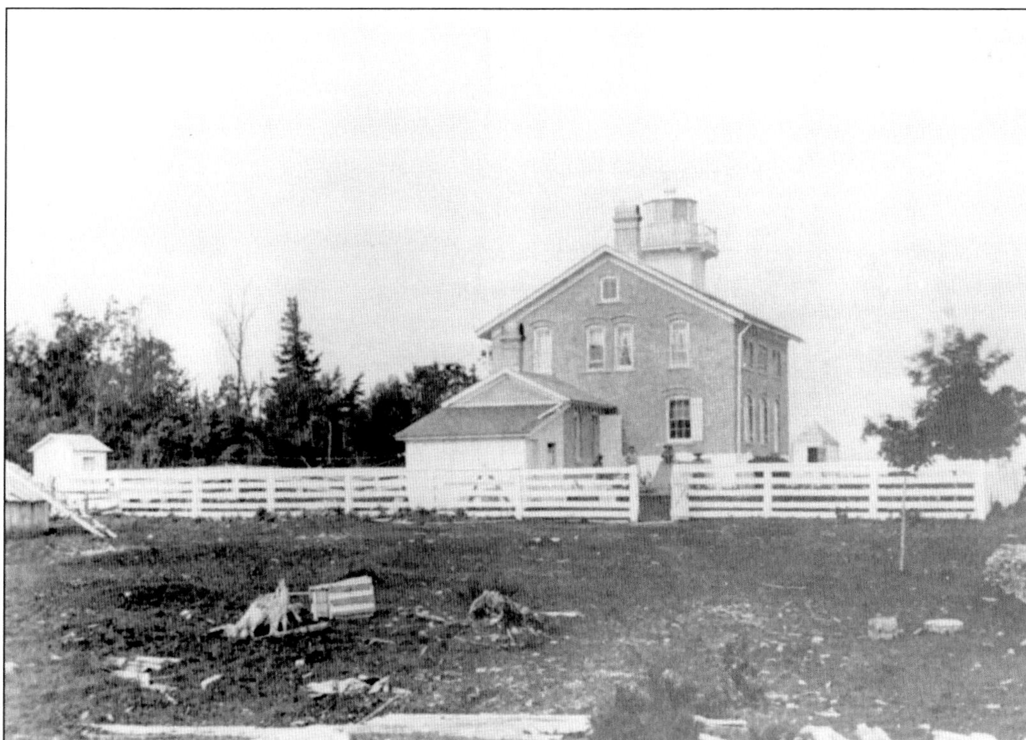

This is the east side of Grand Traverse Lighthouse around 1868. Philo Beers supervised the construction of the second Grand Traverse Lighthouse, which was located west of the original light station. This light was a square, two-story brick dwelling with a nine-sided light tower on the roof. (Courtesy National Archives and Records Administration.)

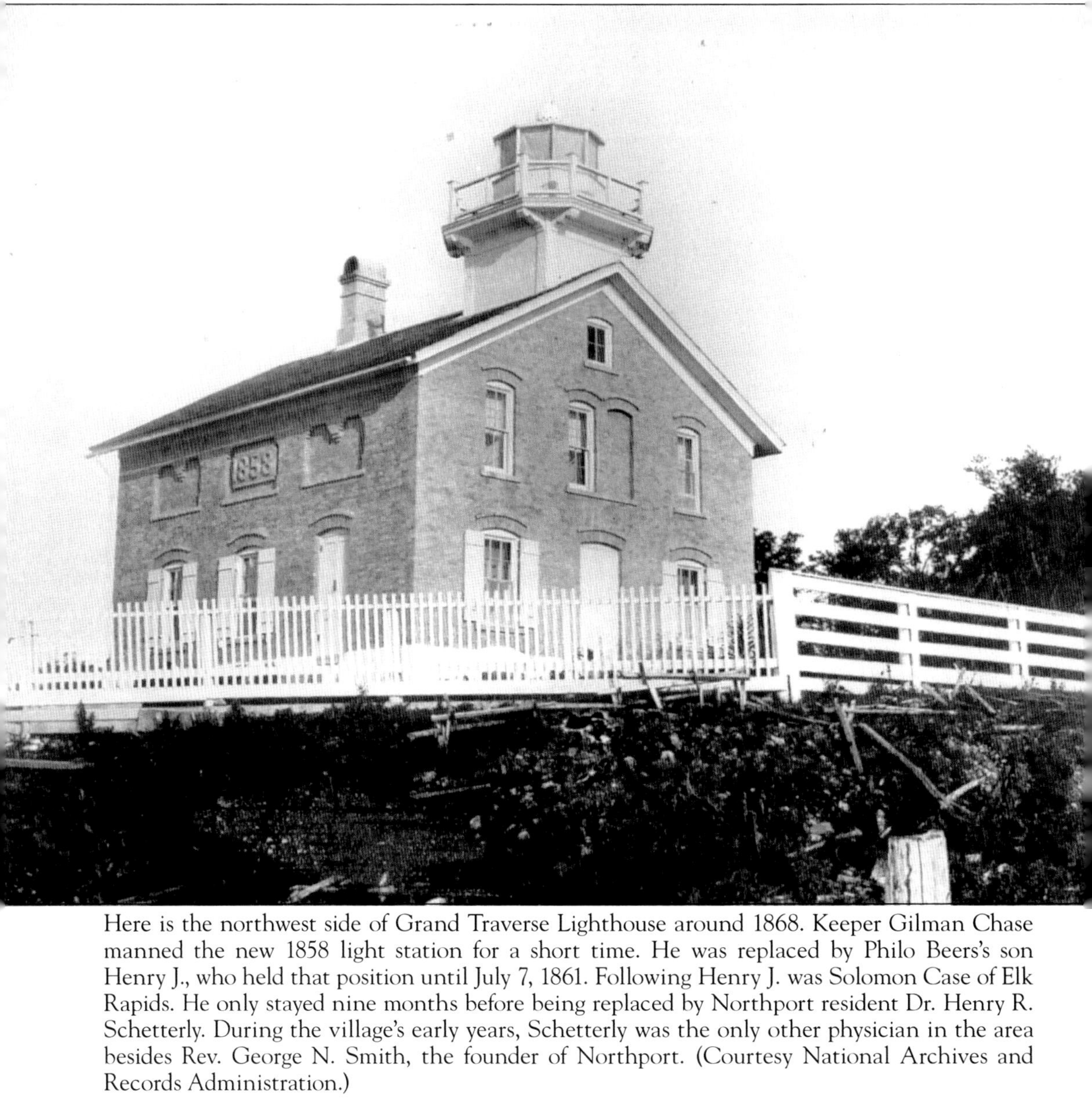

Here is the northwest side of Grand Traverse Lighthouse around 1868. Keeper Gilman Chase manned the new 1858 light station for a short time. He was replaced by Philo Beers's son Henry J., who held that position until July 7, 1861. Following Henry J. was Solomon Case of Elk Rapids. He only stayed nine months before being replaced by Northport resident Dr. Henry R. Schetterly. During the village's early years, Schetterly was the only other physician in the area besides Rev. George N. Smith, the founder of Northport. (Courtesy National Archives and Records Administration.)

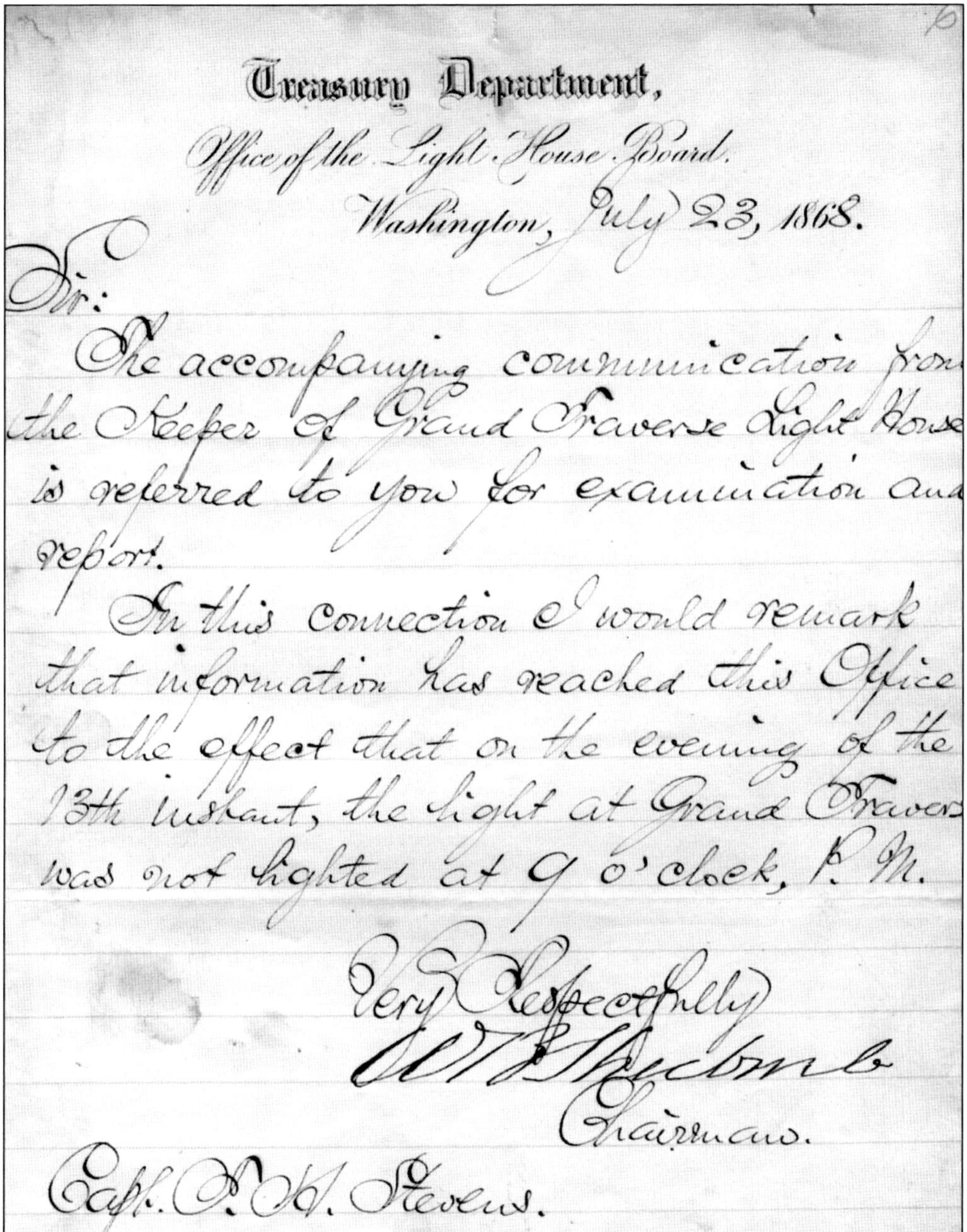

Treasury Department,

Office of the Light-House Board,

Washington, July 23, 1868.

Sir:

The accompanying communication from the Keeper of Grand Traverse Light House is referred to you for examination and report.

In this connection I would remark that information has reached this Office to the effect that on the evening of the 13th instant, the light at Grand Traverse was not lighted at 9 o'clock, P.M.

Very Respectfully

W. B. Shubrick

Chairman.

Capt. O. H. Stevens.

Museum member Steve Voisin donated these letters to the Grand Traverse Lighthouse Museum in 2002. An avid lighthouse and maritime antiques collector, Voisin came across these documents through his aggressive collecting efforts. Both letters are dated 1868, with one written in July and the other in August. These letters relate to charges against the keeper at Grand Traverse Lighthouse regarding the light not being lit in a timely fashion. The keeper at this time was Schetterly. A keeper was considered delinquent in his duties if the light was not lit 30 minutes prior to dusk and kept lit until 30 minutes after sunrise. The sole purpose of a lighthouse keeper was to keep the light on. Many times, demerits, loss of pay, or loss of job resulted from such actions.

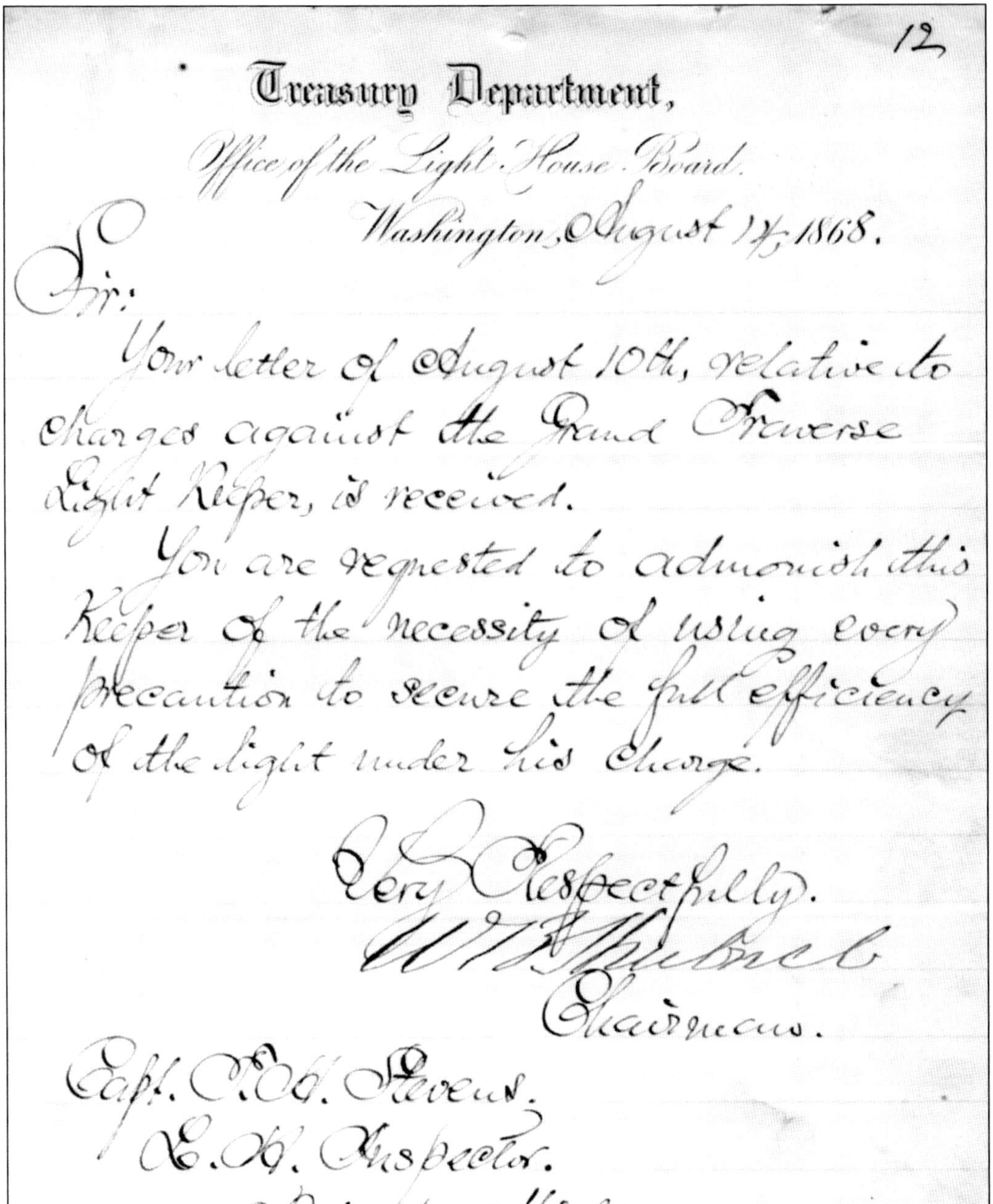

12

Treasury Department,

Office of the Light-House Board.

Washington, August 14, 1868.

Sir:

Your letter of August 10th, relative to charges against the Grand Traverse Light Keeper, is received.

You are requested to admonish this Keeper of the necessity of using every precaution to secure the full efficiency of the light under his charge.

Very Respectfully.

W. B. Shubrick

Chairman.

Capt. T. H. Stevens.
L. H. Inspector.
Detroit. Michigan.

Dr. Henry R. Schetterly assumed his duty as keeper on April 21, 1862, and served until October 10, 1873. Schetterly was married to Susannah Kiley and together they had a son, Benjamin. Susannah died at the lighthouse in 1869. During his time as keeper, Schetterly also operated a mission for the local Native Americans, providing medical treatment.

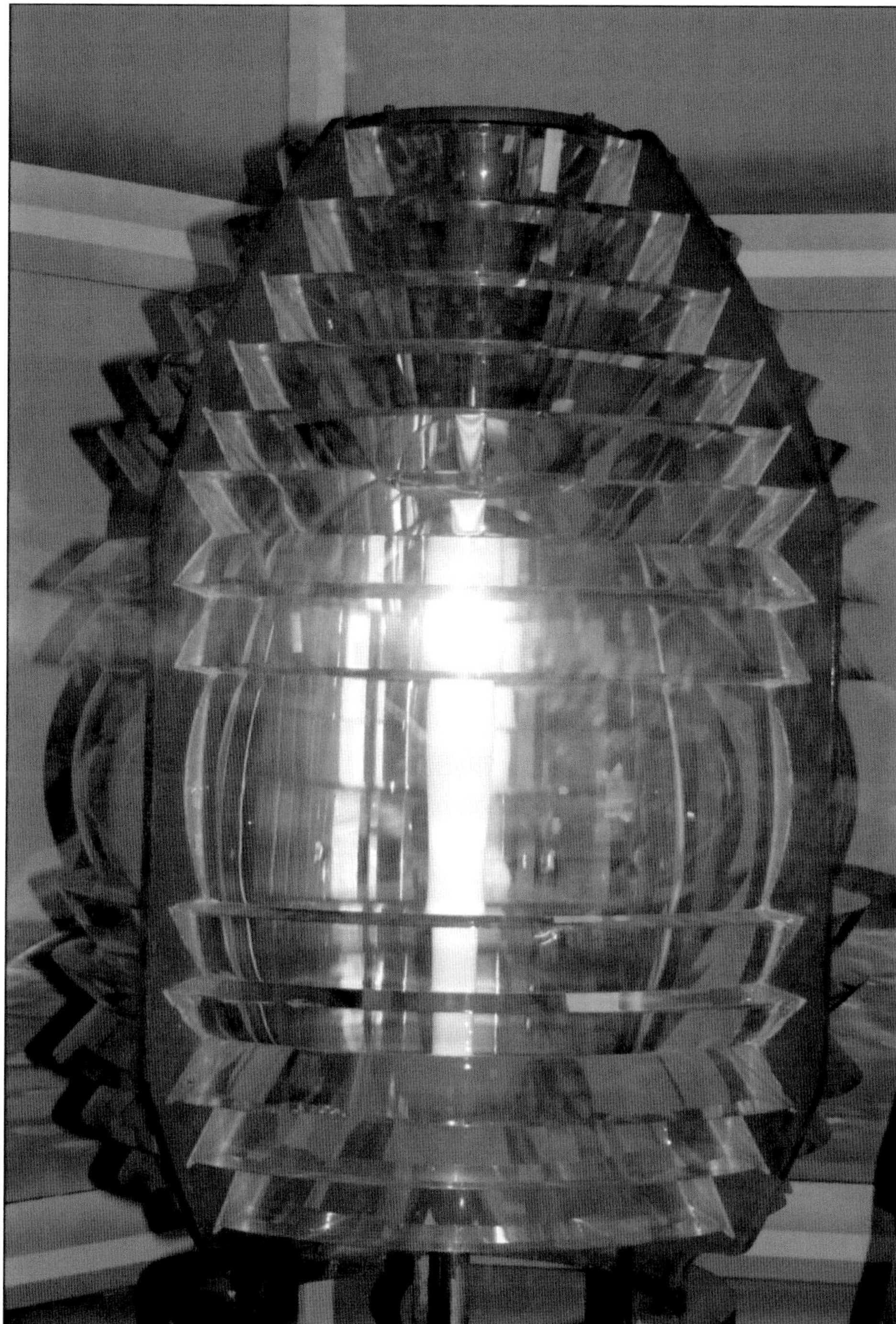

In 1870, the U.S. Lighthouse Service replaced the fifth-order Fresnel lens with a larger, fourth-order Fresnel lens. The majority of the Grand Lakes lighthouses used this size lens. Weighing nearly 600 pounds, the lens cast a beam up to 17 nautical miles. This lens remained in operation until the station was closed and automated in 1972. Its final disposition is unknown. (Courtesy Grand Traverse Lighthouse Museum Collection.)

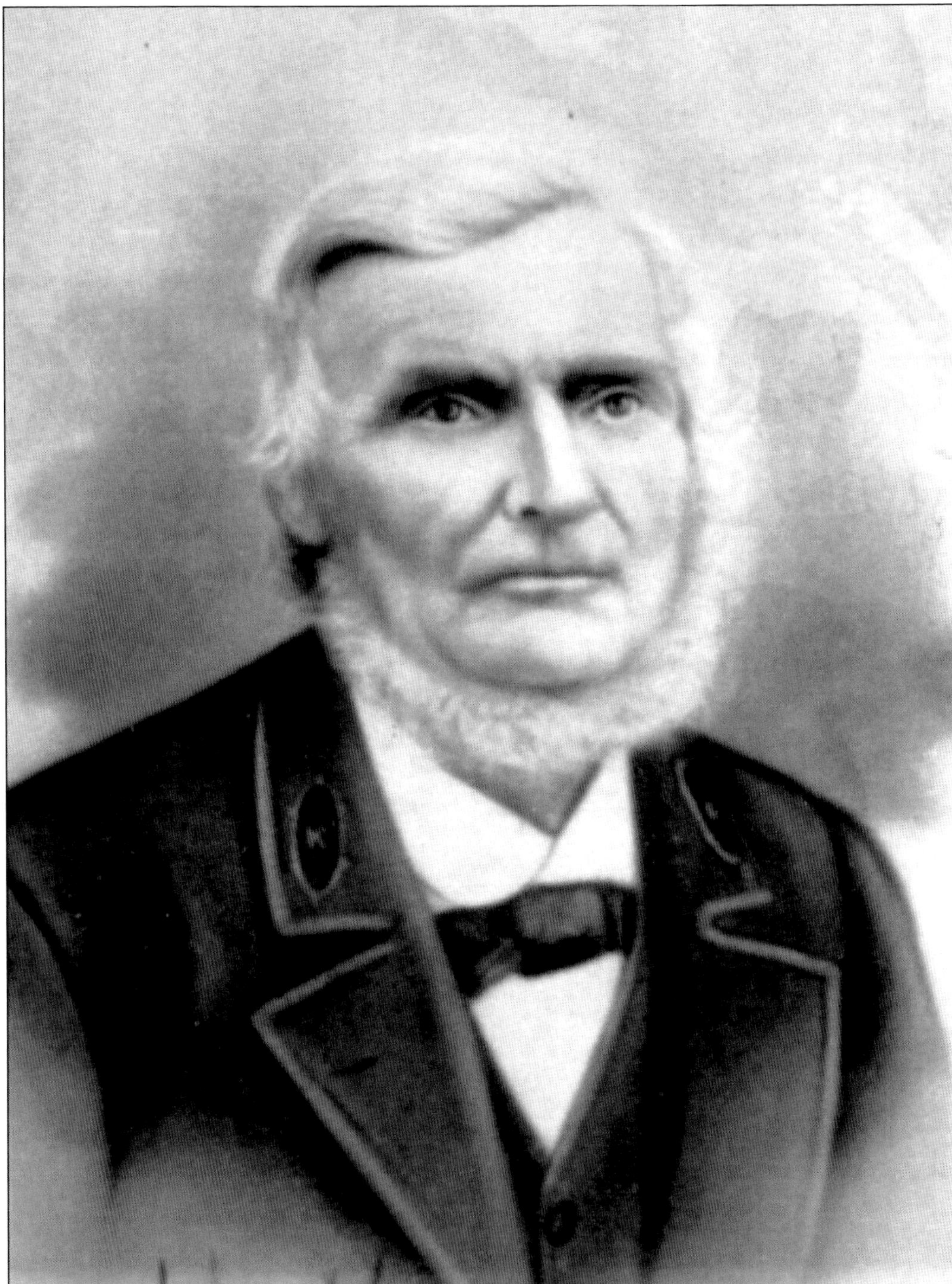

Capt. Peter Nelson, who replaced John C. Hall, was born in Copenhagen, Denmark, in 1811. He came to the United States in 1835 and made his way west to the Great Lakes. In 1851, he brought Perry Hannah and Albert Lay on the vessel *Venus* from Chicago to what is now Traverse City. Nelson settled in the region and worked for the Hannah, Lay and Company for a number of years. (Courtesy Grand Traverse Lighthouse Museum Collection.)

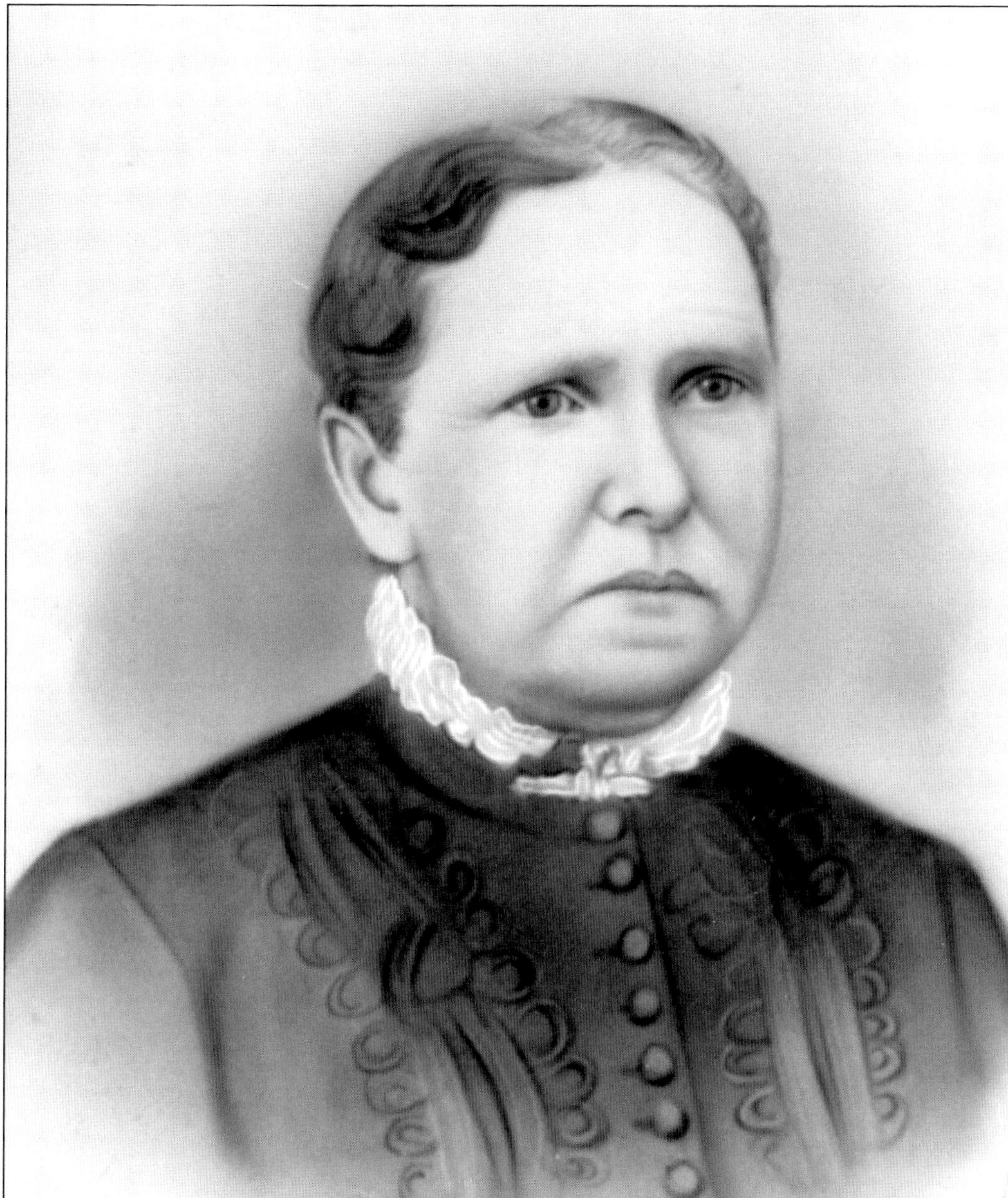

Nelson married Alice Bigelow in 1866. Alice had two children from a previous marriage, and together they had three more children. On October 14, 1874, Nelson was appointed keeper at the Grand Traverse Light Station for $440 per annum. Nelson spent the next 15 years tending the light. (Courtesy Grand Traverse Lighthouse Museum Collection.)

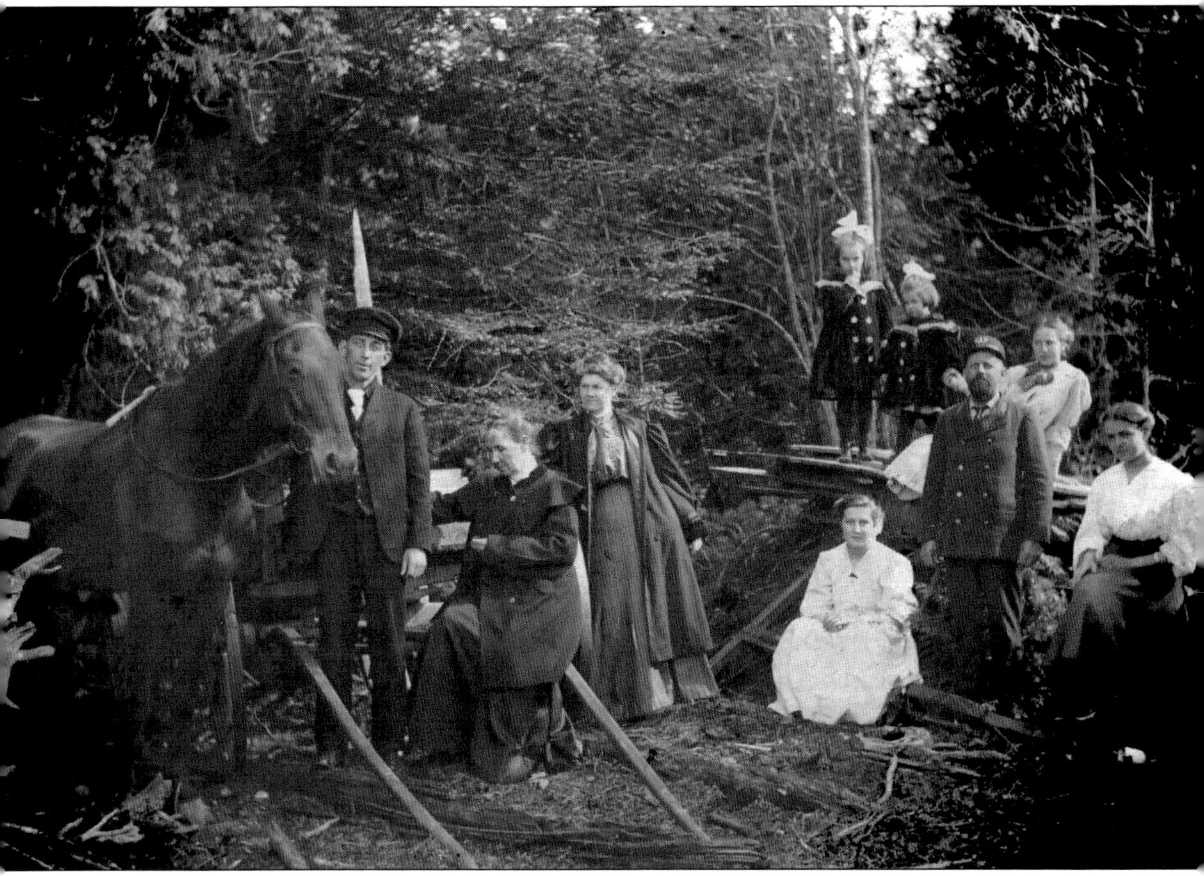

Born in England, George Buttars became the 10th keeper at Grand Traverse Light Station and saw more changes than any other keeper during his 18 years on site. A career man in the U.S. Lighthouse Service, he was married and raised four children while serving as keeper from 1885 until retiring in 1918. Buttars, with family and friends, is the man to the far right. (Courtesy Grand Traverse Lighthouse Museum Collection.)

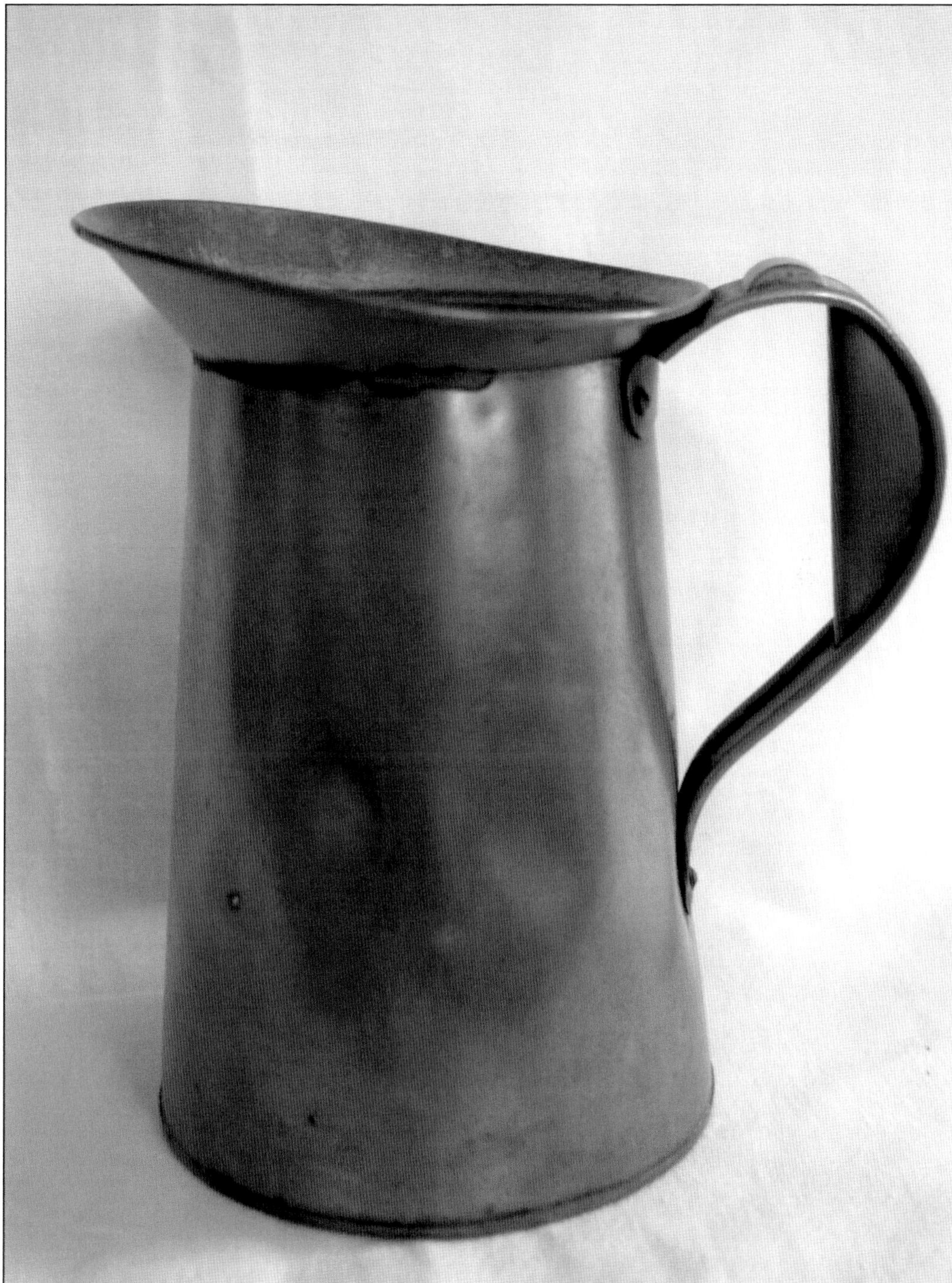

On October 10, 1873, Dr. Henry R. Schetterly died at the Grand Traverse Light Station. His housekeeper, Priscilla Parker, was appointed temporary keeper until a replacement could be found. She only served 30 days and received full keeper pay. John C. Hall stepped in as keeper on November 10, 1873, but was removed on September 26, 1874. (Courtesy Grand Traverse Lighthouse Museum Collection.)

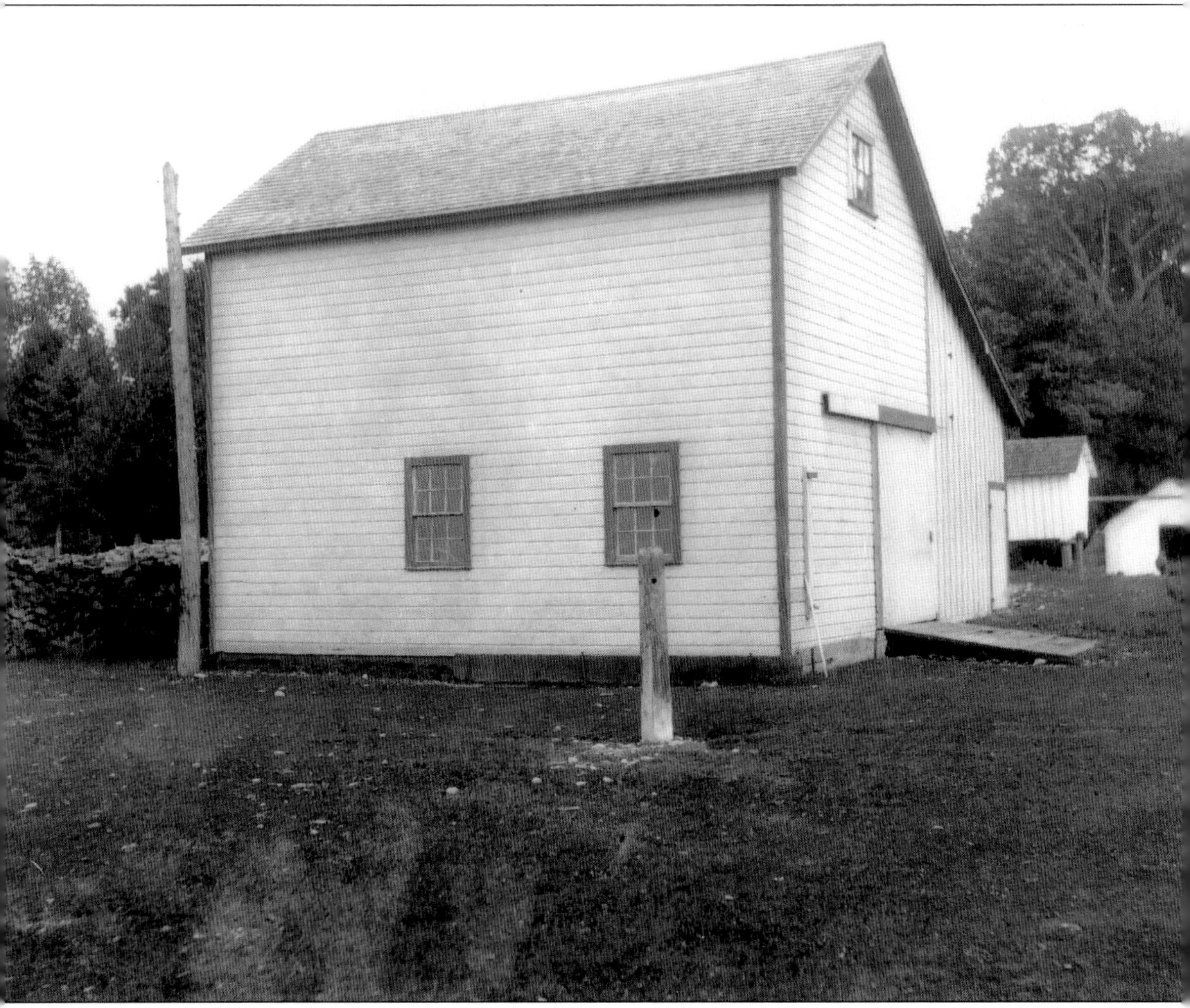

The two-story barn, measuring 18 feet wide, 20 feet long, and 16 feet high with a pitched roof, was built in 1891. Storage of farming implements was certain to be the reason for this structure, since the keepers often grew their own food and tended gardens. An addition was made to the barn in 1895. (Courtesy National Archives and Records Administration.)

In 1895, an oil house was erected just southwest of the keeper's house. Rectangular in plan, it was only 8 feet by 10 feet and constructed of brick. A hipped roof with a ventilator capped the structure that housed the lamp oil and, later, paint. Once the Coast Guard assumed supervision of stations, the structures were typically painted. The upkeep of this finish demanded a great deal of material and storage space. (Courtesy Grand Traverse Lighthouse Museum Collection.)

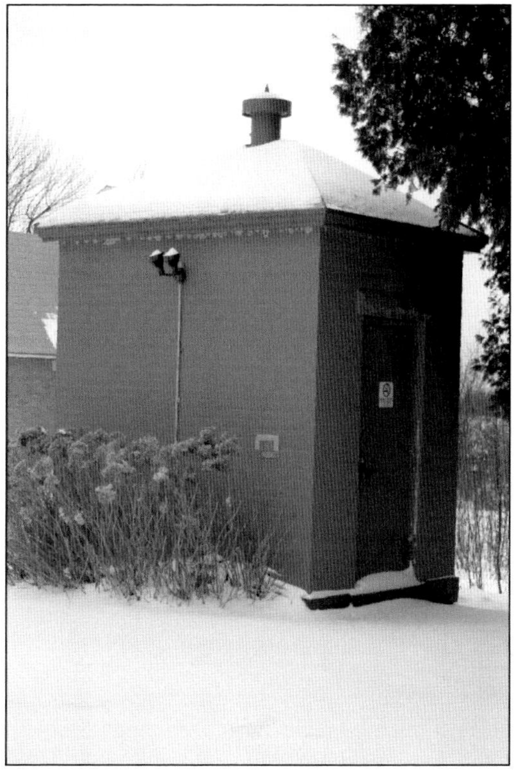

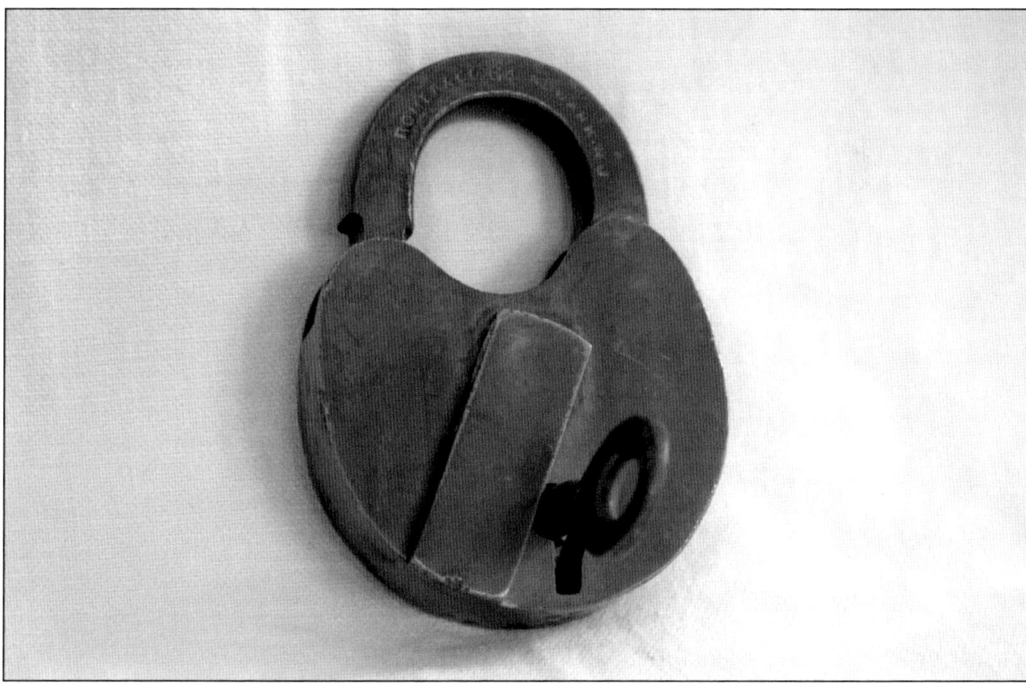

Here is a lock for the oil house dating from about 1900. The skeleton key is inside the lock. This artifact was donated to the Grand Traverse Lighthouse Museum by Doug McCormick. (Courtesy Grand Traverse Lighthouse Museum Collection.)

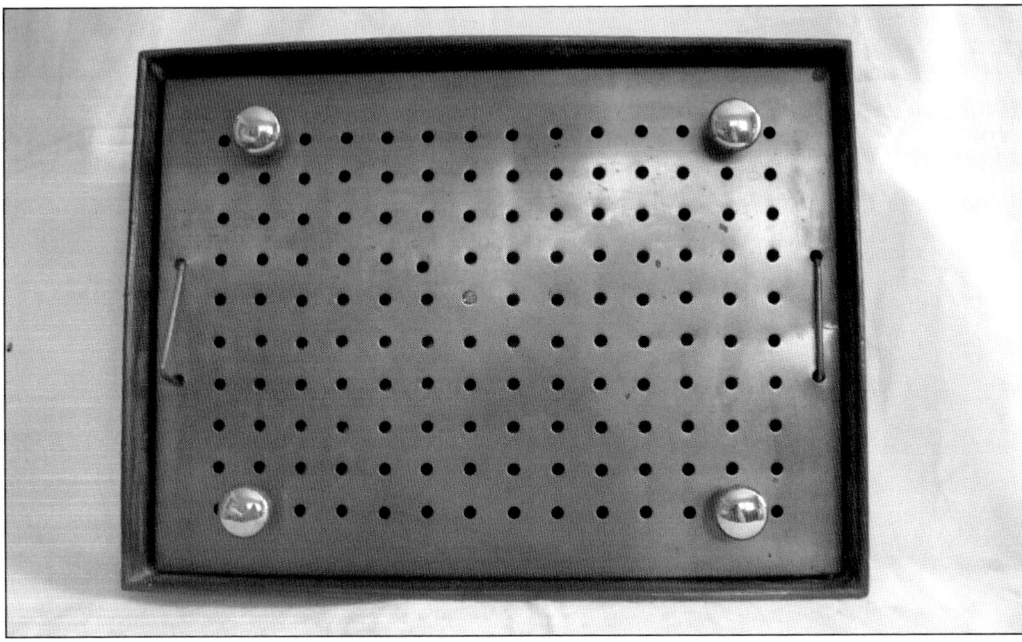

Oil drip pans were used to fill lanterns or small cans. Any oil spilling or overflowing is captured in the pan and then reused by pouring it back into a larger distribution can. The lid is removable and small handles are attached to the top of the pan allowing it to be picked up out of the tray. Small lips under the pan are used to keep the oil from pouring out of one area.

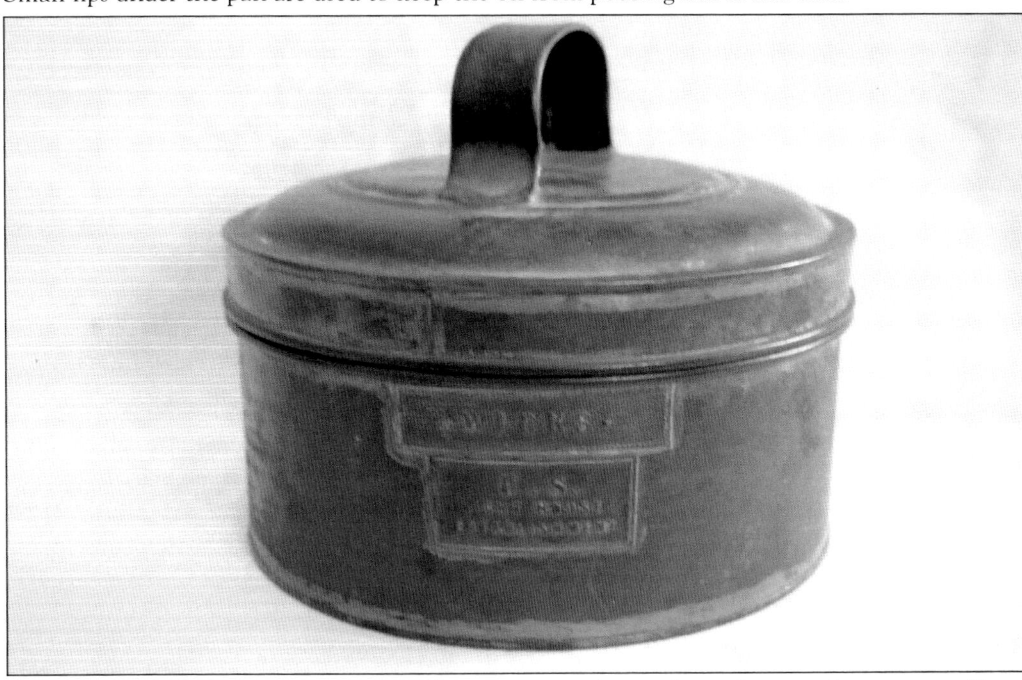

Wick storage containers came in several variations and sizes depending on the purpose. House lanterns required small containers, while several feet of wick for a lantern lens required a much larger container. These containers were designed to keep the wicks in a clean, dry place ready for use.

Three

AN ERA OF CHANGE 1900–1939

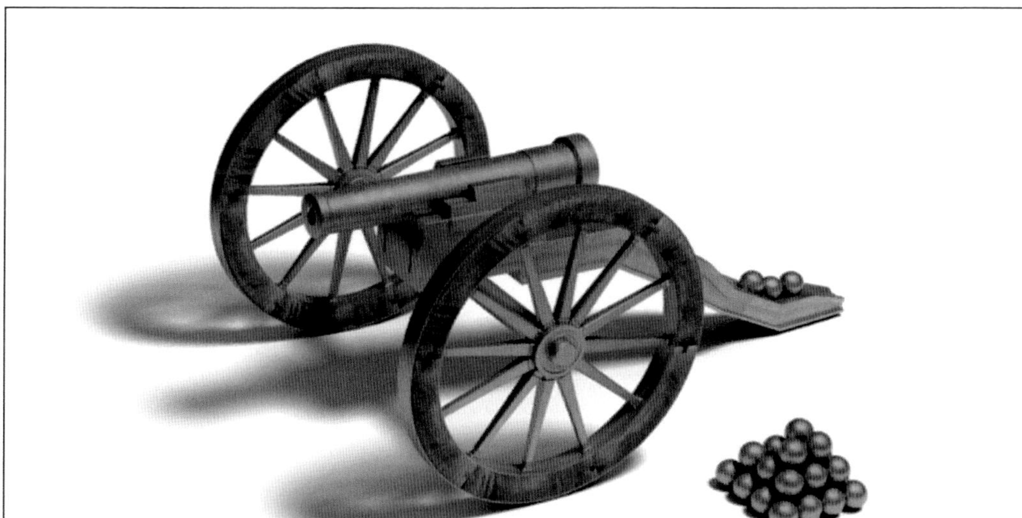

The first lighthouses were constructed as navigational aids for ships traversing the waterways of the world. Shortly after the construction of the first United States lighthouse in Boston in 1716, it became clear that there were certain weather conditions that rendered the lights useless and necessitated another type of navigational aid. This led to the development of the first United States fog signal in 1719. Calling the first fog signal by that name, however, is somewhat misleading. It was not a complicated, technical piece of machinery, but rather the sound of regulated cannon fire that alerted ships of their proximity to land. Gradually, as settlers moved west and trade grew, lighthouses became increasingly necessary as navigational tools along every coastline. Over the next century, hundreds of lighthouses would come to exist on the waterways of the United States. This does not mean, however, that fog signals were also installed at all of these lighthouses. Undoubtedly some lighthouses were built with fog signals, but the vast majority would not receive a fog signal until decades after their construction.

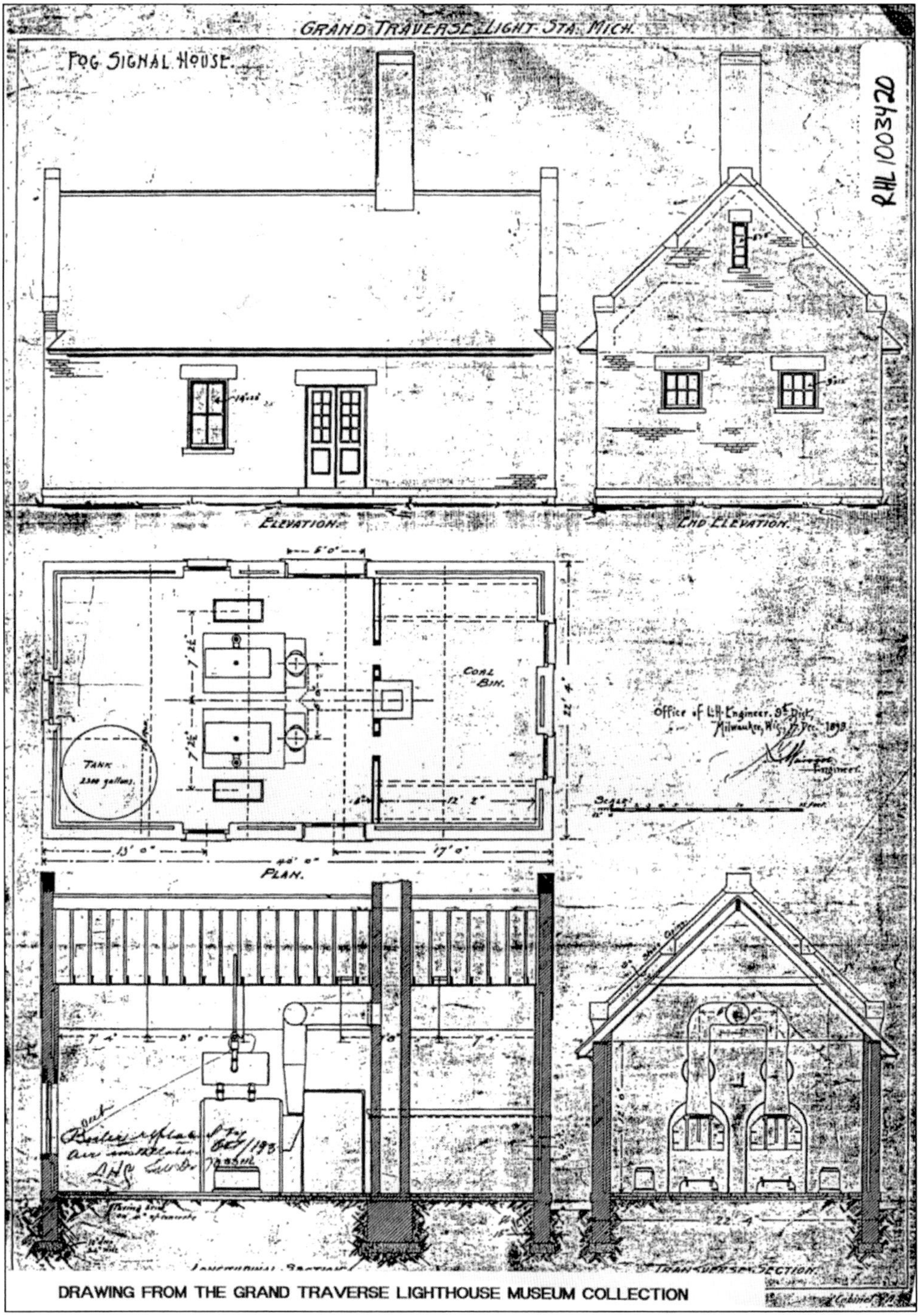

DRAWING FROM THE GRAND TRAVERSE LIGHTHOUSE MUSEUM COLLECTION

In 1889, the Lake Carrier's Association drafted a proposal to install a fog signal at the Grand Traverse Lighthouse. For 10 years this proposal was denied, leaving the entrances of Grand Traverse Bay and the Manitou Passage silent. Then on July 1, 1898, a sum of $5,500 was appropriated for the construction of a fog signal building. Rectangular in plan, it was to be 22 feet by 40 feet and constructed of brick. (Courtesy National Archives and Records Administration.)

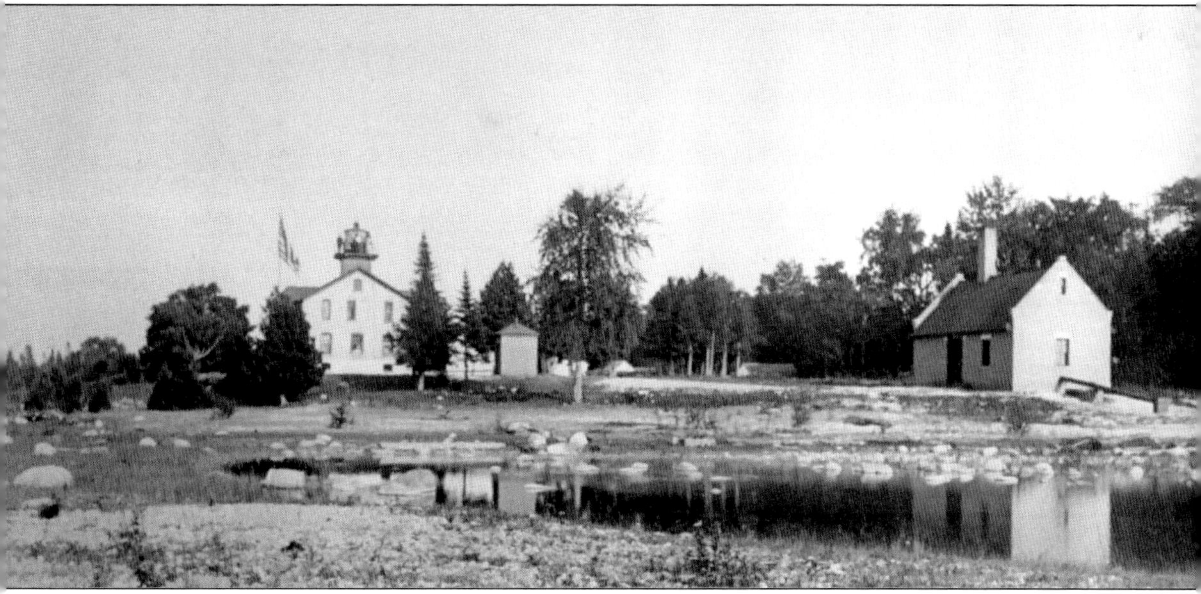

The first fog signal at Grand Traverse Lighthouse was powered by steam. Two immense boilers were located inside the building where they were lit when the fog rolled in. From the moment the first fire was lit under one of the massive tanks, 55 minutes passed before enough steam had built up in the boiler for the fog signal to sound. In this photograph taken from the water's edge, notice the keepers on the catwalk of the lighthouse. (Courtesy Grand Traverse Lighthouse Museum Collection.)

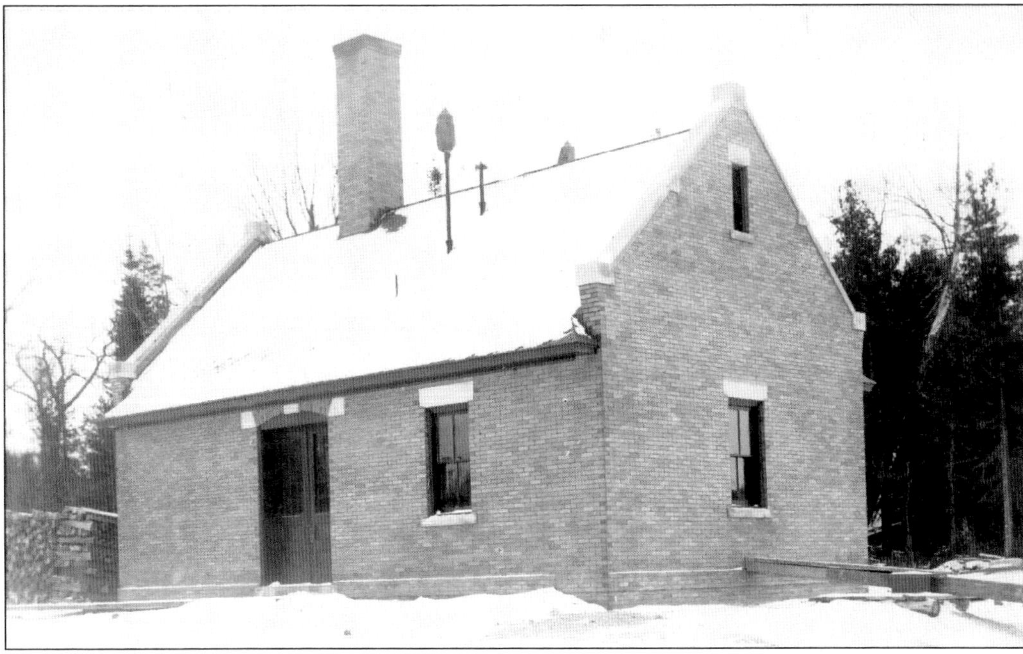

The first fog signals at Grand Traverse Lighthouse were two 10-inch steam whistles that stood 37 feet above the water level. This is one of the earliest known photographs of the Fog Signal Building, taken shortly after construction in 1899. Notice the original wood double-hung windows with two/two lights. (Courtesy Grand Traverse Lighthouse Museum Collection.)

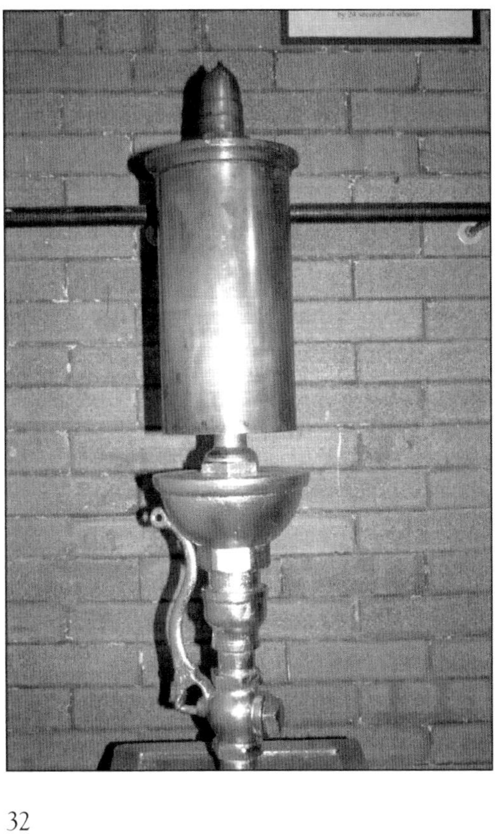

The photograph on the left is an example of a steam whistle similar to the one used at Grand Traverse Light from 1899 to 1933. This whistle is on loan from the National Park Service and is on display in the Grand Traverse Lighthouse Fog Signal Building. (Courtesy Grand Traverse Lighthouse Museum Collection.)

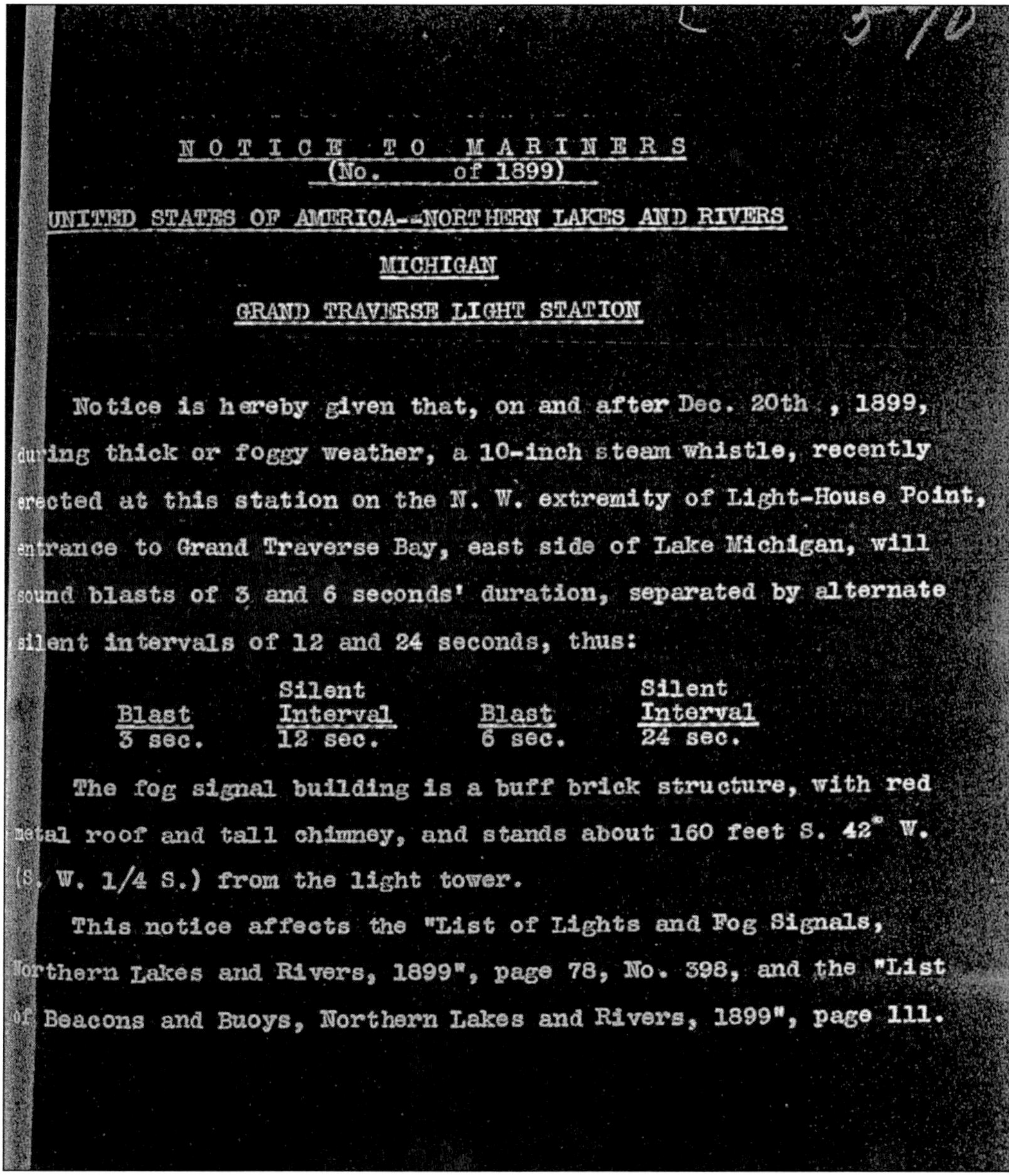

NOTICE TO MARINERS
(No. of 1899)

UNITED STATES OF AMERICA--NORTHERN LAKES AND RIVERS

MICHIGAN

GRAND TRAVERSE LIGHT STATION

Notice is hereby given that, on and after Dec. 20th , 1899, during thick or foggy weather, a 10-inch steam whistle, recently erected at this station on the N. W. extremity of Light-House Point, entrance to Grand Traverse Bay, east side of Lake Michigan, will sound blasts of 3 and 6 seconds' duration, separated by alternate silent intervals of 12 and 24 seconds, thus:

Blast	Silent Interval	Blast	Silent Interval
3 sec.	12 sec.	6 sec.	24 sec.

The fog signal building is a buff brick structure, with red metal roof and tall chimney, and stands about 160 feet S. 42° W. (S. W. 1/4 S.) from the light tower.

This notice affects the "List of Lights and Fog Signals, Northern Lakes and Rivers, 1899", page 78, No. 398, and the "List of Beacons and Buoys, Northern Lakes and Rivers, 1899", page 111.

Every fog signal in the country had a specific sequence of sound and silence intervals that was characteristic to that specific location. At the Grand Traverse Lighthouse that sequence was a three second blast followed by 12 seconds of silence and a six second blast followed by 24 seconds of silence. Then it was repeated. This characteristic was located on the nautical charts and used by mariners to identify their location. (Courtesy Grand Traverse Lighthouse Museum Collection.)

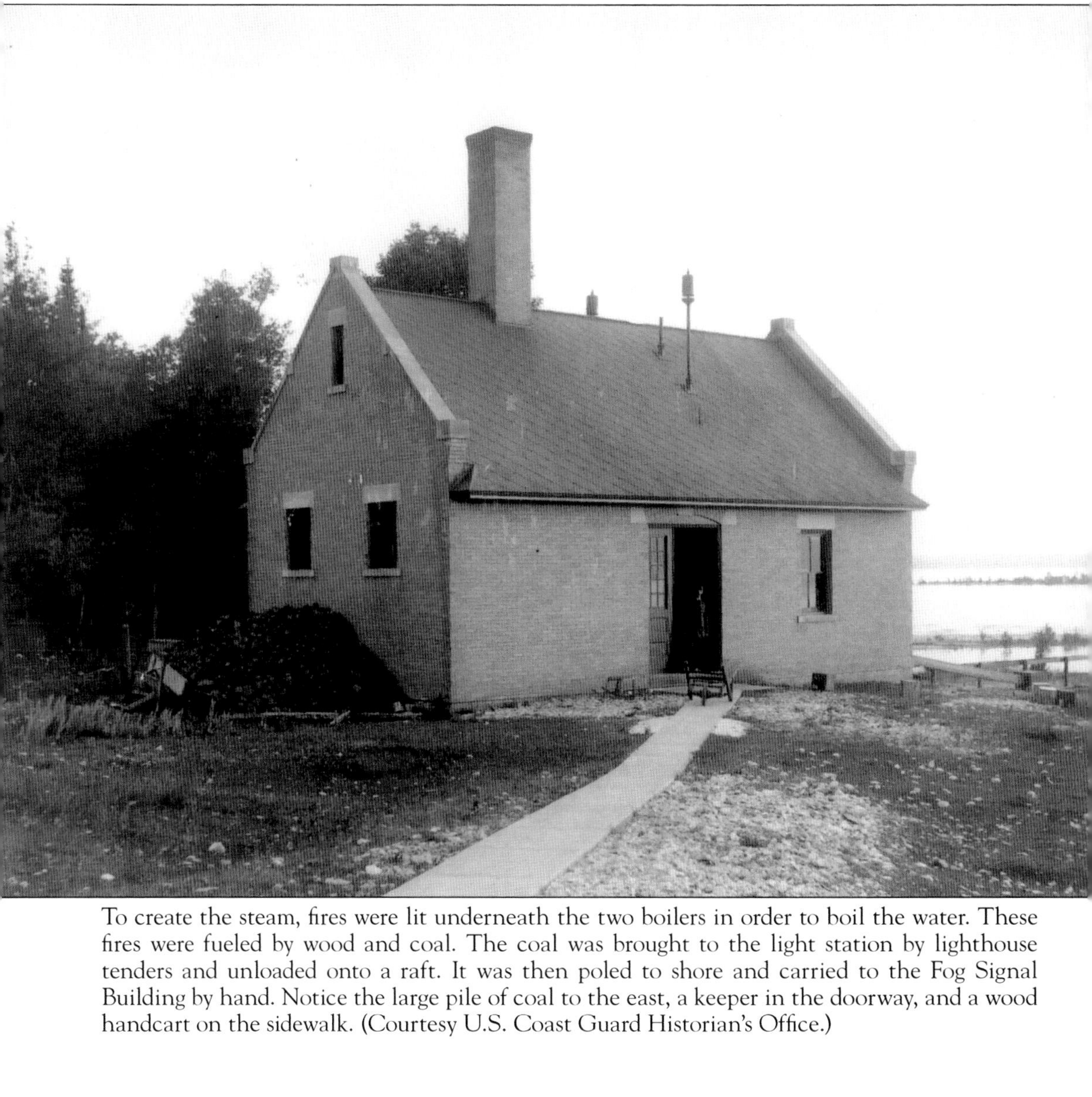

To create the steam, fires were lit underneath the two boilers in order to boil the water. These fires were fueled by wood and coal. The coal was brought to the light station by lighthouse tenders and unloaded onto a raft. It was then poled to shore and carried to the Fog Signal Building by hand. Notice the large pile of coal to the east, a keeper in the doorway, and a wood handcart on the sidewalk. (Courtesy U.S. Coast Guard Historian's Office.)

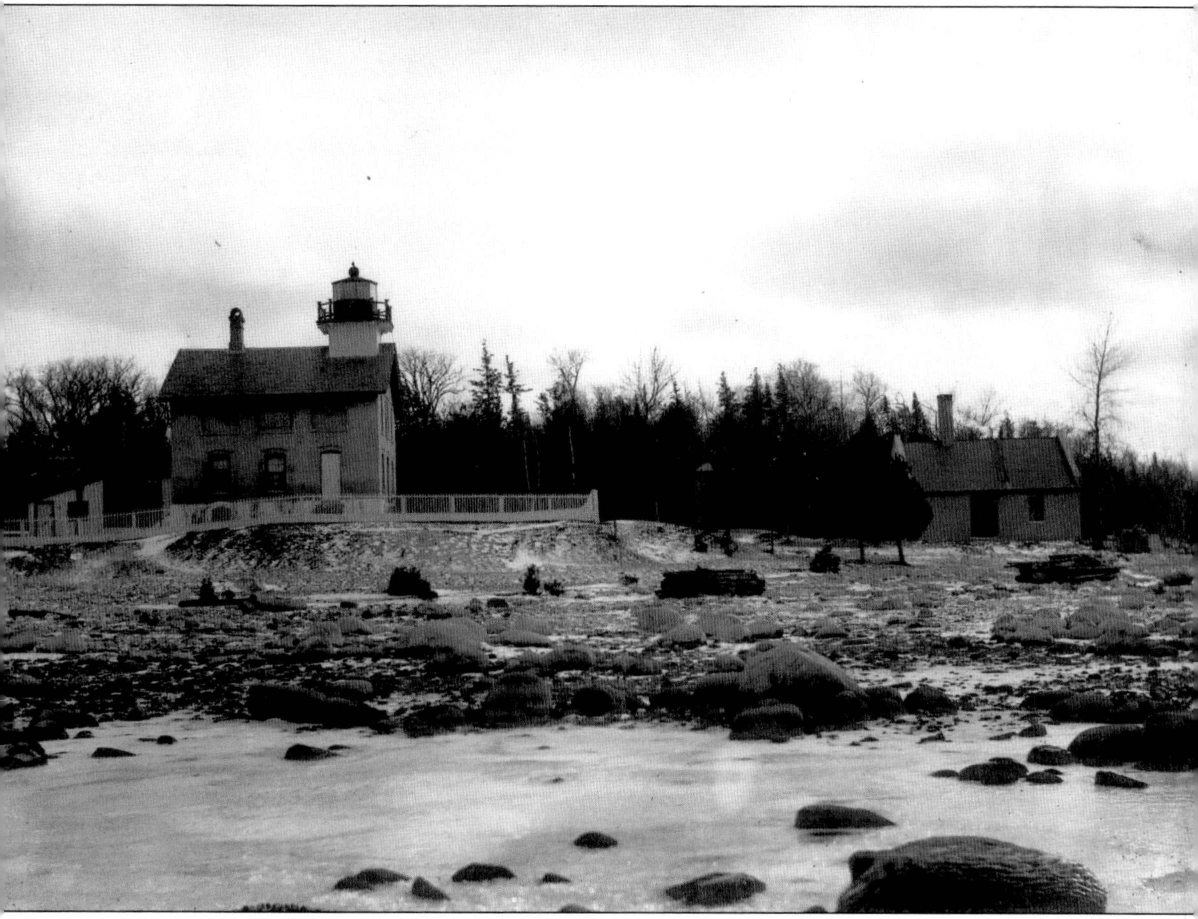

A view from the north, as shown in this photograph from early 1900, highlights the original, white entrance door to the dwelling that is surrounded by a white, wooden fence. To the rear or east side of the building, a kitchen is attached. There is a white storage shed, and the second-floor window frames are bricked in. (Courtesy U.S. Coast Guard Historian's Office.)

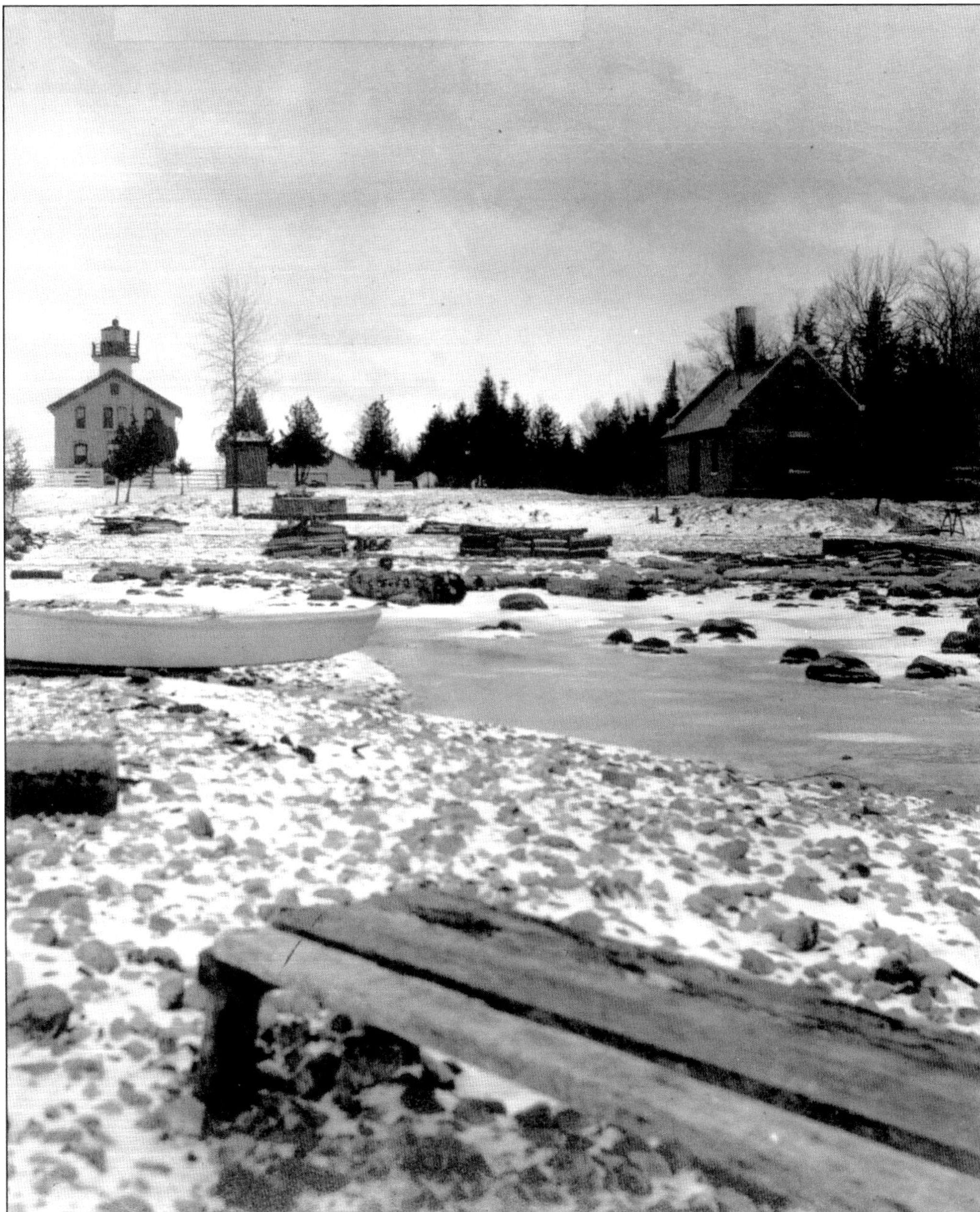

This early-1900 photograph from the west provides an overall view of all the buildings on the site. They include the dwelling, oil house, barn, crib, hen coop, and Fog Signal Building. In the foreground at the water's edge is a wooden bench and white rowboat most likely used for fishing. (Courtesy U.S. Coast Guard Historian's Office.)

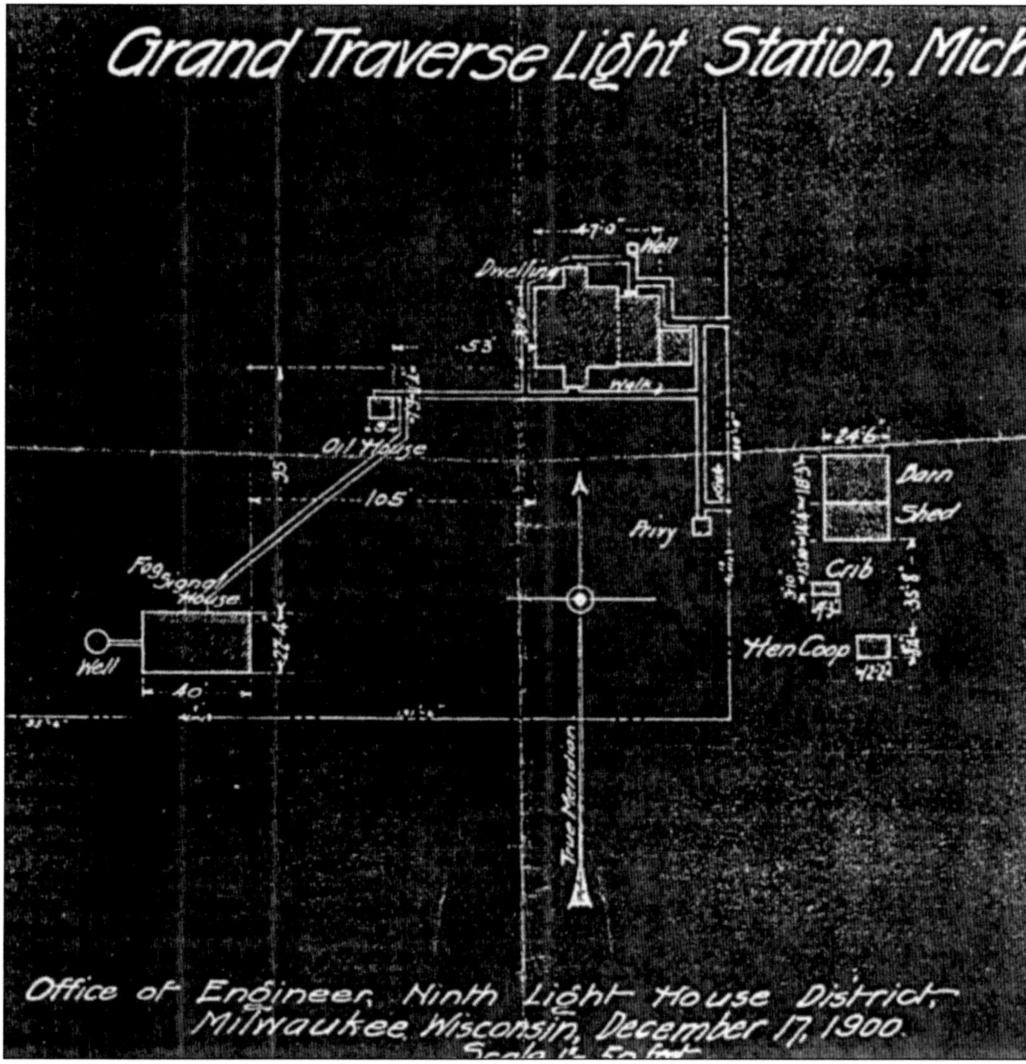

The addition of a fog signal building required the work of a second keeper. The first assistant keeper, William Porter Wilson, was hired to perform these added responsibilities. Wilson had offered to build a house on the site at his own expense, as he was being transferred from the South Fox Island Light Station. The U.S. Lighthouse Service instead made plans to alter the existing lighthouse into two separate dwellings to house both keepers. (Courtesy U.S. Coast Guard.)

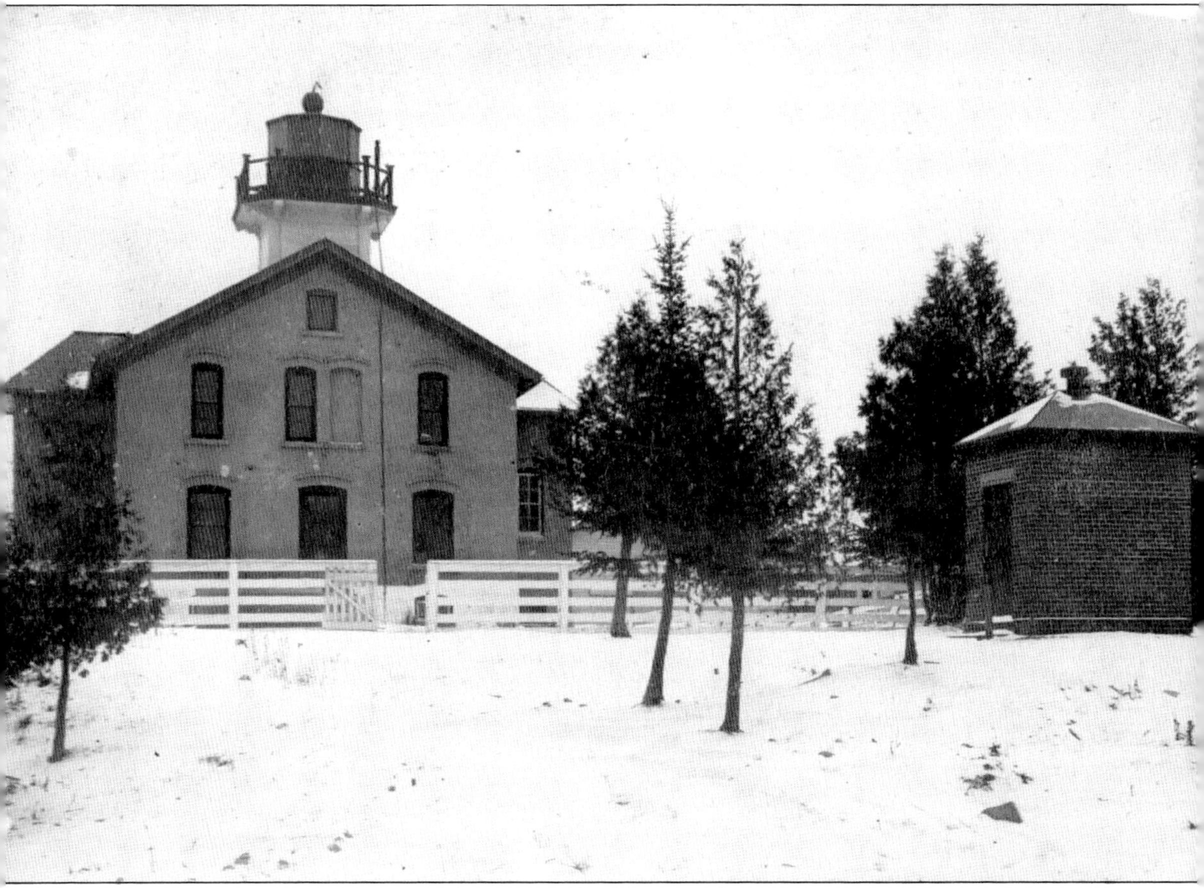

The main house was divided in half from east to west. New two-story stairwell "wings" were added to the exterior of the footprint to replace the original stairs and allow accessibility to the second floor from each apartment. These new wings were capped with a small, hipped roof and created a small vestibule entry for each of the families. (Courtesy Grand Traverse Lighthouse Museum Collection.)

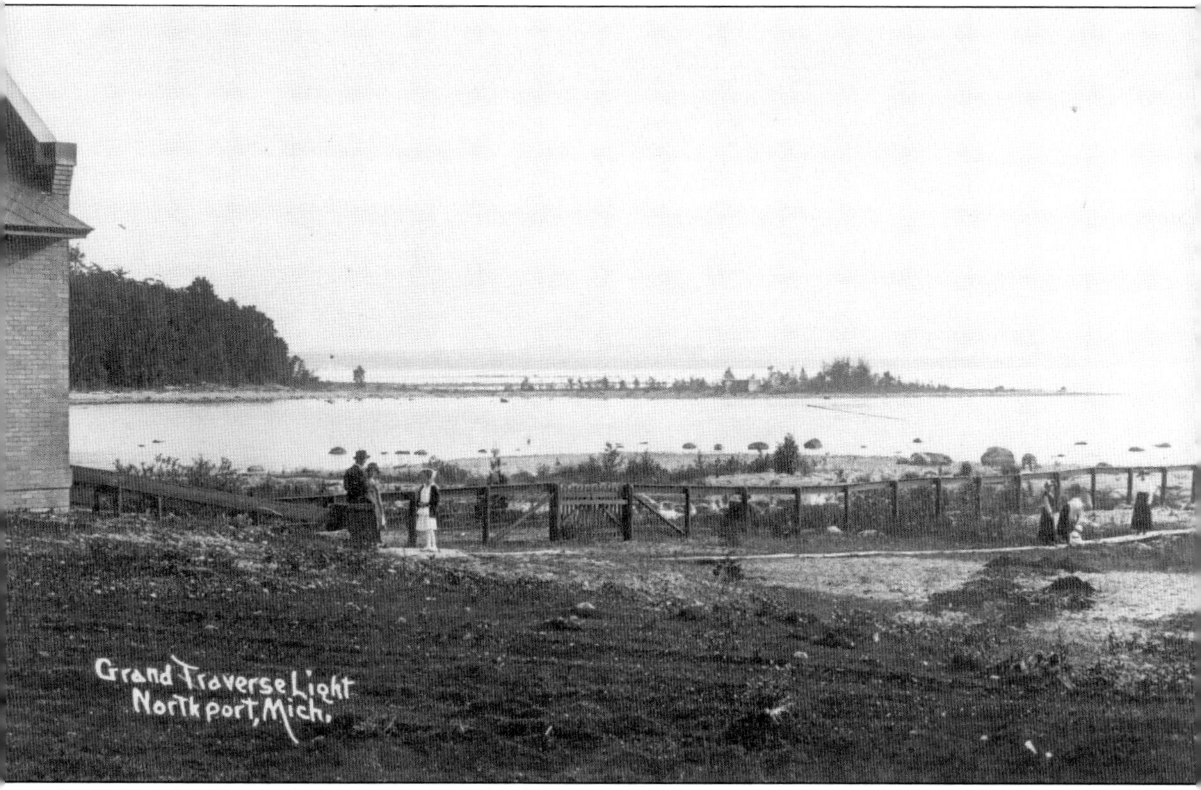

In 1903, a landing crib was erected in the lake west of the Fog Signal Building. It was used for off-loading wood, coal, and other supplies delivered by the lighthouse tender. A tramway was used to move the supplies up to the buildings. A closer look at the photograph shows people meandering along the crib toward the lake. It is uncertain if they are lighthouse families or visitors. (Courtesy Grand Traverse Lighthouse Museum Collection.)

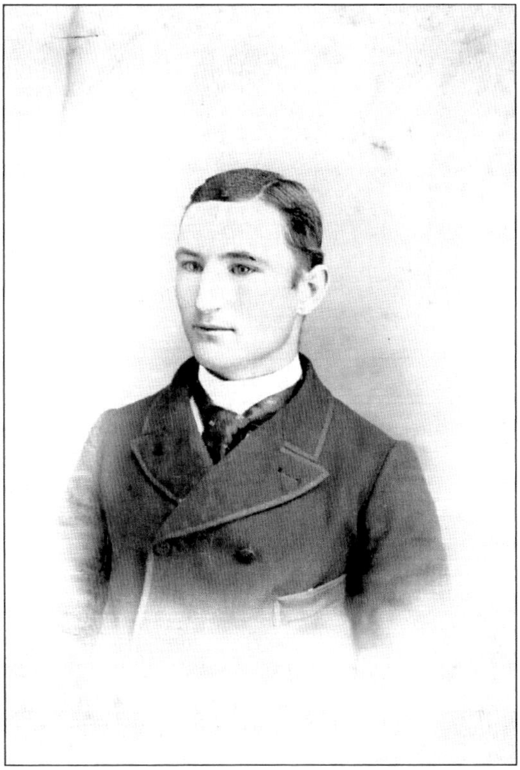

Oscar Dame, a resident of Northport, served as assistant keeper at Grand Traverse Light twice. He began in 1907, married Ella Estella Fuller in 1909, and returned in 1928. Retiring after 35 years of U.S. Lighthouse Service, he passed away at age 73 in Northport. Of the lights he called home, three were Kenosha South Port Light in Wisconsin, South Fox Island Light in Michigan, and Grand Traverse Light. (Courtesy Grand Traverse Lighthouse Museum Collection.)

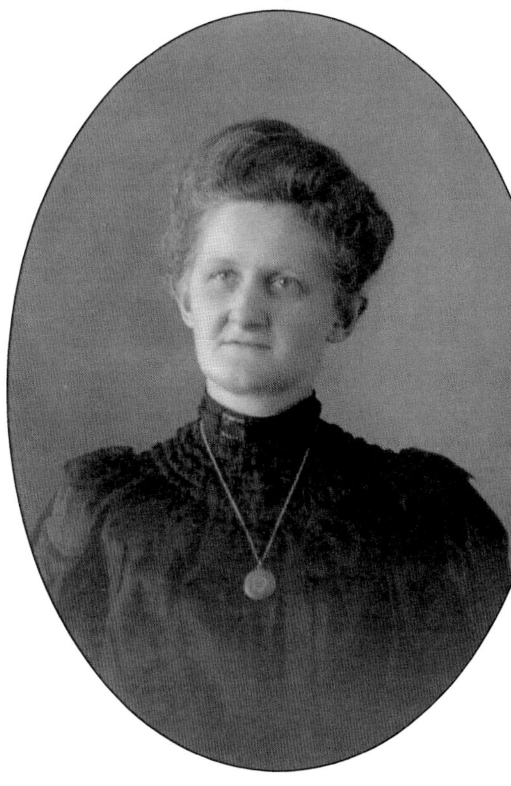

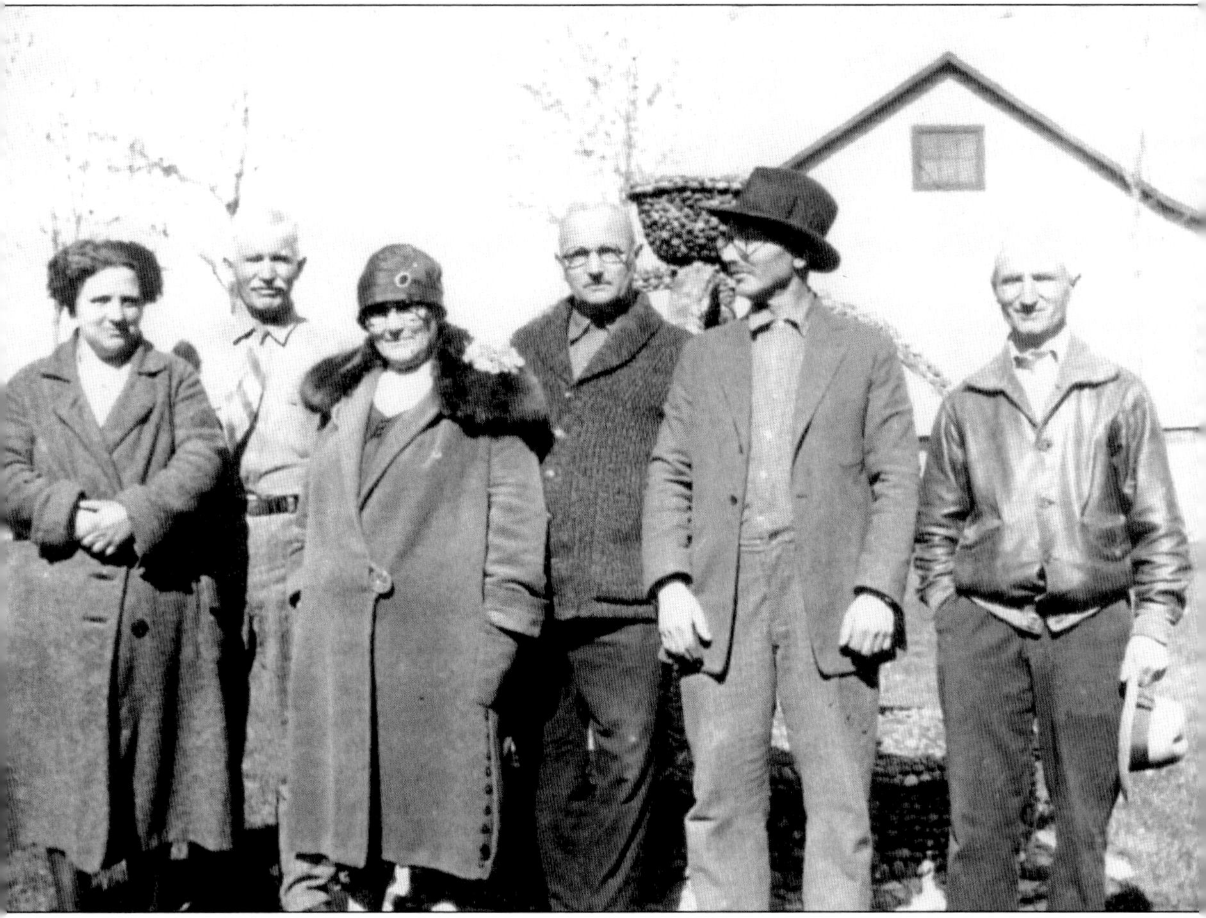

This photograph from about 1928 pictures the children of Eusebius and Ella Dame and the grandchildren of Deacon Joseph and Ursula Dame. From left to right are Pearl Dame Voice, Gilman Marston Dame, Myrta Dame Johnston, Seba Dame, Isa Dame, and Oscar. Joseph established the town of Northport in the early 1850s. (Courtesy Grand Traverse Lighthouse Museum Collection.)

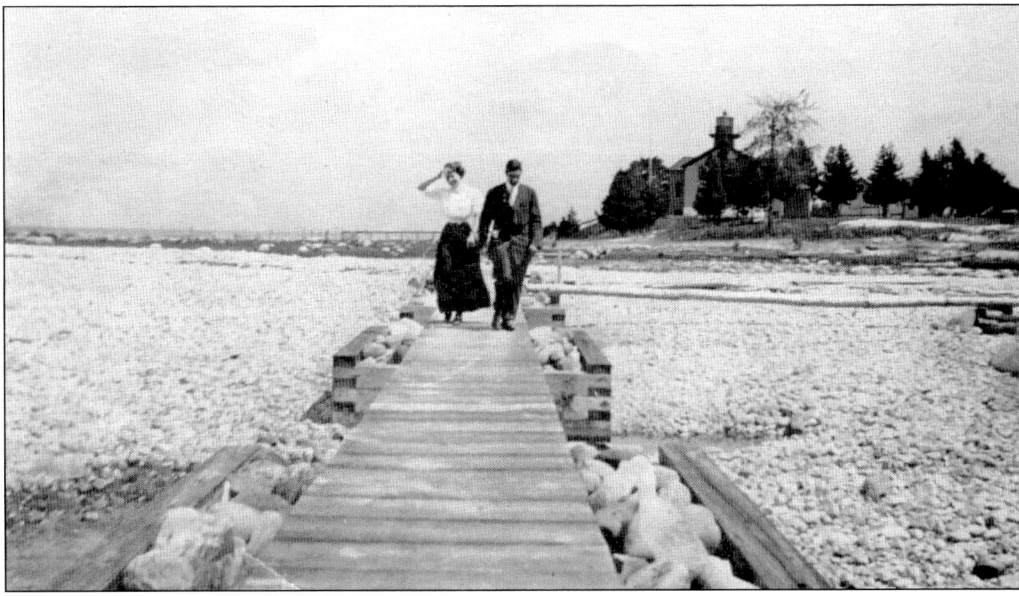

Enjoying its natural setting among the woodlands and the peacefulness of the atmosphere, many local people visited the lighthouse as a day excursion from Northport. The Thieses were no exception. The waterline around the dawn of the 20th century was quite low. Notice how far they are out on the dock, walking west of the lighthouse. (Courtesy Grand Traverse Lighthouse Museum Collection.)

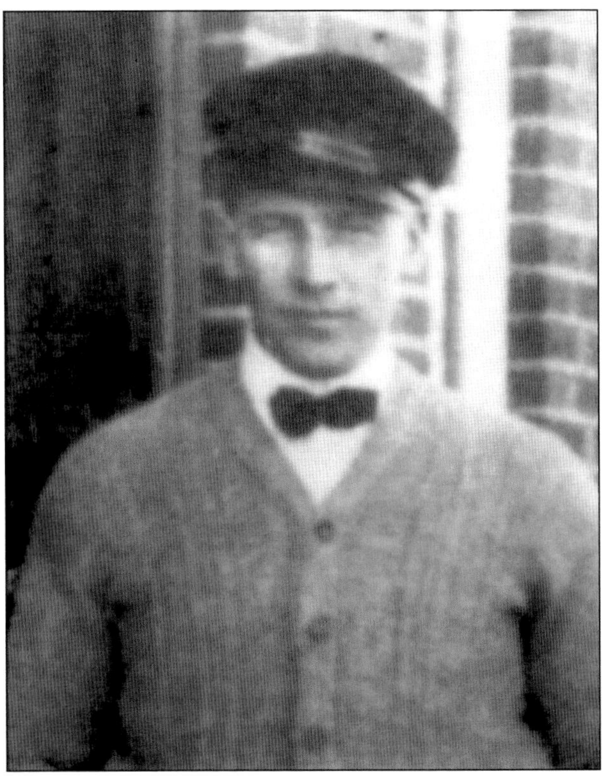

Nels Nelson, pictured around 1907, served as the fifth assistant keeper at Grand Traverse Lighthouse. Nelson began his service career at the North Manitou Light in April 1907. He was promoted and transferred to Grand Traverse Light one month later. Staying only two months, he was transferred back to North Manitou Light. During his 35 years of service, he tended lights at South Manitou, South Fox Island, Point Betsie, St. Helena Island Light, the Chicago Coast Guard station, and the Frankfort Coast Guard station before retiring in 1947. (Courtesy Grand Traverse Lighthouse Museum Collection.)

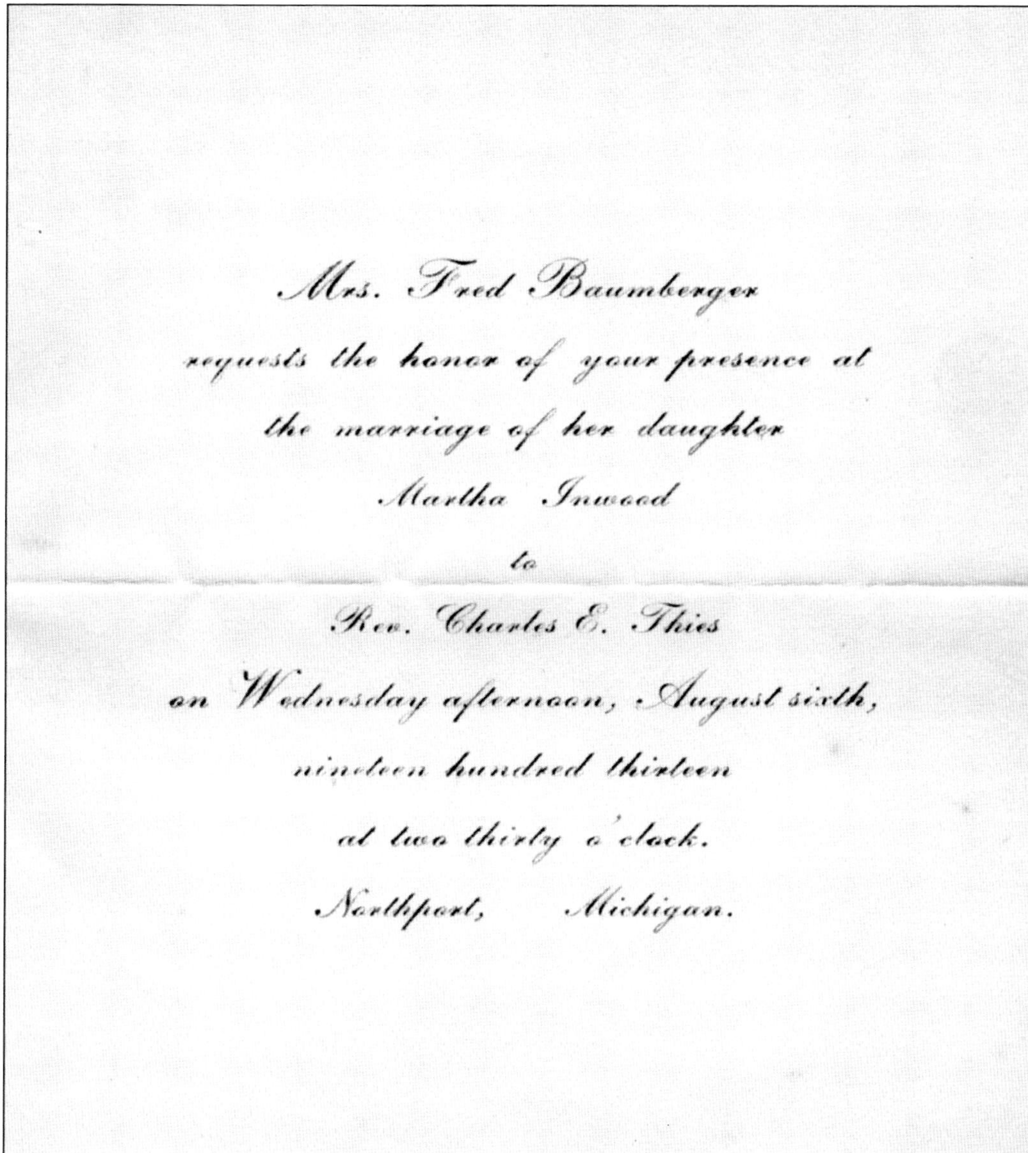

Mrs. Fred Baumberger
requests the honor of your presence at
the marriage of her daughter
Martha Inwood
to
Rev. Charles E. Thies
on Wednesday afternoon, August sixth,
nineteen hundred thirteen
at two thirty o'clock.
Northport, Michigan.

This wedding invitation announcing the marriage of Martha Inwood Baumberger to Charlie Thies is a wonderful historical document that was handed down from generation to generation. It is now part of the archival collections of the Grand Traverse Lighthouse Museum. It was donated by Martha L. Roberts of Northport. Roberts, the current president of the Grand Traverse Lighthouse Museum, was named after Martha. (Courtesy Grand Traverse Lighthouse Museum Collection.)

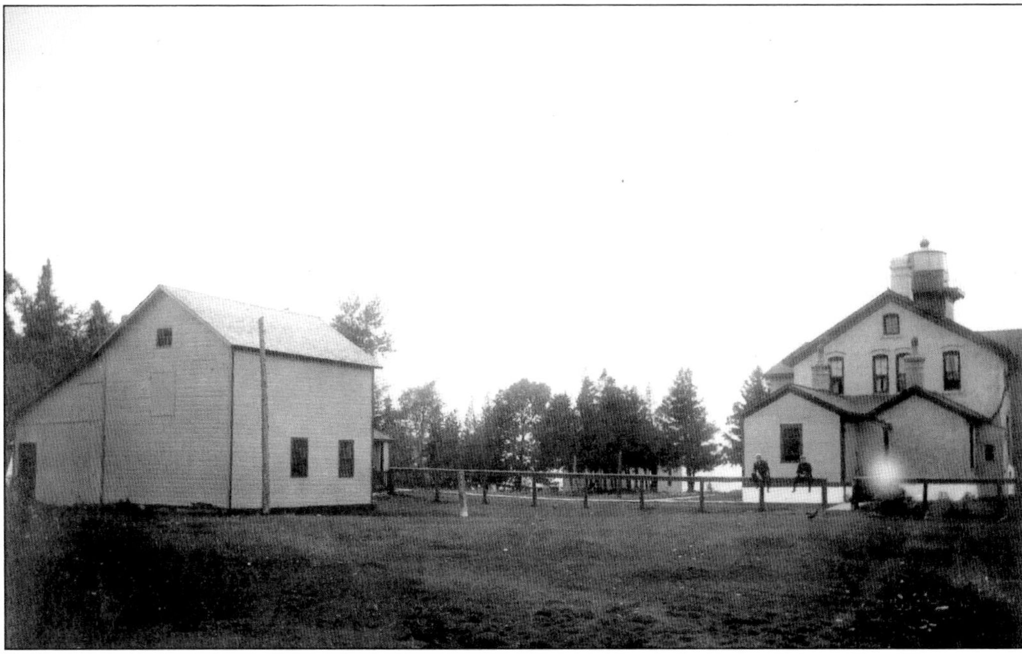

Seated on the fence, keeper George Buttars and assistant keeper Ira Flagstad take a break from their daily chores on August 15, 1914. The 1891 barn can be seen to the south, and the fence has changed to only a top rail and was either painted or stained a dark color. (Courtesy U.S. Coast Guard Historian's Office.)

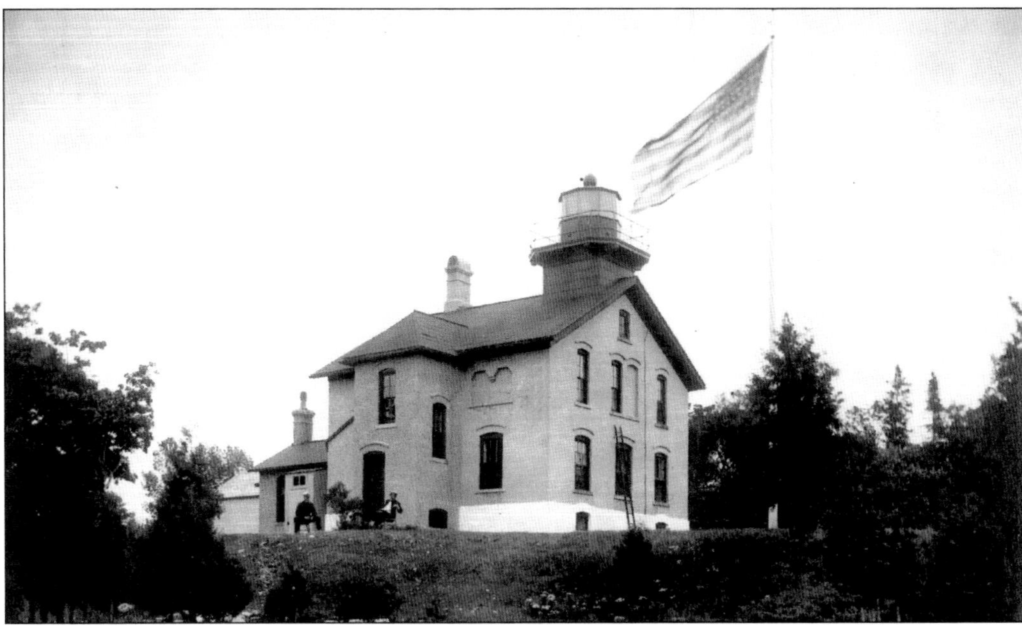

The lighthouse has now undergone more changes, including permanent kitchen additions for both apartments located on the east end. Notice the ladder leaning against the building on the west side. Keeper George Buttars and assistant keeper Ira Flagstad appear to be taking a respite from washing windows. Keeping the light station clean and tidy for inspection was an ongoing duty. (Courtesy U.S. Coast Guard Historian's Office.)

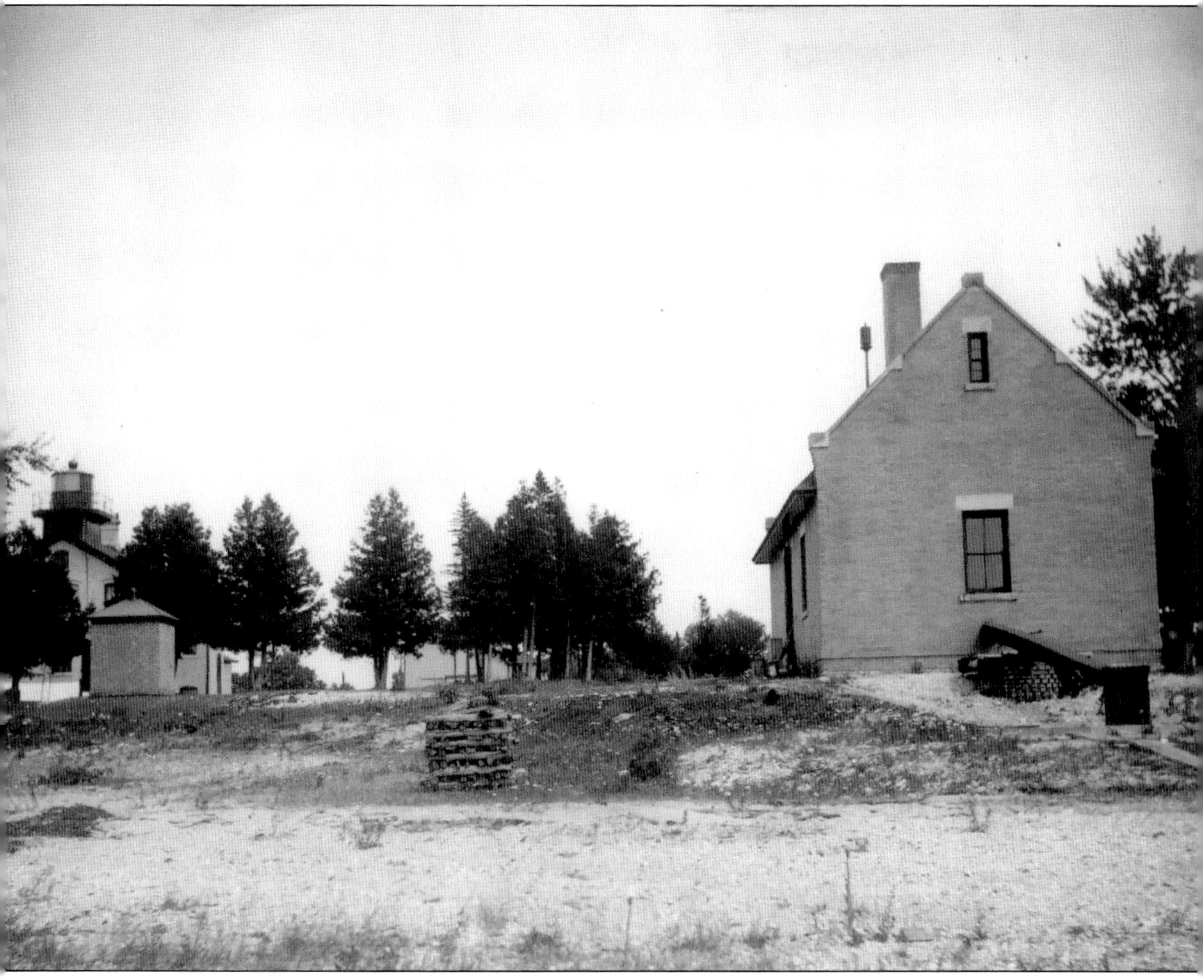

This photograph was taken on August 15, 1914. In the lighthouse tower, the shades are drawn to protect the lens from the natural light during daylight hours. The ball atop the tower's roof provides ventilation for the heat radiating from the lamp when lit during the night. The dwelling also shows a white-painted strip around the lower bottom four feet. (Courtesy U.S. Coast Guard Historian's Office.)

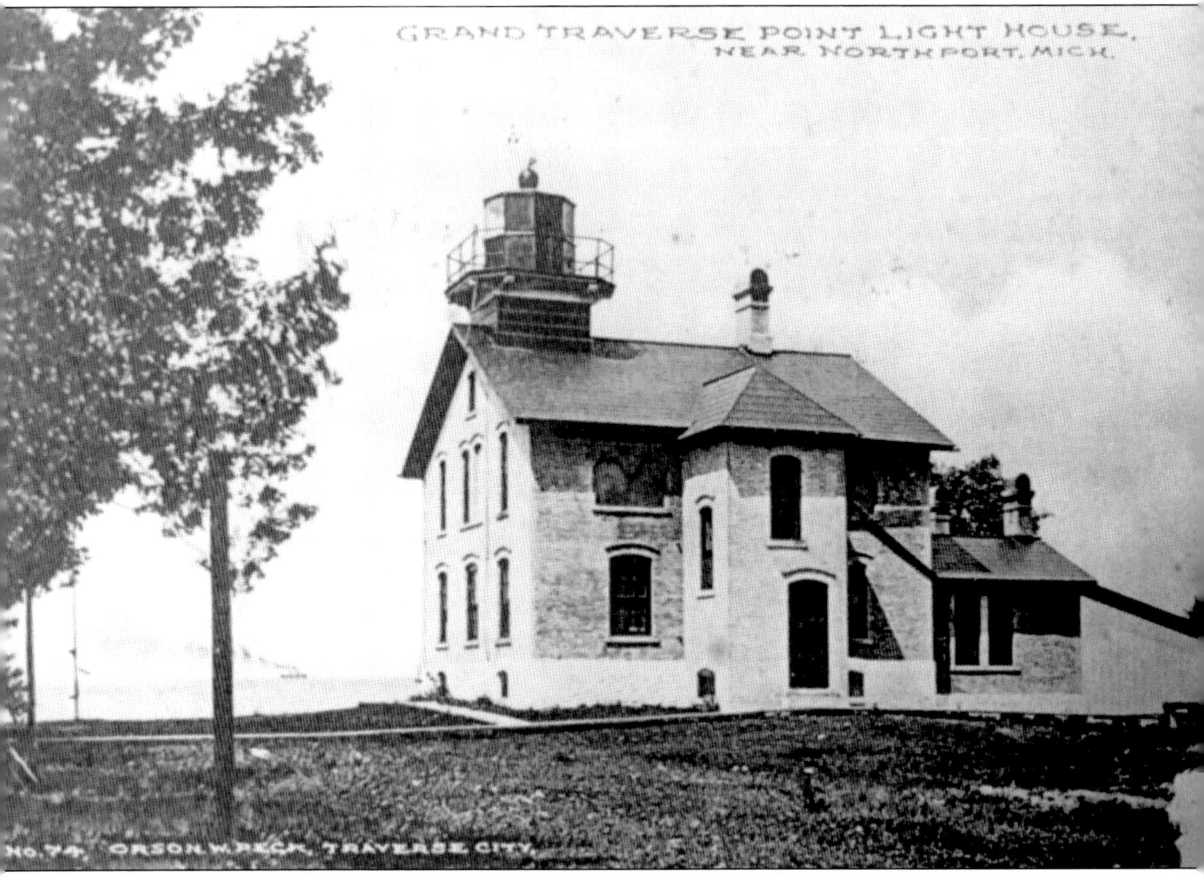

Many photographs have been taken of the Grand Traverse Lighthouse over the last 150 years. This one, taken between 1901 and 1916, is unusual because it shows very little vegetation and trees immediately surrounding the building. Life was very simple then, and this lonely lighthouse stood majestically at the tip of the peninsula guiding sailors to their destinations. (Courtesy Grand Traverse Lighthouse Museum Collection.)

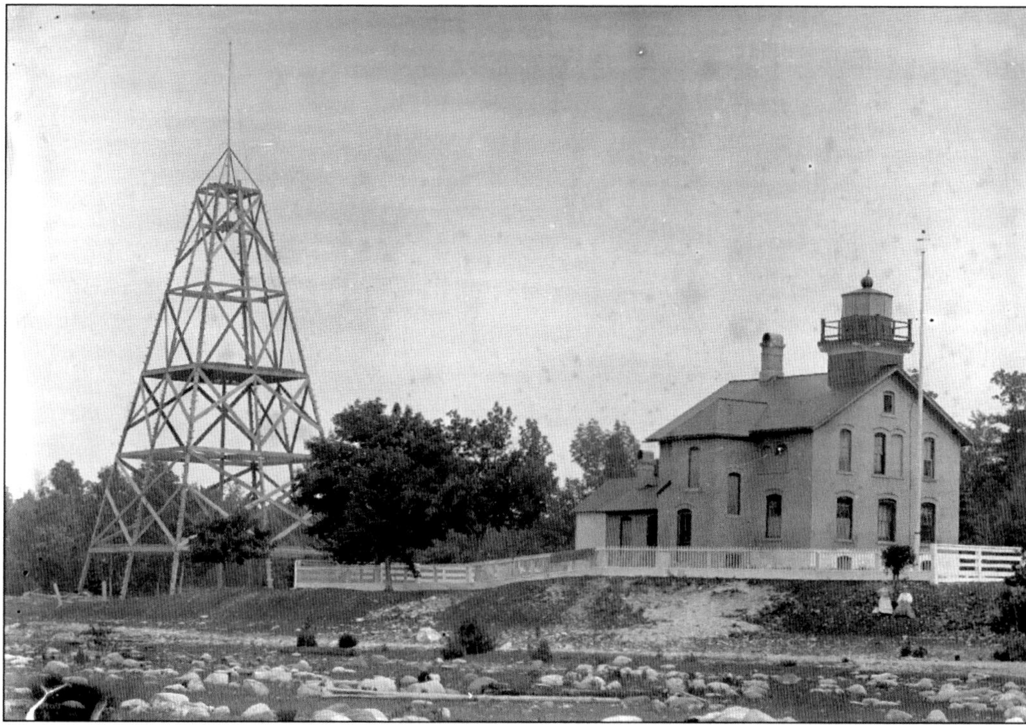

A survey tower once stood to the northwest of the lighthouse from about 1910 until about 1920. The survey vessel *Margaret* used the tower to take bearings that provided water depth. These surveys were done throughout the Great Lakes and provided data used for mariners' charts, marking the water depths of the lakes. This is the survey vessel *Margaret* around 1918. (Courtesy Grand Traverse Lighthouse Museum Collection.)

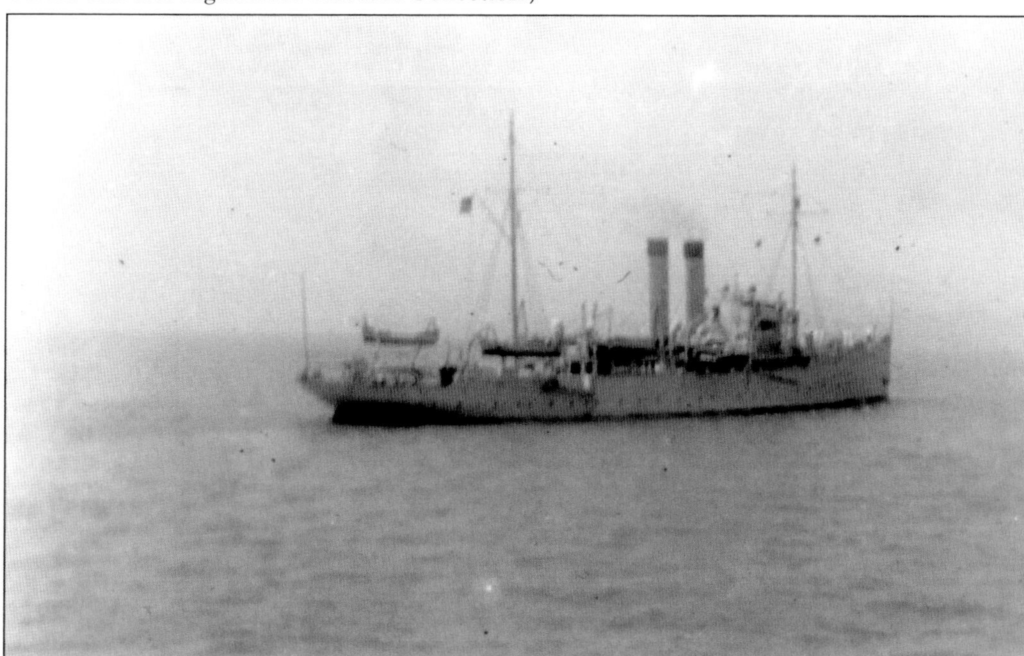

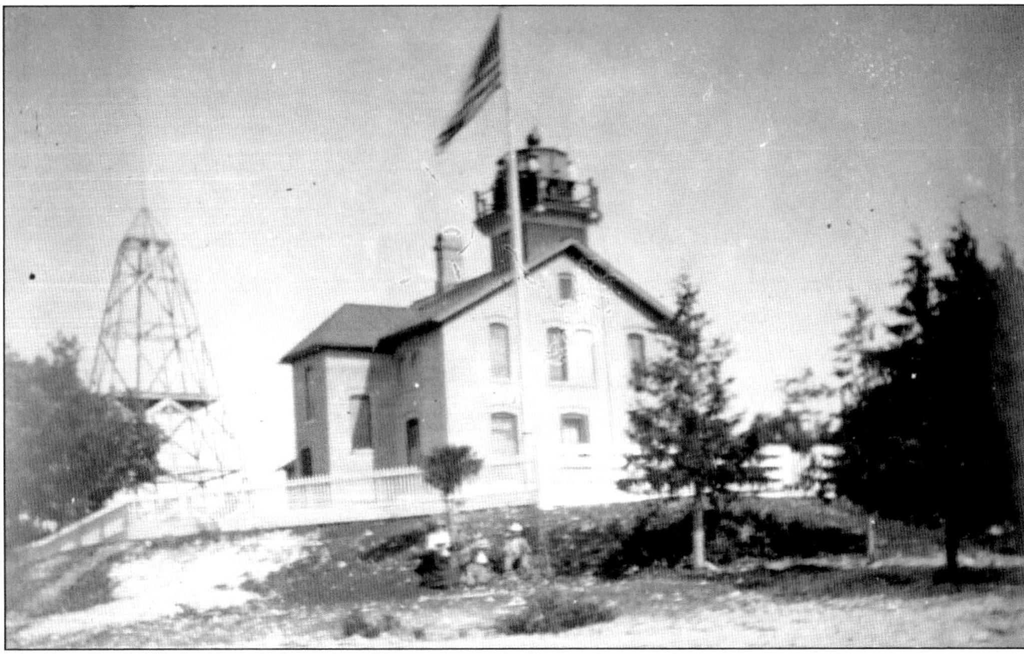

Sunday was the day when villagers from nearby towns ventured out on the rough road to the lighthouse and rocky shore. Greeted by the keeper, they were given a tour of the grounds and lighthouse proper. In this photograph, take note of the people sitting below the flagpole in the foreground, while a keeper highlights the sights from the catwalk of the tower to his guests.

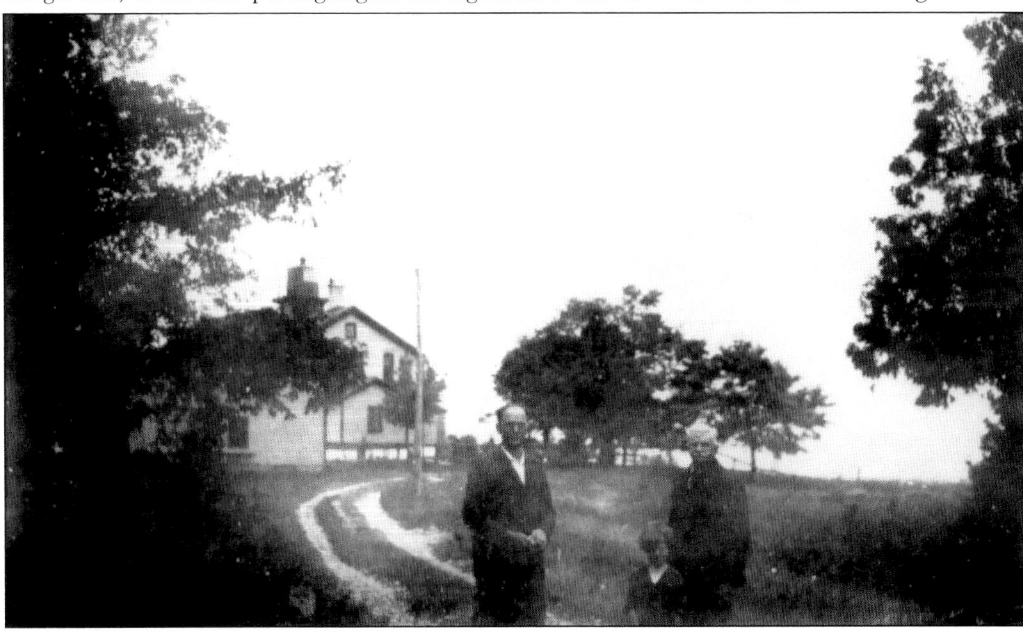

This photograph has a very different view than most photographers would have chosen. Notice the dirt road that comes from the east. The barn is barely visible to the south of the lighthouse. These visitors from Northport, believed to be members of the Thomas family, are posing in the forefront. This photograph was donated by Virginia Thomas of Northport, who found it in her family's photo album. (Courtesy Grand Traverse Lighthouse Museum Collection.)

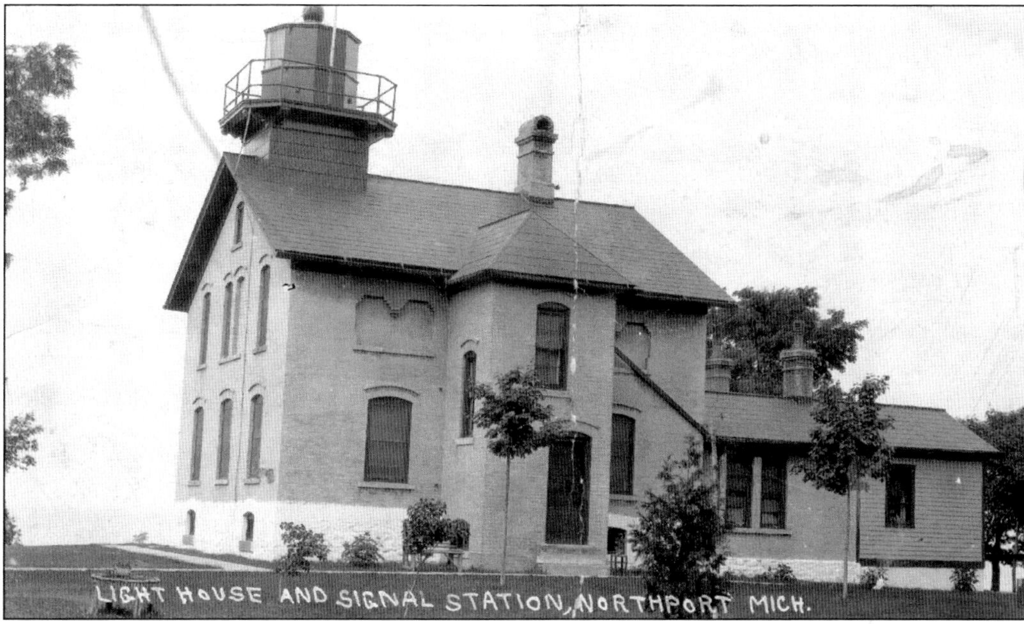

This postcard, dated August 26, 1926, was addressed to U.S. Forest Service employee Ruth Macnab of St. Regis, Montana, from Scott James. James writes, "After attempting to climb a forest watch tower in Northern Michigan, I've decided I don't want in the forestry service. Envy your Brook Trout. They are certainly hard to catch here." (Courtesy Archives of Michigan, Negative 11829.)

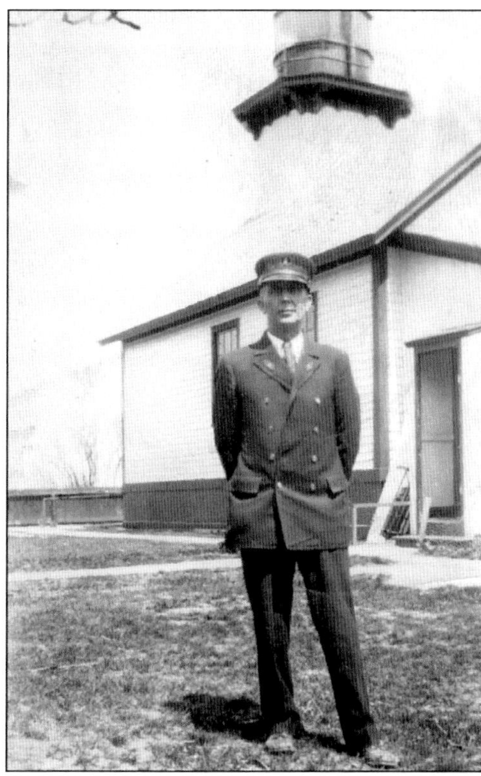

Emil Conrad Johnson was born on November 12, 1884, in Sweden. He was a career lighthouse keeper stationed at Chicago Harbor, Grand Traverse, Holland, Calumet Pierhead, and Mission Point. He came to Grand Traverse twice, in 1908 and in 1924. His first wife died in 1925, and later that year, he met and married Northport native Evelyn Haynes Brow. He died in 1934 in Chicago. (Courtesy Grand Traverse Lighthouse Museum Collection.)

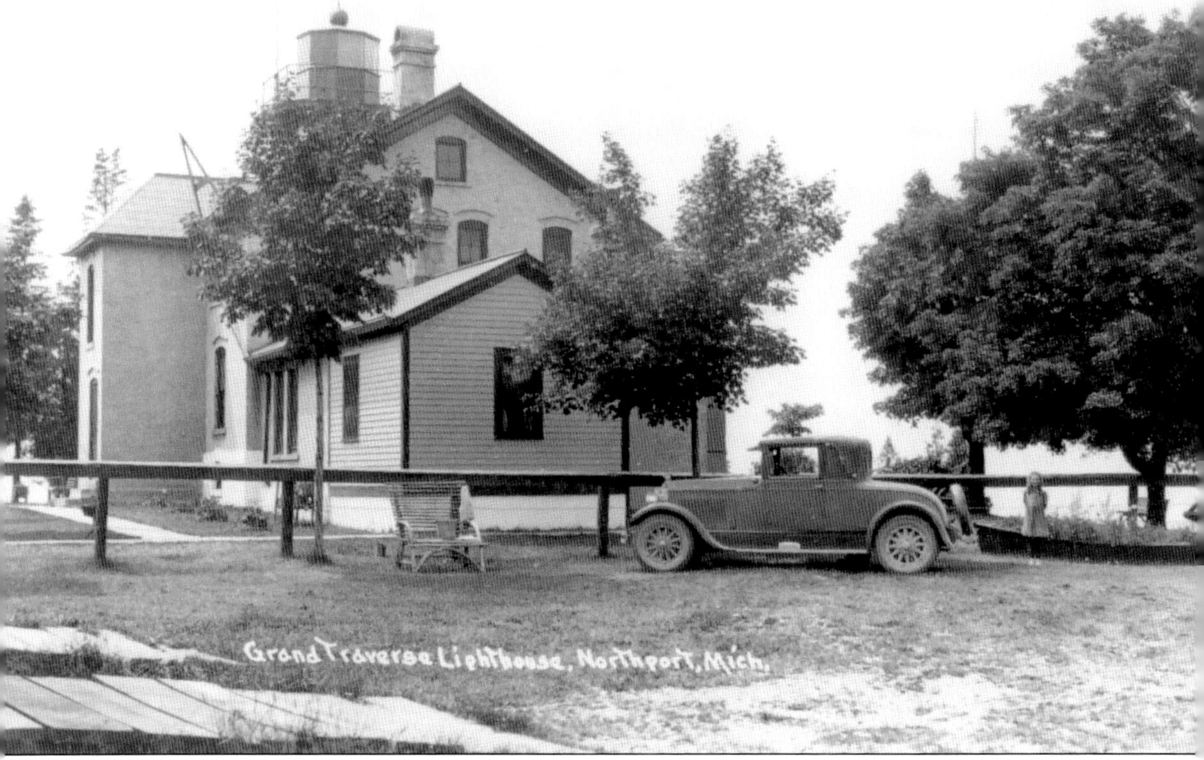

One morning during the 1930s, Mary McCormick spied a rowboat washed up on the beach. At her request, keeper James McCormick checked the boat and reported it empty with a hole in the bottom. She asked if he could drag it up to the yard for a flower planter. Granting her wish, he moved it for her, thus starting the flower boat tradition. The boat is shown here to the right filled with flowers. The car is a Buick coupe from about 1927. (Courtesy Archives of Michigan, Negative 11828.)

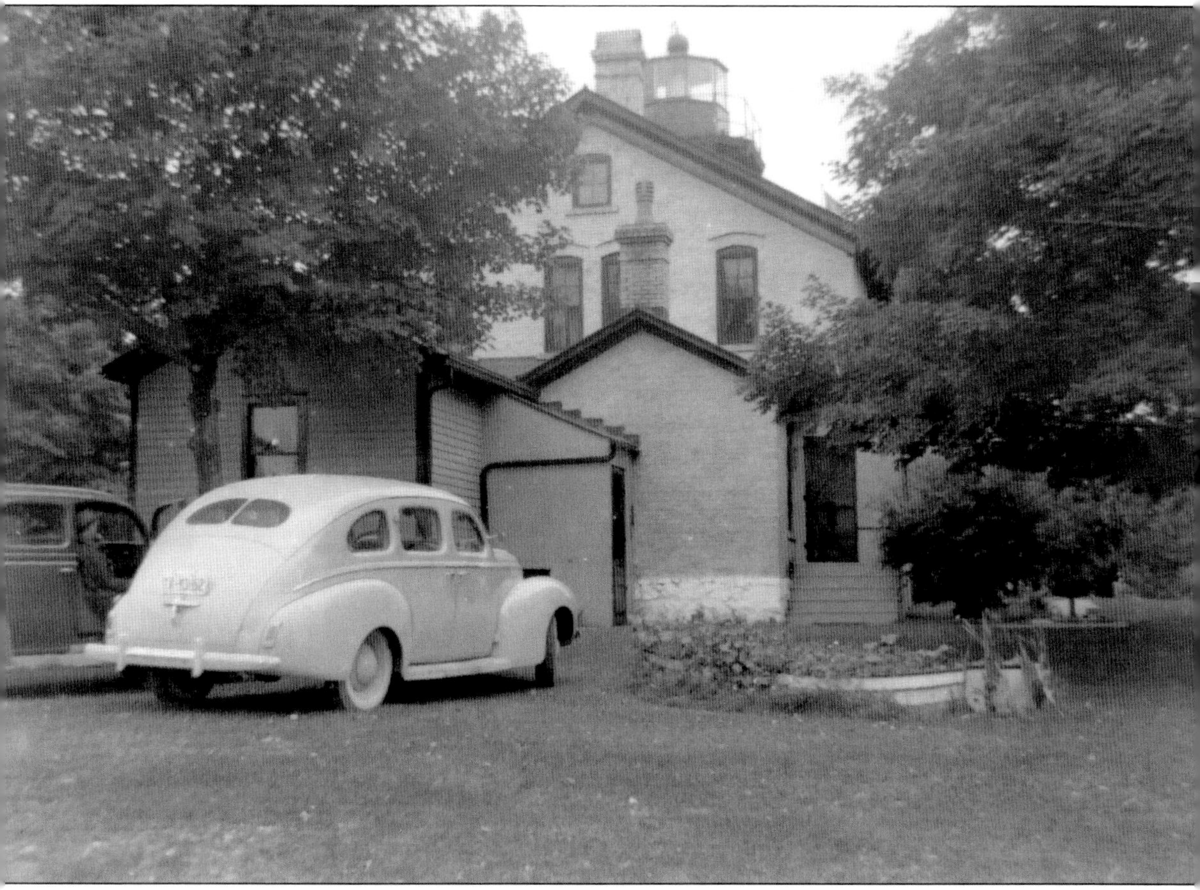

Initially all materials came to the station via water vessels. With the evolution of roads and motor vehicles, supplies could be obtained from retail stores as close as the village of Northport. In 1931, it was approved that 31 acres of the reserved lighthouse property be deeded to the State of Michigan as a park, leaving 14 acres for lighthouse use. (Courtesy Grand Traverse Lighthouse Museum Collection.)

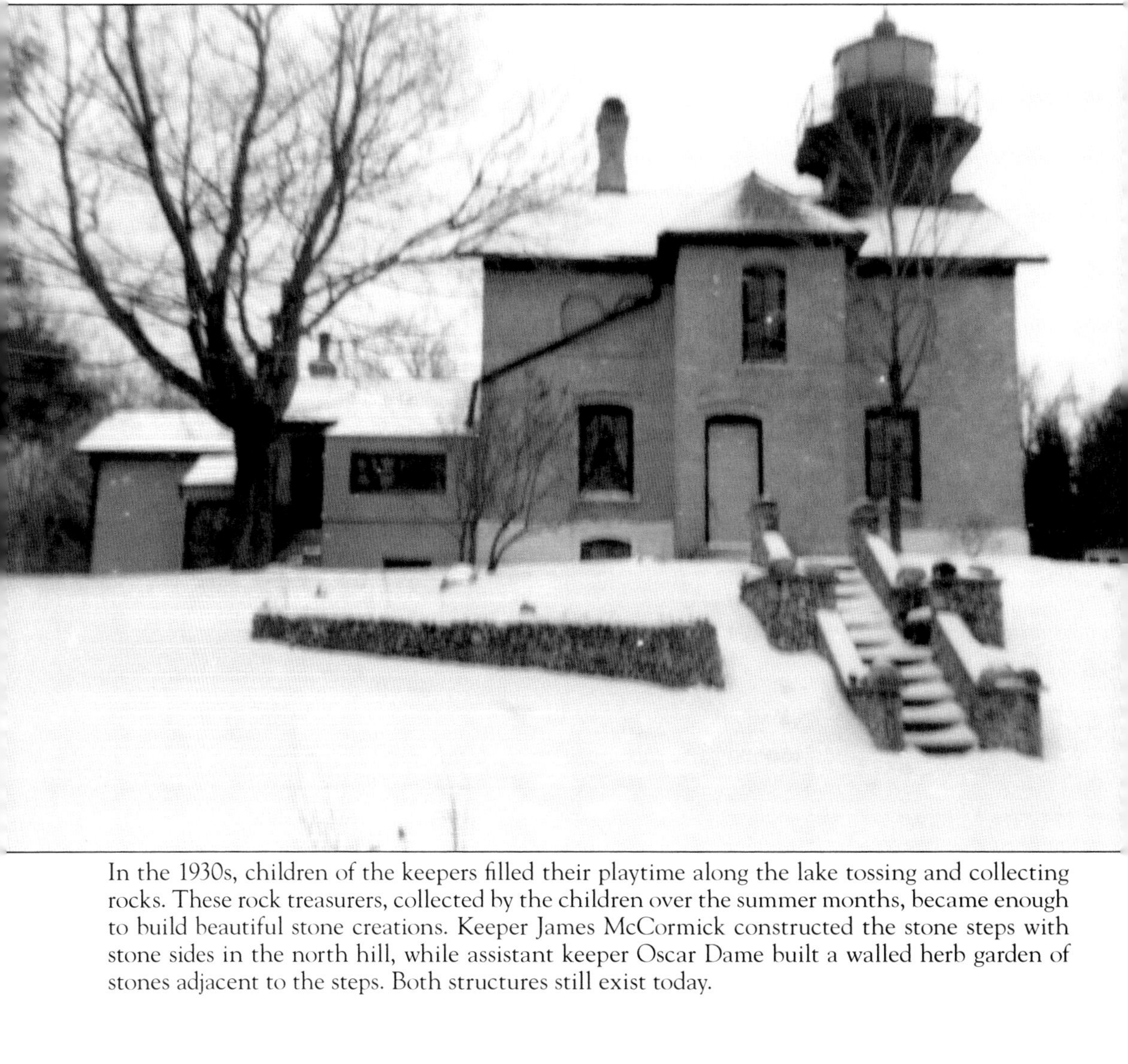

In the 1930s, children of the keepers filled their playtime along the lake tossing and collecting rocks. These rock treasurers, collected by the children over the summer months, became enough to build beautiful stone creations. Keeper James McCormick constructed the stone steps with stone sides in the north hill, while assistant keeper Oscar Dame built a walled herb garden of stones adjacent to the steps. Both structures still exist today.

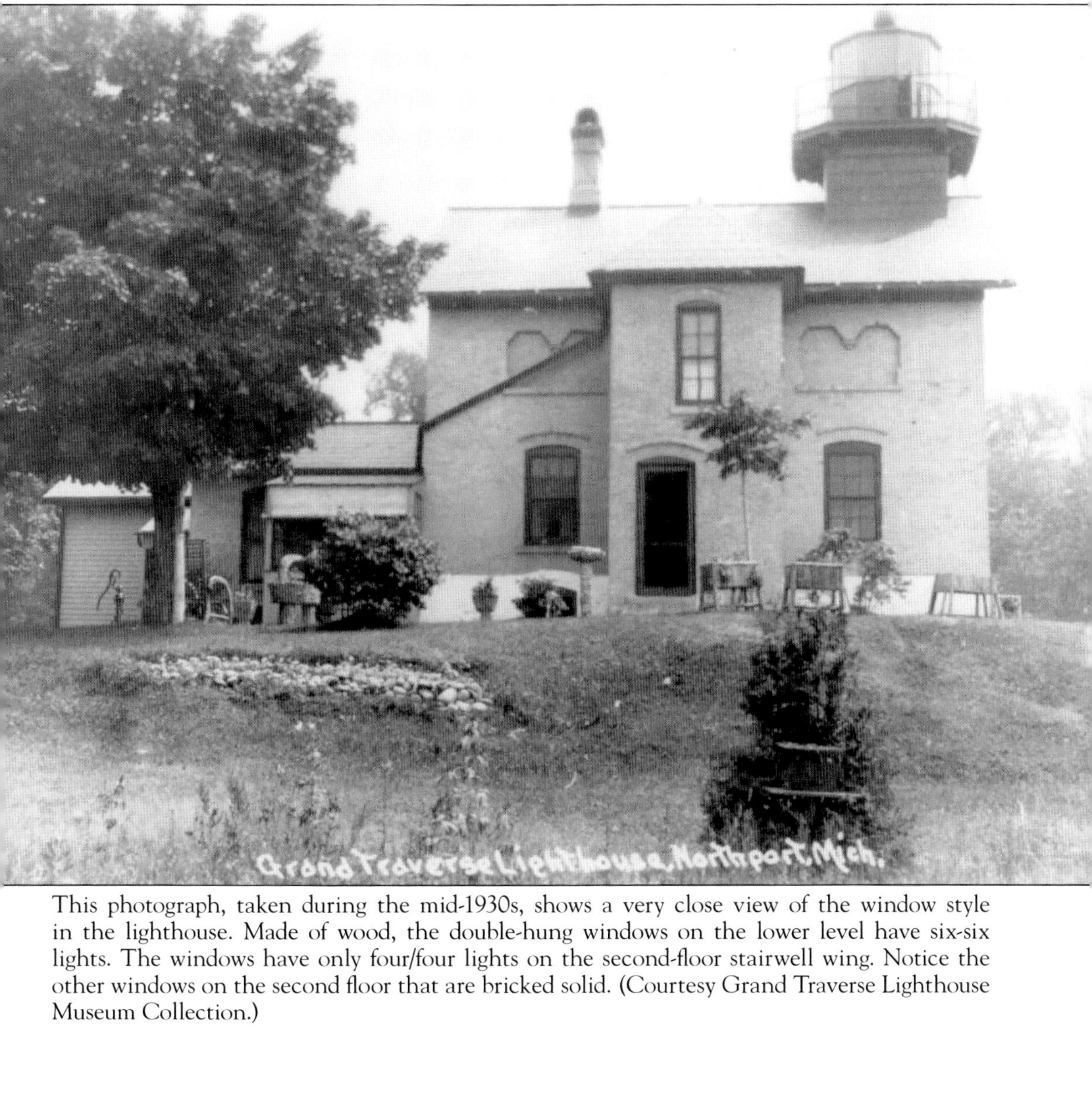

This photograph, taken during the mid-1930s, shows a very close view of the window style in the lighthouse. Made of wood, the double-hung windows on the lower level have six-six lights. The windows have only four/four lights on the second-floor stairwell wing. Notice the other windows on the second floor that are bricked solid. (Courtesy Grand Traverse Lighthouse Museum Collection.)

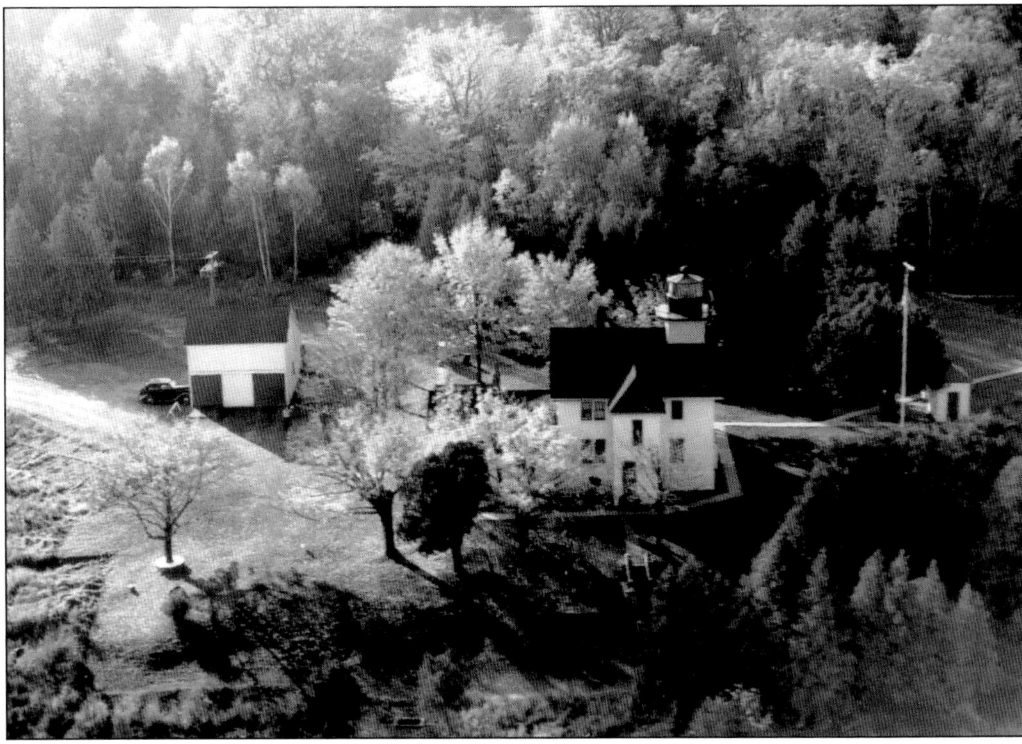

While the lighthouse was operational, there were very few trees in the immediate vicinity surrounding the structures. Any obstruction could hinder the sailors from seeing and identifying the light correctly and confirming their position on the lake. The existing trees included pine, cedar, and maple. (Courtesy U.S. Coast Guard Historian's Office.)

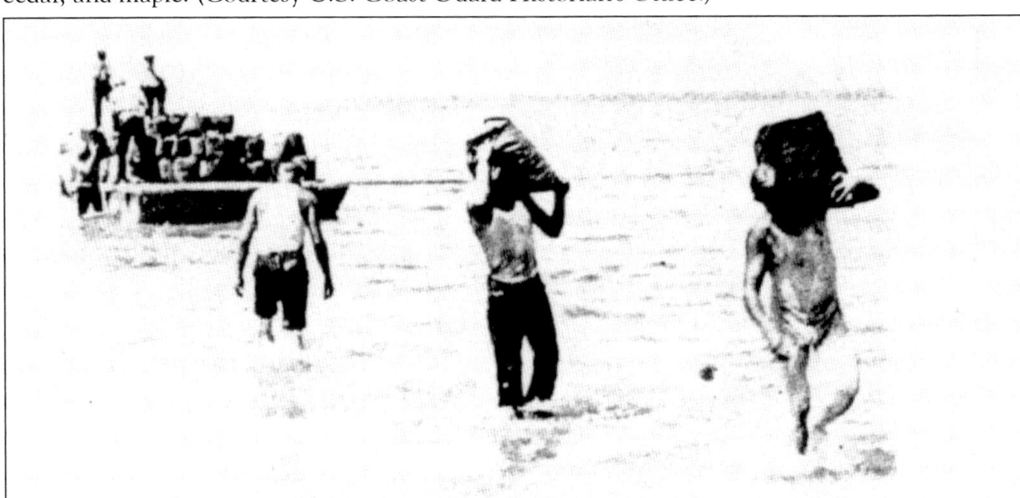

The lighthouse tender *Hyacinth* is anchored east of Grand Traverse Light. Don McCormick, son of keeper James McCormick, is the man in the middle carrying a container of coal. The U.S. Lighthouse Service provided supplies to the light station via lighthouse tenders that visited every three months. The coal was loaded onto a small scow and then pulled by the launch toward shore. The crew then carried the coal in small containers to its final destination. (Courtesy Grand Traverse Lighthouse Museum Collection.)

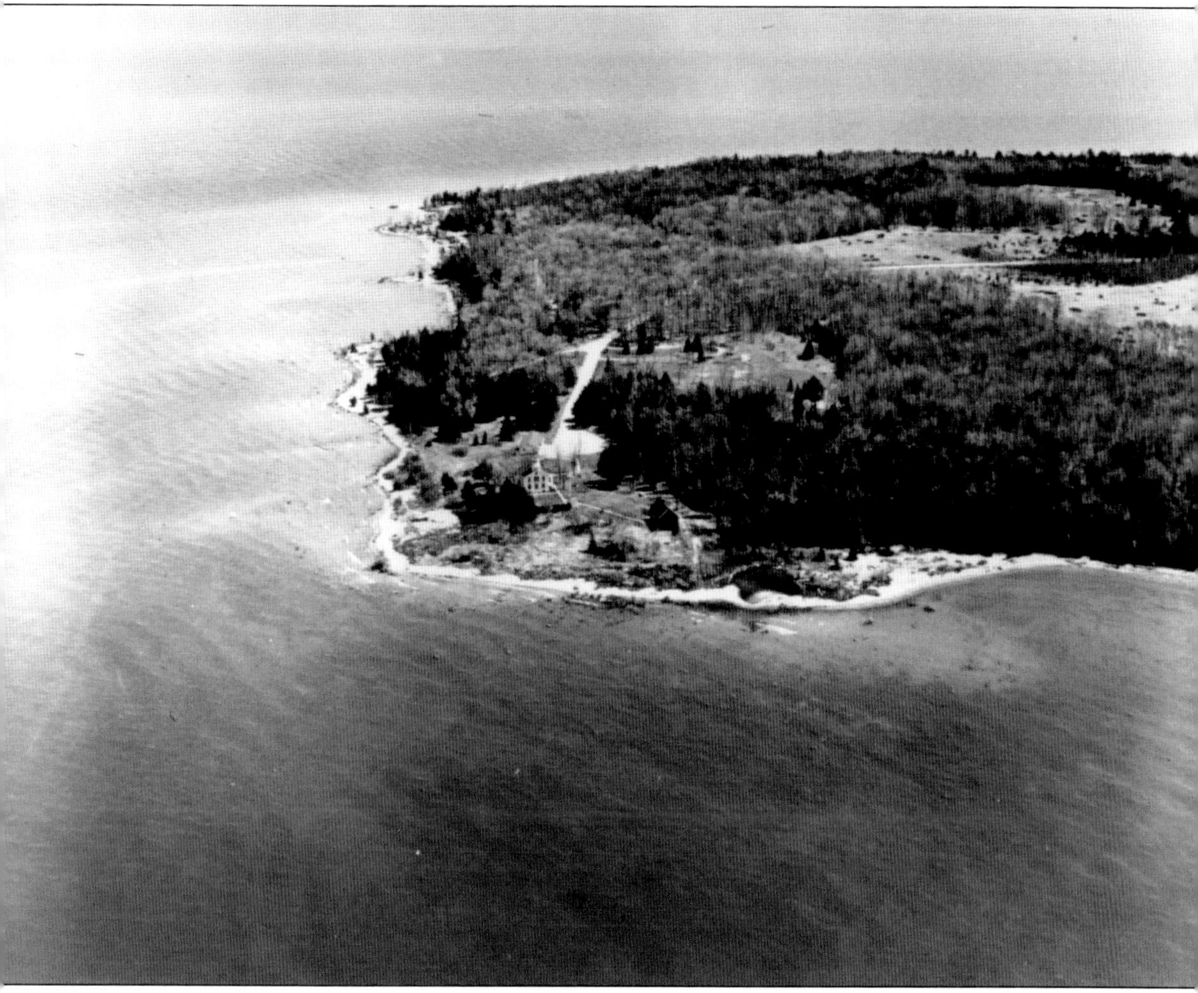

The writing at the bottom of this photograph is cut off. It should read, "Cathead Point Light House, Northport, Mich." Grand Traverse Light was often called Cathead Point Light by the mariners in the early years. This nickname caught on because the landmark of Cathead Point is only five miles to the southwest of the lighthouse. (Courtesy Archives of Michigan, Negative 10378.)

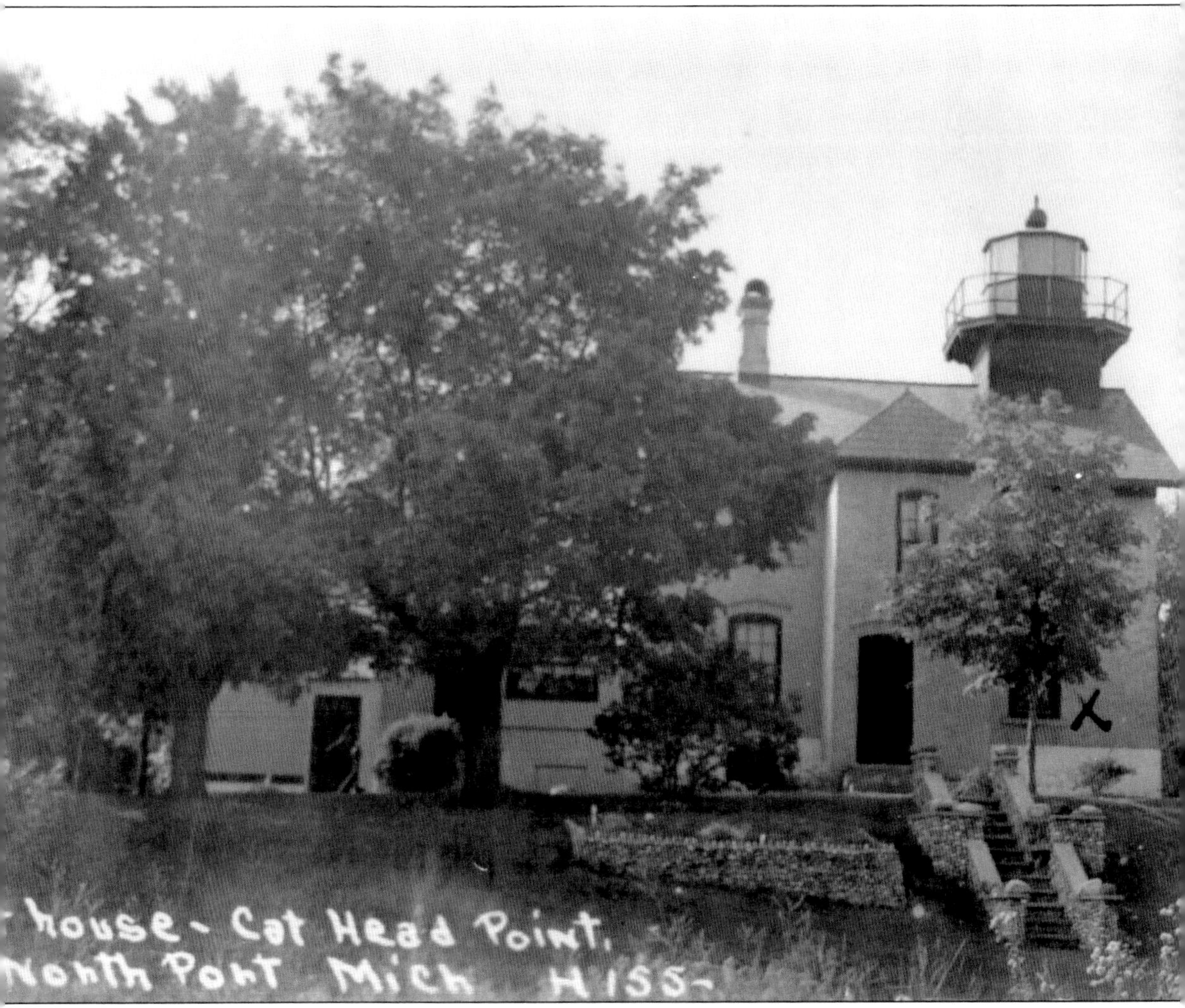

Northport resident Guyles Dame took this photograph in 1925. Dame was an avid photographer and documented many things in the area. He once operated a radio repair shop in Northport and was the first in town to receive radio broadcasts and signals. The Dame family made many important contributions to Northport and its history. During this time, Dame's brother Oscar was an assistant keeper and the *x* probably identifies his bedroom. When the building was first constructed, this window was actually a door and was the original entrance into the structure. (Courtesy Grand Traverse Lighthouse Museum Collection.)

Families were an important part of life at the Grand Traverse Light. Pictured in this photograph are the grandchildren of assistant keeper Guy Patterson. Evelyn Paton is sitting on the hill and her brother Delmer Paton is running up near the lighthouse. (Courtesy Grand Traverse Lighthouse Museum Collection.)

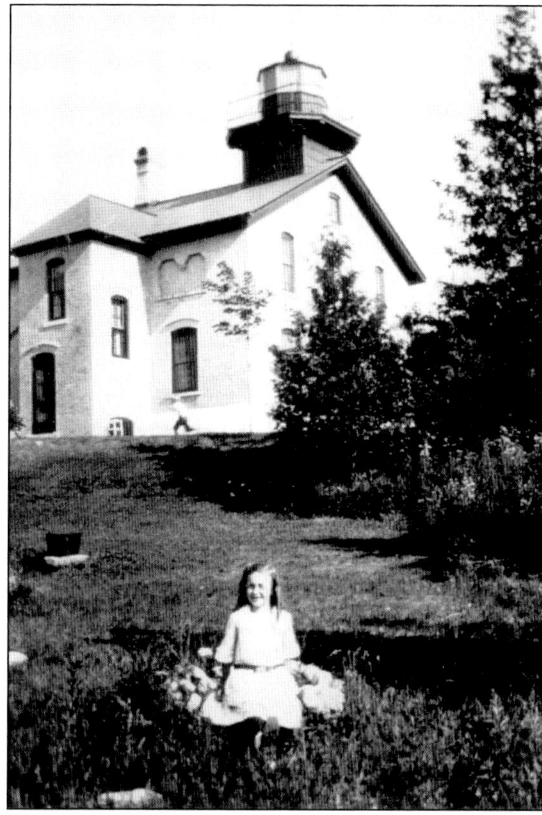

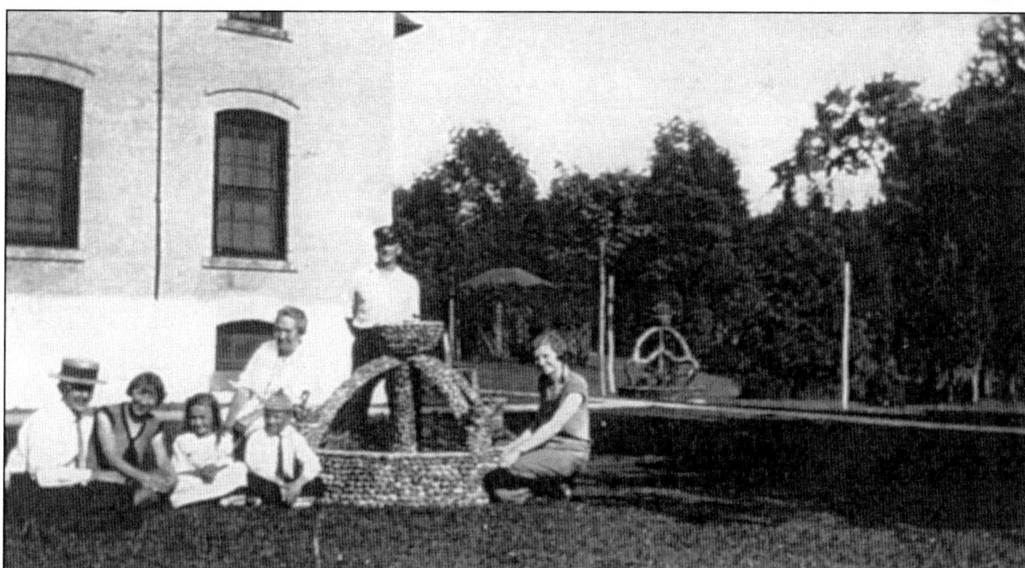

This is a Patterson family photograph taken in 1925. Included are assistant keeper Guy Patterson and his wife, Mina, to his left, as well as their grandchildren Evelyn and Delmer, who lived with them at the lighthouse. The others are visitors who stopped by during the day. The stone planter was built by assistant keeper Reinhold Johnson in 1920. (Courtesy Grand Traverse Lighthouse Museum Collection.)

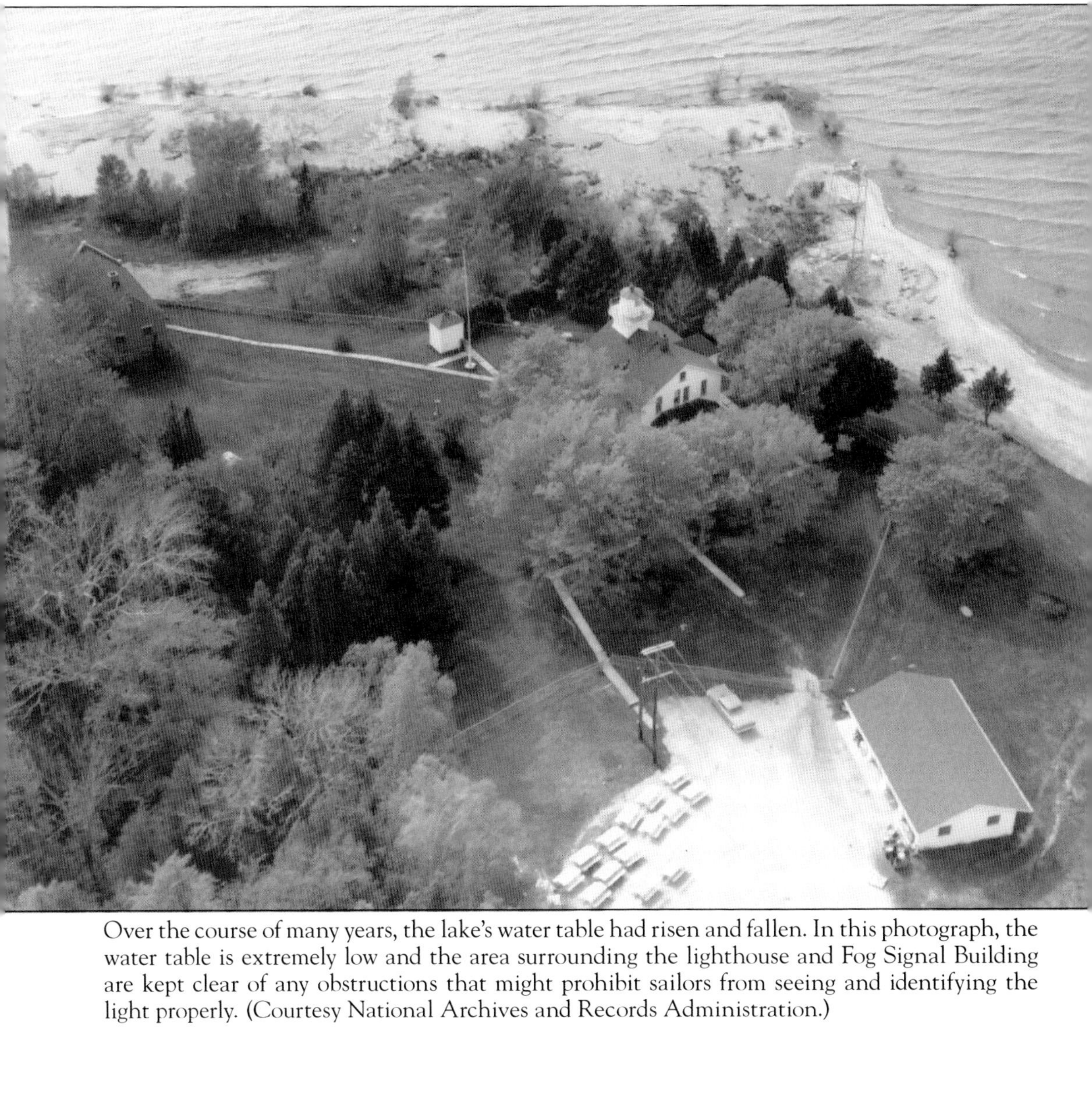

Over the course of many years, the lake's water table had risen and fallen. In this photograph, the water table is extremely low and the area surrounding the lighthouse and Fog Signal Building are kept clear of any obstructions that might prohibit sailors from seeing and identifying the light properly. (Courtesy National Archives and Records Administration.)

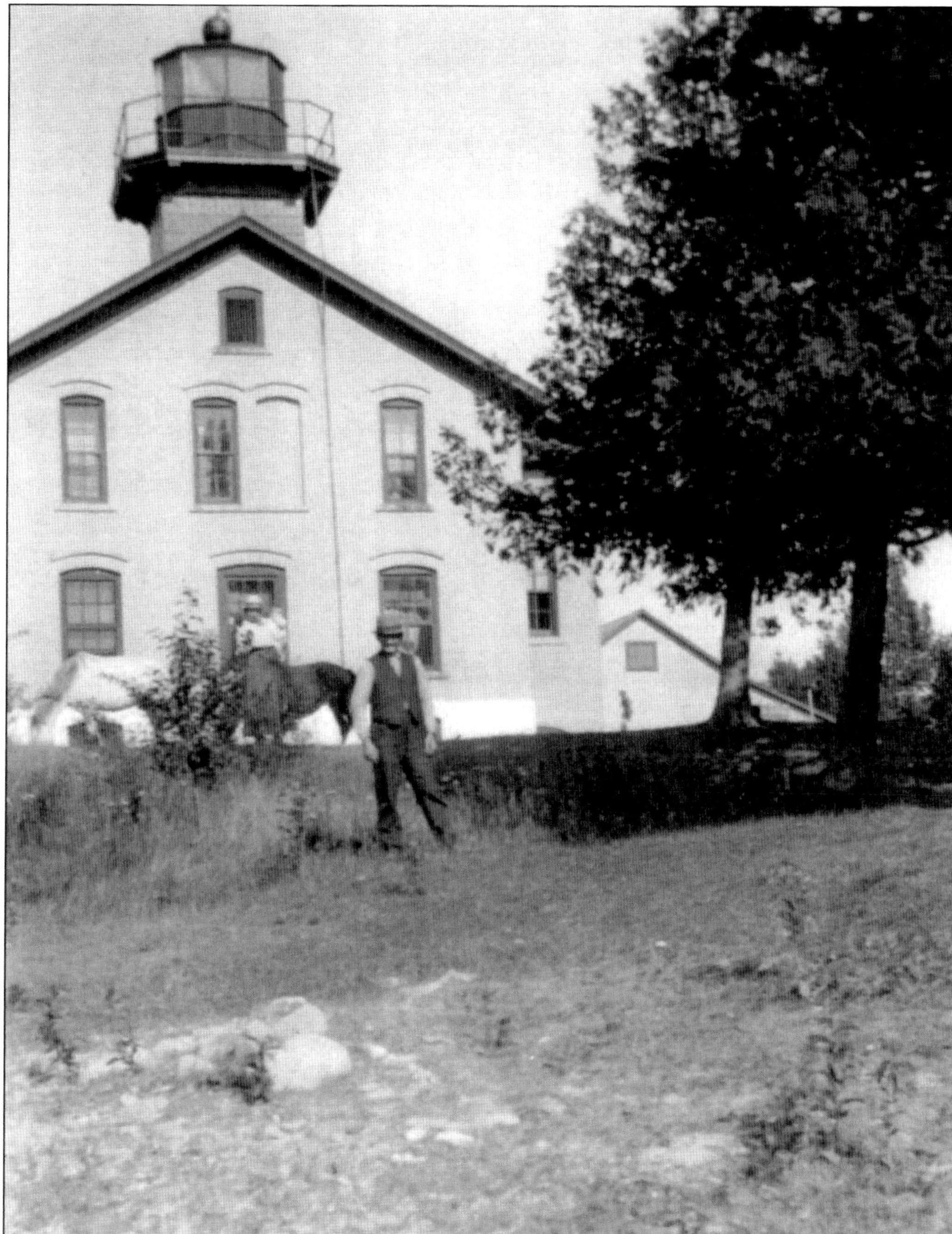

This interesting photograph shows a man with two horses standing next to the lighthouse. This is probably a local resident visiting on a warm summer's day. The McCormick children often tell the story of having to walk about three quarters of a mile to catch the horse-drawn school bus. The winter school bus (a sleigh) had two sets of runners. In the dead of winter, hot bricks or soap stones wrapped in burlap were placed on top of the straw on the floor to keep it warm. (Courtesy Grand Traverse Lighthouse Museum Collection.)

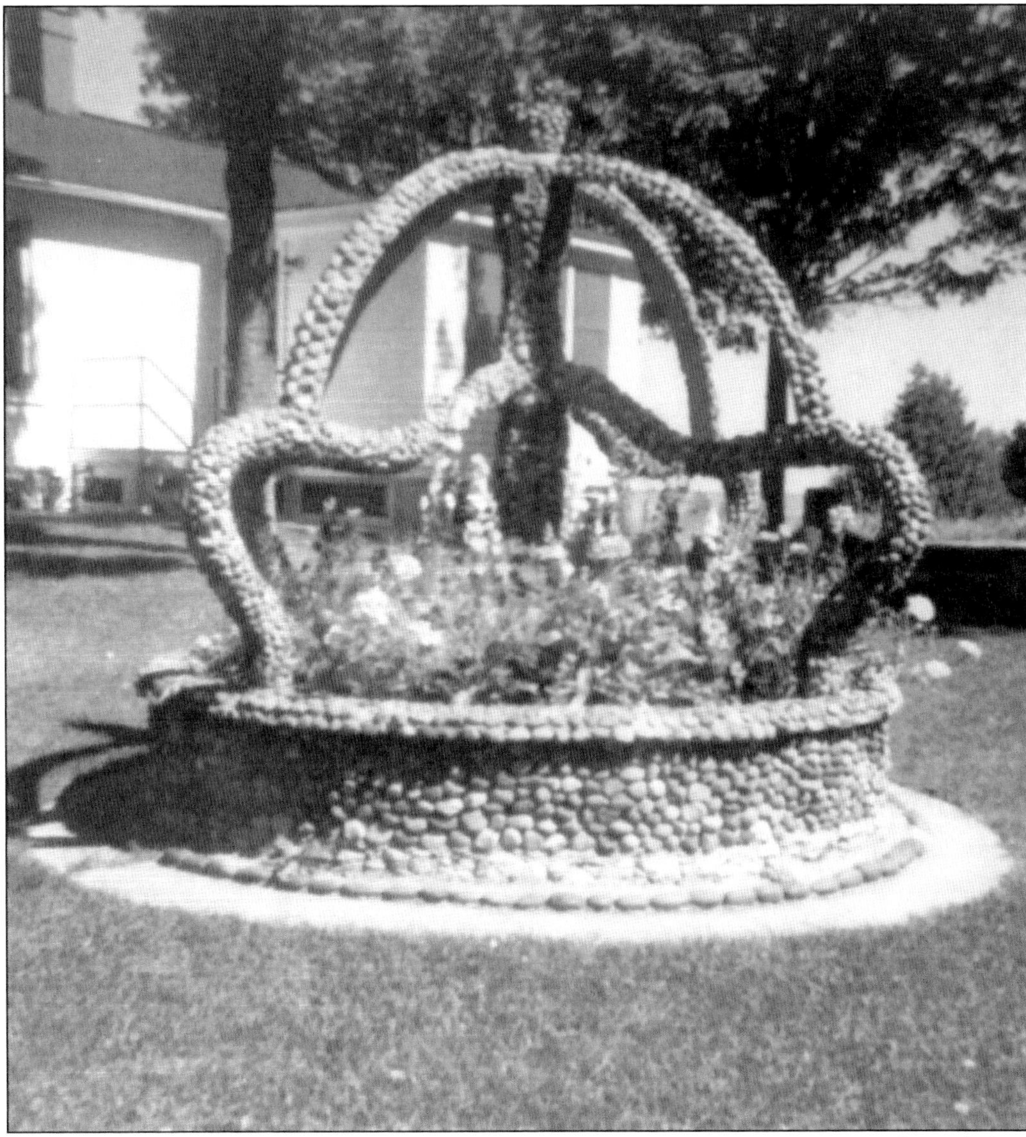

Keeper James McCormick built this stone crown structure in 1926. Rocks were collected along the shoreline by the family. During the winter months when time permitted, McCormick constructed this structure in pieces in the basement of the lighthouse. Underneath the rocks and mortar is a steel piece that gives it a crown-shaped form. Freezing and thawing over the last 80 years have caused the rocks and mortar to fall away from the steel piece. (Courtesy Grand Traverse Lighthouse Museum Collection.)

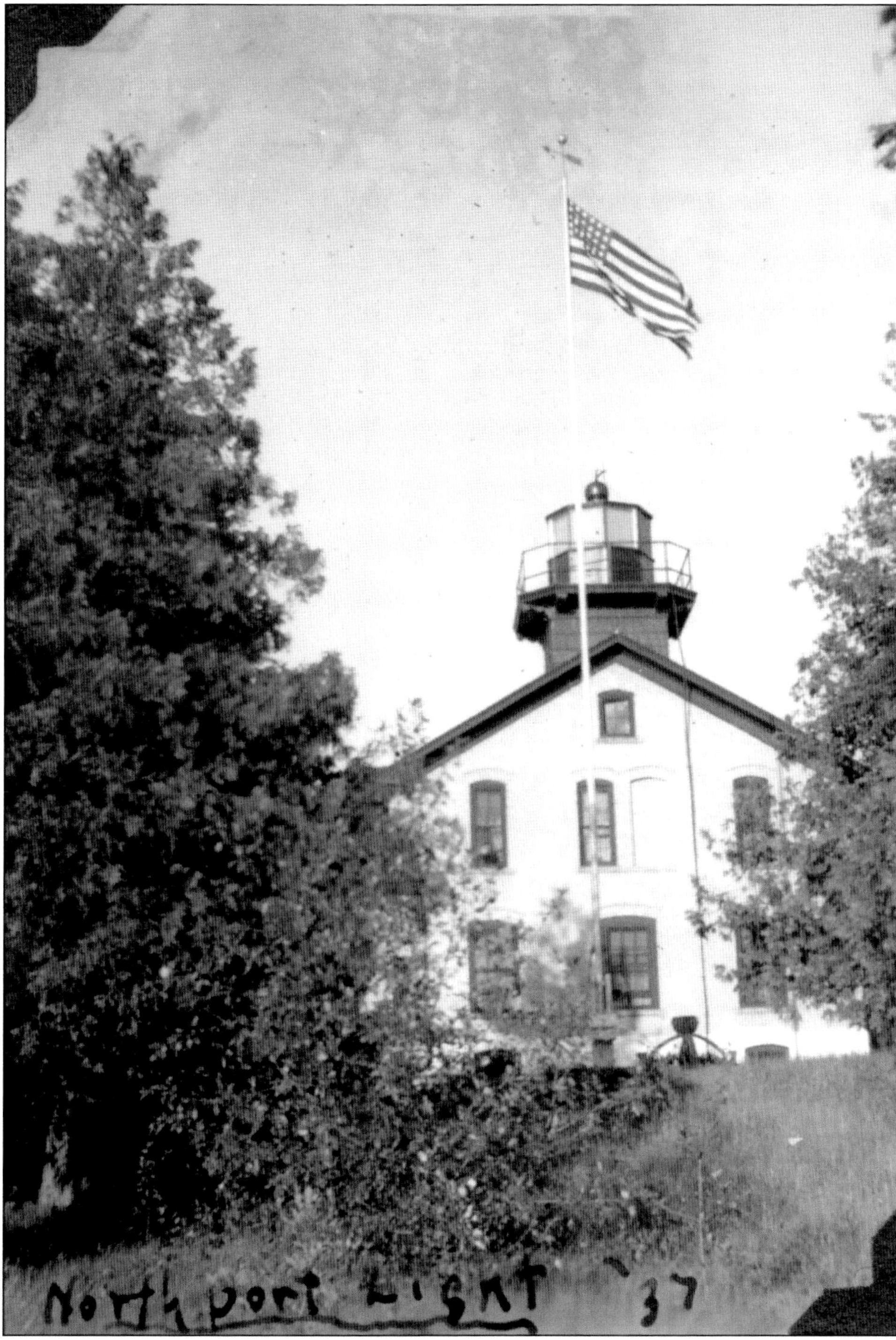

This photograph shows the American flag flying proudly on the west side of the lighthouse. The flagpole was erected by keeper James McCormick. The duty of raising and lowering the flag was important. This tradition exists today with the volunteer lighthouse keepers who stay and maintain the Grand Traverse Light. (Courtesy Grand Traverse Lighthouse Museum Collection.)

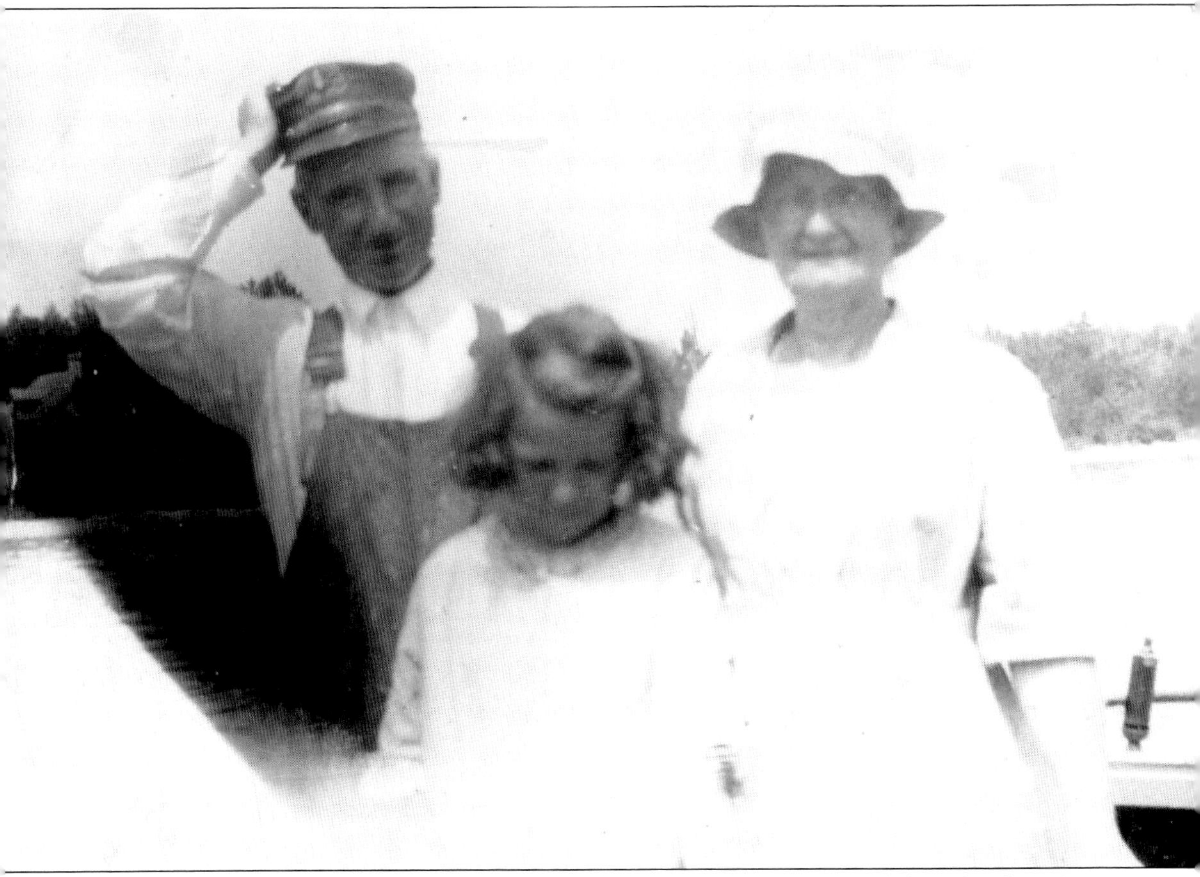

This rare photograph of assistant keeper Oscar Dame, his wife, Ella, and their daughter, Vivian, was donated to the lighthouse museum in 2005. Vivian, the only child of Oscar and Ella, died of heart disease in 1928 at the age of 15. She was always known to have a smile on her face, full of hope that she would soon be well. (Courtesy Grand Traverse Lighthouse Museum Collection.)

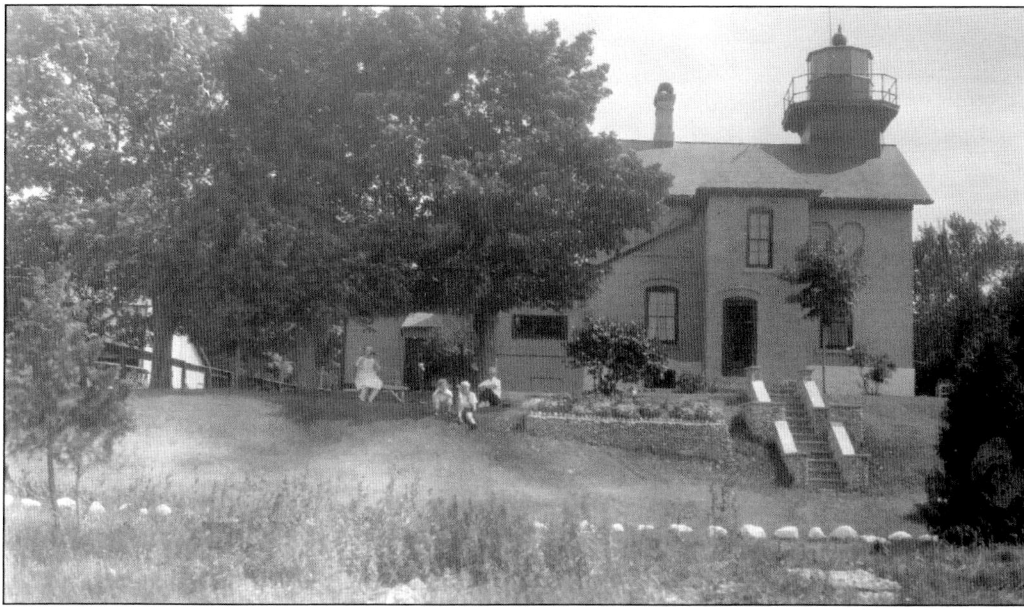

Grand Traverse Light Station was considered a family station. The house was divided into two apartments, one for the keeper and the other for the assistant keeper. Many lighthouse keeper families were large, consisting of six or more children. The McCormick family had 12 children. Many of them grew up to become lighthouse keepers or wives of lighthouse keepers. (Courtesy Grand Traverse Lighthouse Museum Collection.)

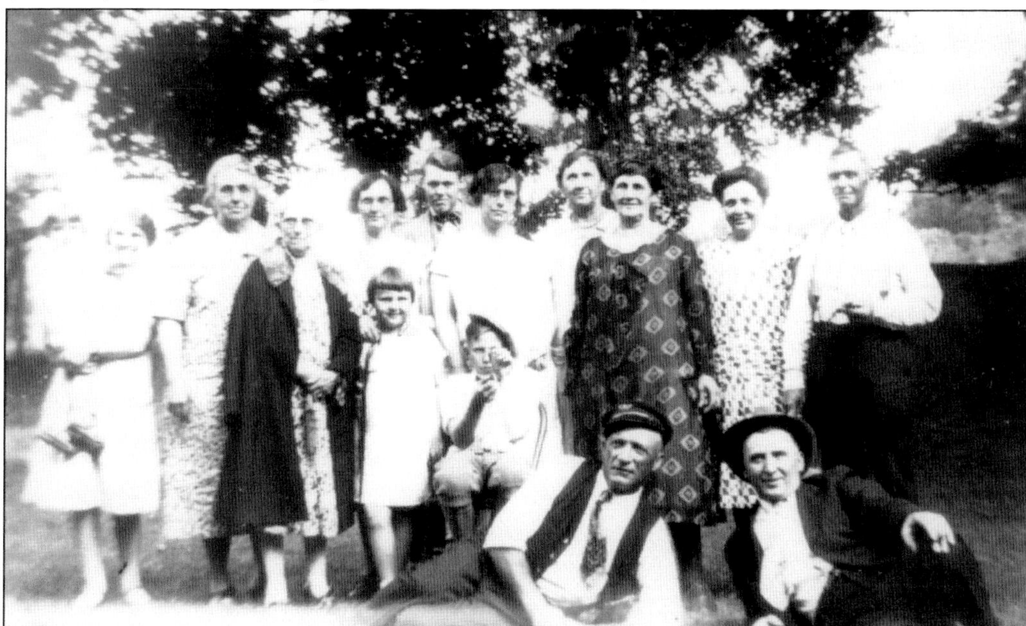

This is the Patterson family reunion on the grounds of the Grand Traverse Lighthouse. Assistant keeper Guy Patterson is sitting in the front with the lighthouse keeper hat and vest. Keepers were required to wear a uniform, whether formal or work related, at all times. The uniform consisted of a coat, vest, trousers, belt, shoes, and cap. (Courtesy Grand Traverse Lighthouse Museum Collection.)

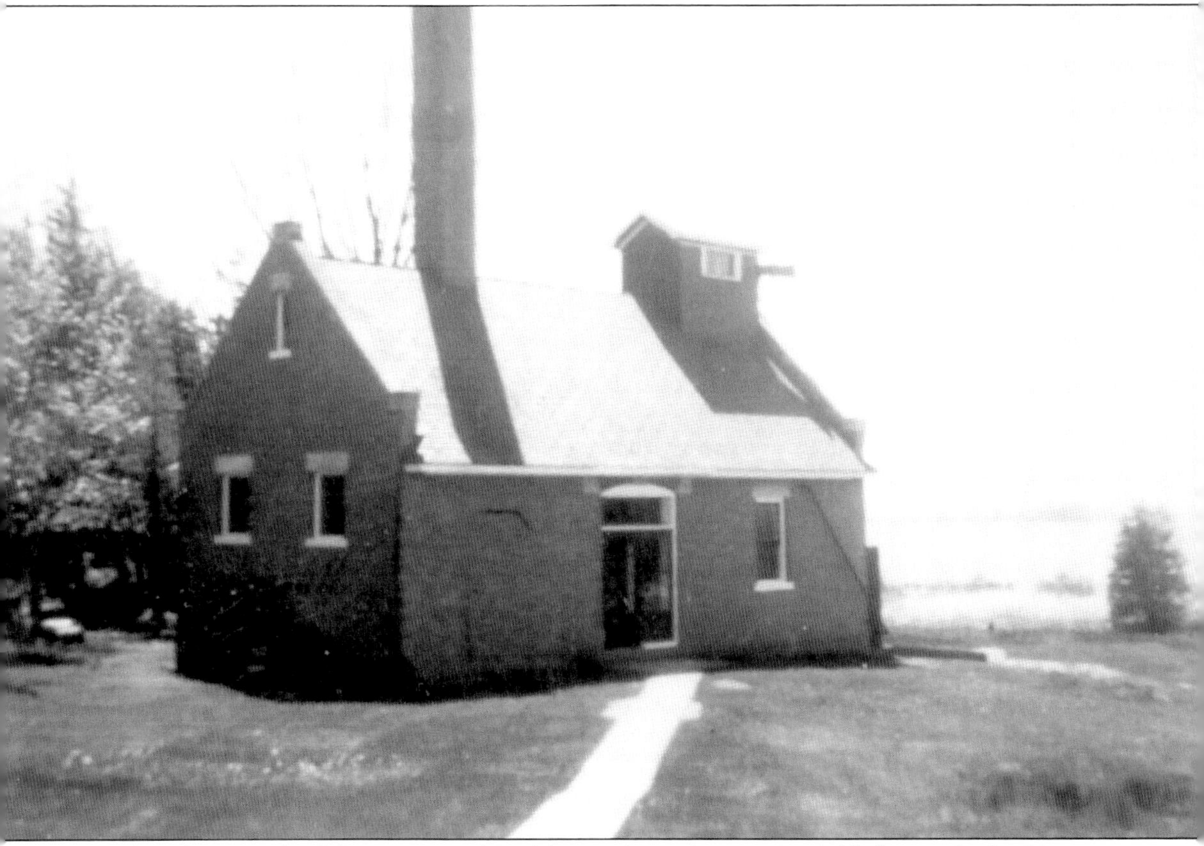

This photograph of the Fog Signal Building is from about 1933. Added atop the building are a very tall chimney and a cupola. Sticking out of the cupola is the Type F air diaphone foghorn. This horn was so loud when blown that it could be heard nine miles away in Northport. It was this signal that replaced the steam whistles. It used compressed air run by a diesel-powered air compressor. (Courtesy Grand Traverse Lighthouse Museum Collection.)

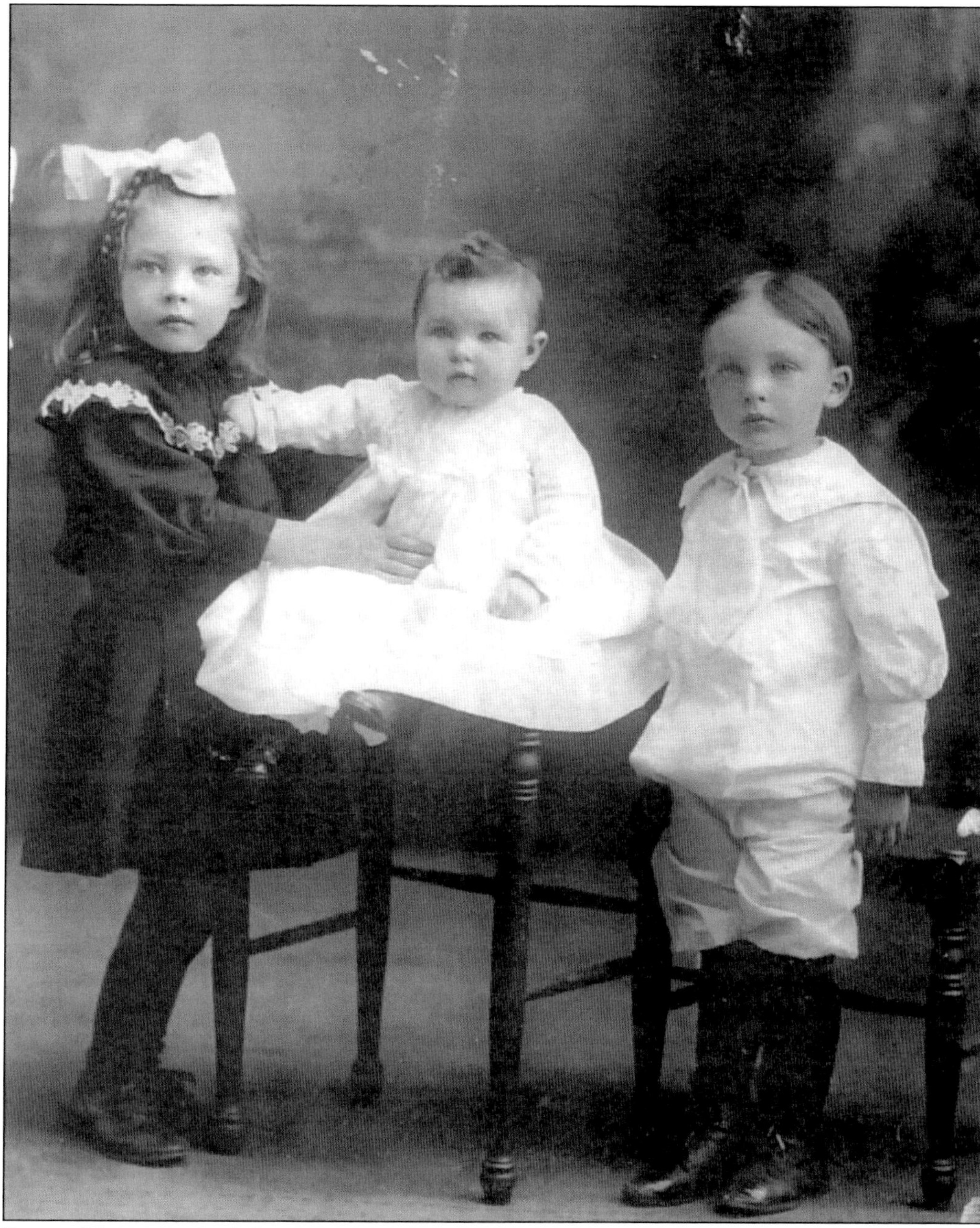

Pictured here are 3 of the 12 McCormick children. From left to right are Violet M., Justine, and James D. Violet married Irving Carlson, who was a fisherman in Leland before he joined the U.S. Lighthouse Service. He served at Poverty Island Light, South Fox Light Station, and Skillagalee Island (Ile Aux Galets Light) in Lake Michigan. Justine married Mike Maclosky, who worked for Continental Motors in Muskegon, where he built engines and was a sailor. They lived in Muskegon. James worked at the Shingle Mill on South Fox Island. He joined the U.S. Coast Guard and was stationed in Frankfort for four years. He moved to Muskegon to work for Continental Motors before coming home to Northport, where he was a fisherman on the tug *Major*. (Courtesy Grand Traverse Lighthouse Museum Collection.)

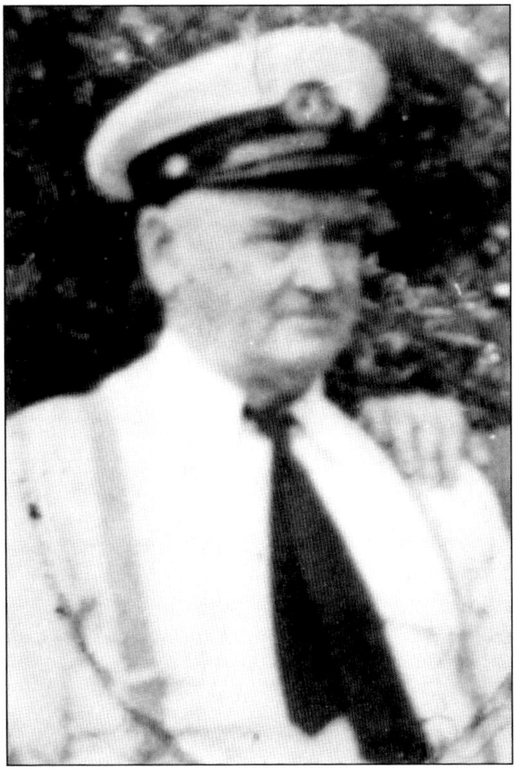

James McCormick was the keeper of the Grand Traverse Lighthouse from 1922 to 1938. He was a career man, having also served at Poverty Island Light, South Fox Island Light Station, and Beaver Island Light Station. It is rumored that when he retired in 1938, the federal government offered him the Mission Point Lighthouse, which was closed in 1933, for $1. He declined their offer. (Courtesy Grand Traverse Lighthouse Museum Collection.)

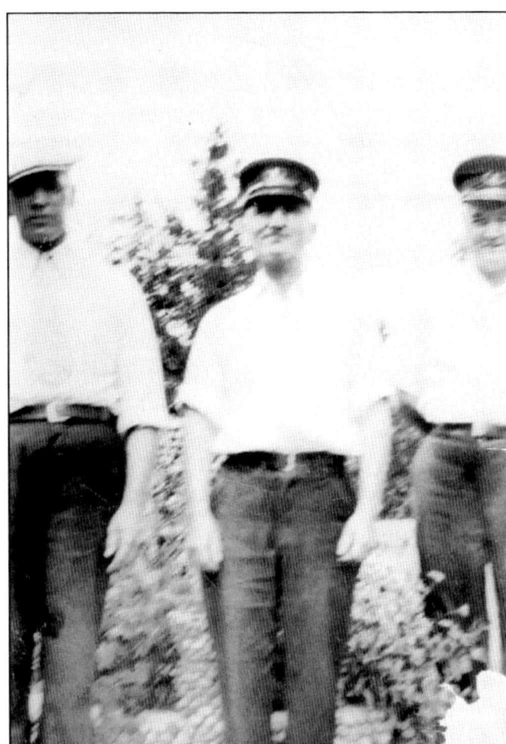

Here are, from left to right, Nels Nelson, Oscar Dame, and McCormick at Grand Traverse Lighthouse. In 1931, the U.S. Secretary of Commerce authorized the disposal of 31.01 acres of the 45-acre lighthouse reservation to the State of Michigan for the sole purpose of a public park. The United States retained 14 acres, which included the lighthouse and its surrounding property for use as aids to navigation.

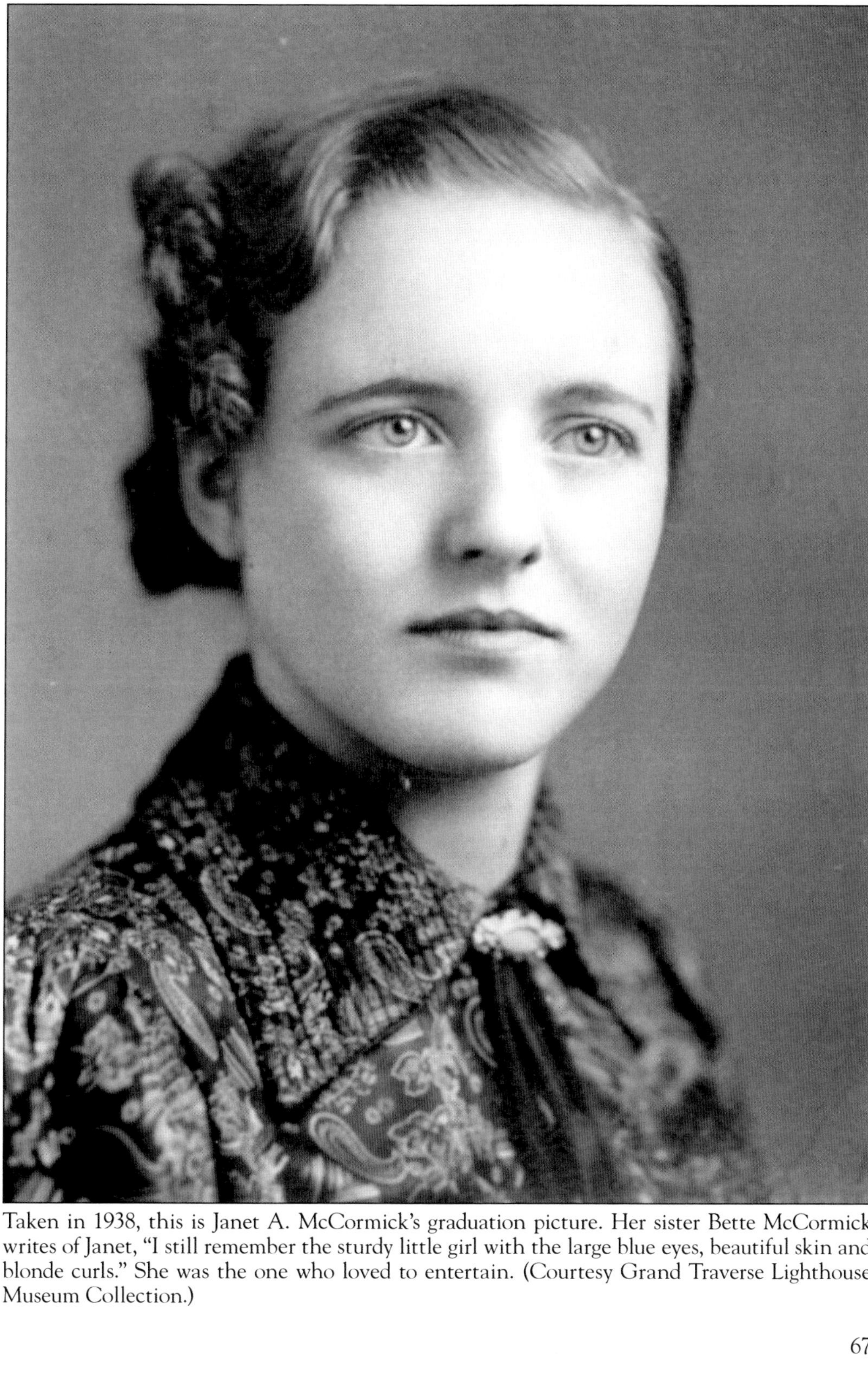

Taken in 1938, this is Janet A. McCormick's graduation picture. Her sister Bette McCormick writes of Janet, "I still remember the sturdy little girl with the large blue eyes, beautiful skin and blonde curls." She was the one who loved to entertain. (Courtesy Grand Traverse Lighthouse Museum Collection.)

Ode To A Lighthouse Keeper

They called him James when he came to this place,
Nee McCormick, to David and Grace.
In 1900, he took him a wife,
A wee little lass to share in his life.

There at the Beavers to the lighthouse they came,
That Jim and Mary, for that was her name.
They worked & they toiled from morning til night,
She tended the family, while he kept the light.

Many children they reared...one, two, three, four,
Then there were six, and then six more.
All took to the water like ducks to the sea,
They grew to adulthood by the rock and the lee.

Jim was kept busy keeping signal and light,
He'd toil in the day and yet half the night.
Then in the morning in the light of half dawn,
Out to the garden, at once he was gone.

He fished and he sailed and tales he could tell,
Of his shipwreck at sea, and the big buoy bell.
For forty-eight hours he drifted in shivering cold,
Snatched from the water by a big freighter bold.

He blew the fog signal in the days and the nights,
For thirty-four years he tended the lights.
He polished the brass and the lenses he shined,
He filled all the ledgers and they were signed.

Then came the day when work was no more,
The wind became still; no waves at his door.
But, then the wind blows and the fog rolls in,
There in the lighthouse, I think, there's Mary and Jim.

This poem, "Ode to A Lighthouse Keeper," was written by Janet A. (McCormick) Luczyk.

Grace, the youngest of the 12 McCormick children, is pictured here with her son James (known as Nipper), a grandson to James McCormick. Her sister Bette McCormick recalls Grace as "the lover of all creatures great and small." Grace loved nature and, as a child, sported the deepest tan of all the girls each summer. (Courtesy Grand Traverse Lighthouse Museum Collection.)

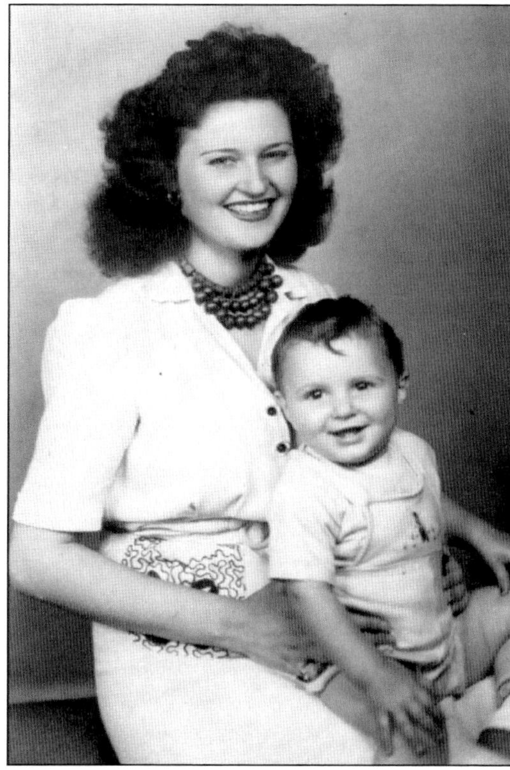

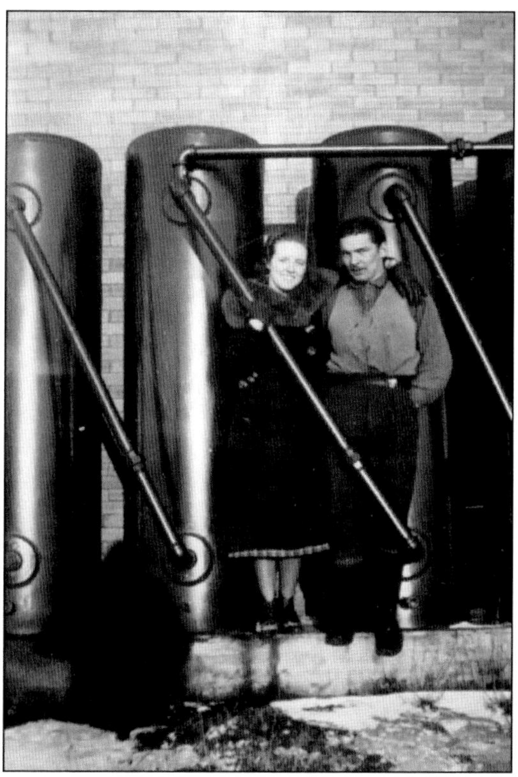

Janet A. McCormick and brother Don McCormick are standing next to the air tanks outside the Fog Signal Building to the west. The air was pressurized in these four tanks and used to blow the Type F air diaphone foghorn that was located inside the building's cupola. The foghorn was used to guide sailors through the fog. (Courtesy Grand Traverse Lighthouse Museum Collection.)

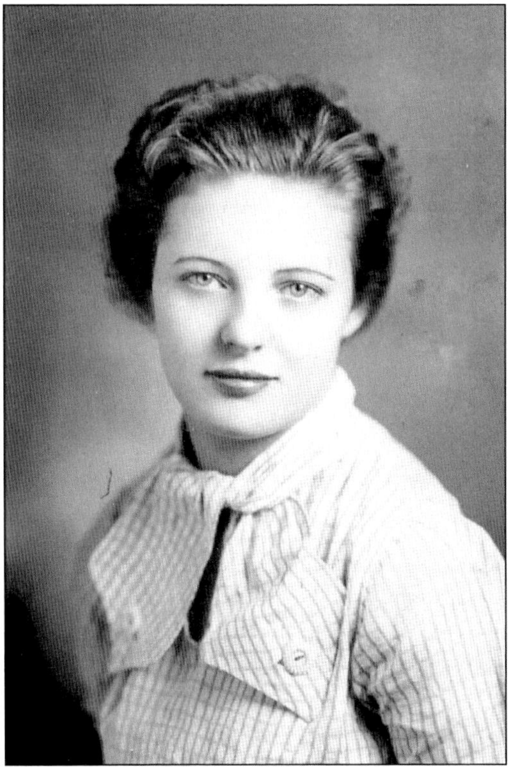

Bette McCormick's graduation picture was taken in October 1934 for her graduation in May 1935. In 1990, Bette authored a book titled, *The Way It Was: Memories of My Childhood at Grand Traverse Lighthouse*, highlighting a keeper's duties and what a typical Christmas was like at the lighthouse. (Courtesy Grand Traverse Lighthouse Museum Collection.)

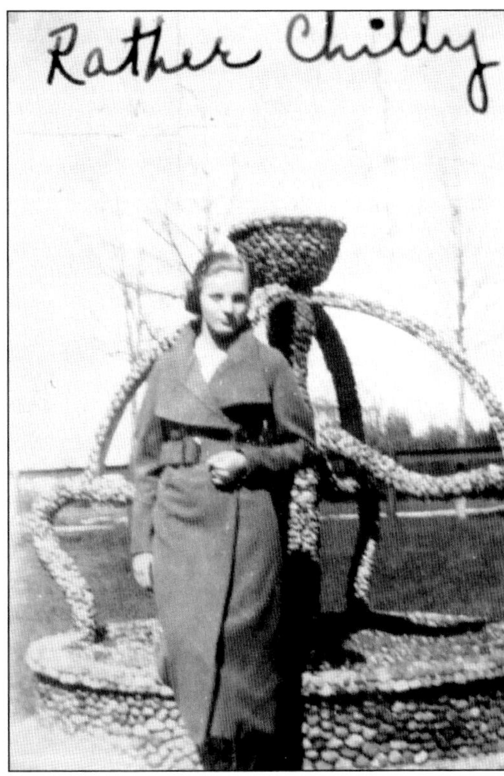

Bette is standing near the crown planter in the 1930s. After she graduated from high school, she lived on South Fox Island with her sister Violet and family at the lighthouse prior to moving to Chicago for a short time. She then moved to Grand Marias to teach, where she met and married Mr. Olli. Together they had one child named Vern. Today she is living in Gwinn.

Here is David Douglas (Doug) McCormick's graduation picture. He graduated from Northport High School in 1934 and was the president of his class. Post graduation, he worked around Northport. In May 1935, he enlisted in the U.S. Coast Guard, where he spent the next 30 years. In 1965, he went to Burlington, Vermont, and was a master on the ferries before going to Wisconsin as a charter boat captain. In 1982, he returned to Traverse City and became involved in the restoration of Grand Traverse Light. (Courtesy Grand Traverse Lighthouse Museum Collection.)

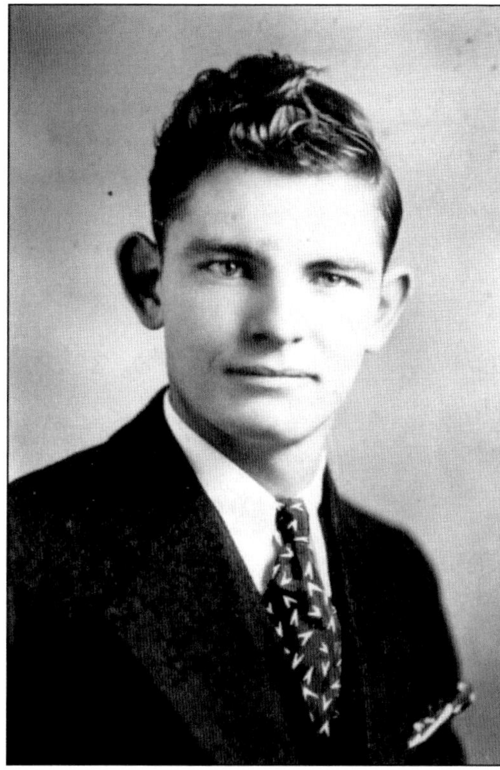

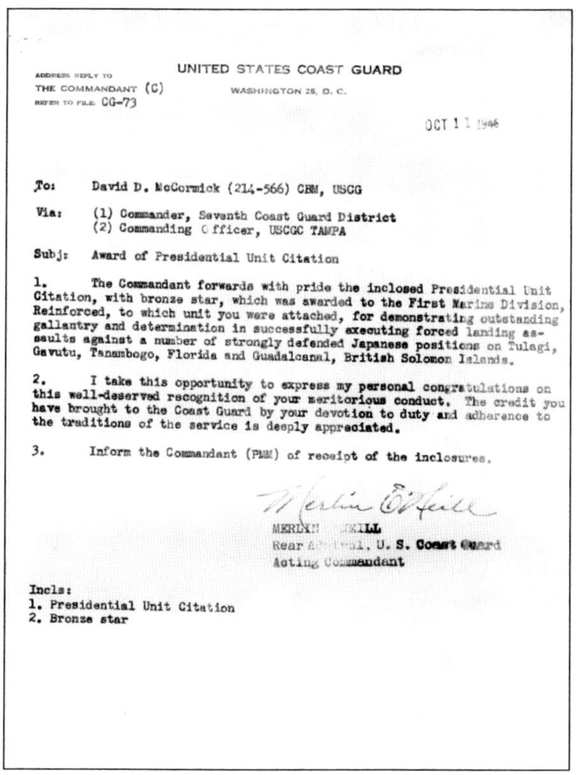

UNITED STATES COAST GUARD

ADDRESS REPLY TO
THE COMMANDANT (C)
REFER TO FILE CG-73

WASHINGTON 25, D. C.

OCT 11 1946

To: David D. McCormick (214-566) CBM, USCG

Via: (1) Commander, Seventh Coast Guard District
(2) Commanding Officer, USCGC TAMPA

Subj: Award of Presidential Unit Citation

1. The Commandant forwards with pride the inclosed Presidential Unit Citation, with bronze star, which was awarded to the First Marine Division, Reinforced, to which unit you were attached, for demonstrating outstanding gallantry and determination in successfully executing forced landing assaults against a number of strongly defended Japanese positions on Tulagi, Gavutu, Tanambogo, Florida and Guadalcanal, British Solomon Islands.

2. I take this opportunity to express my personal congratulations on this well-deserved recognition of your meritorious conduct. The credit you have brought to the Coast Guard by your devotion to duty and adherence to the traditions of the service is deeply appreciated.

3. Inform the Commandant (PMM) of receipt of the inclosures.

Merlin O'Neill

MERLIN [illegible]ILL
Rear Ad[illegible]al, U. S. Coast Guard
Acting Commandant

Incls:
1. Presidential Unit Citation
2. Bronze star

During Doug McCormick's tenure in the U.S. Coast Guard, World War II broke out, and the Coast Guard was temporarily absorbed into the U.S. Navy. Doug was sent oversees to fight against the Japanese. In 1946, he was awarded the Presidential Unit Citation and Bronze Star, for demonstrating gallantry and determination in successfully executing forced landing assaults against a number of Japanese positions. (Courtesy Grand Traverse Lighthouse Museum Collection.)

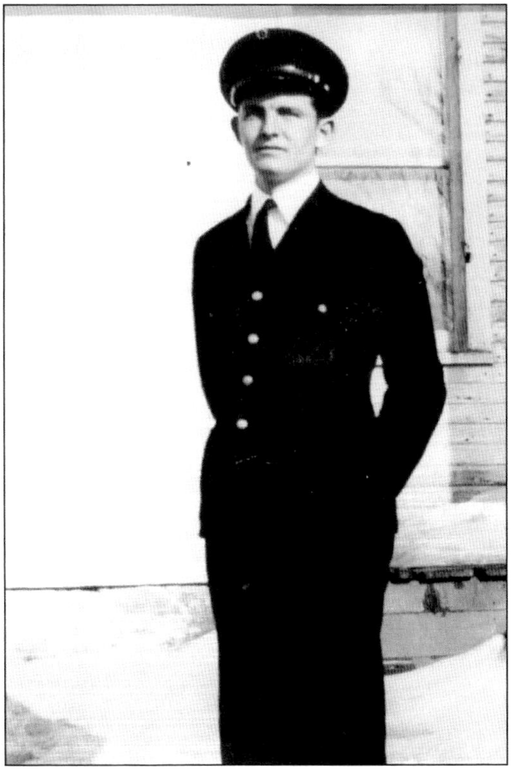

Here is surfman Doug McCormick on Washington Island in Wisconsin around 1936. To most people, he is known as either Doug or Mac. In 2008, at the age of 94, he still resides in Traverse City. (Courtesy Grand Traverse Lighthouse Museum Collection.)

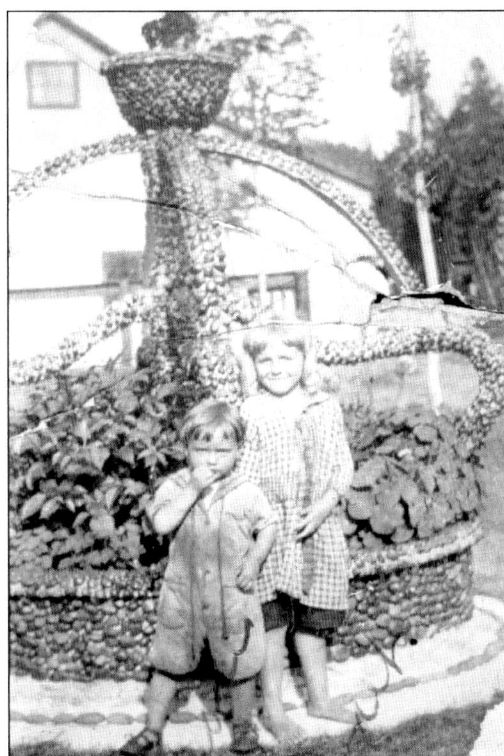

Janet and Grace McCormick are standing near the stone crown planter. Behind them is the 1891 barn. This barn still exists today, relocated just three miles south of the lighthouse on private property. The barn was an important structure on the site with 10 other structures, including the dwelling, oil house, Fog Signal Building, privy, barn, corncrib, hen coop, two laundry sheds, and the old site. (Courtesy Grand Traverse Lighthouse Museum Collection.)

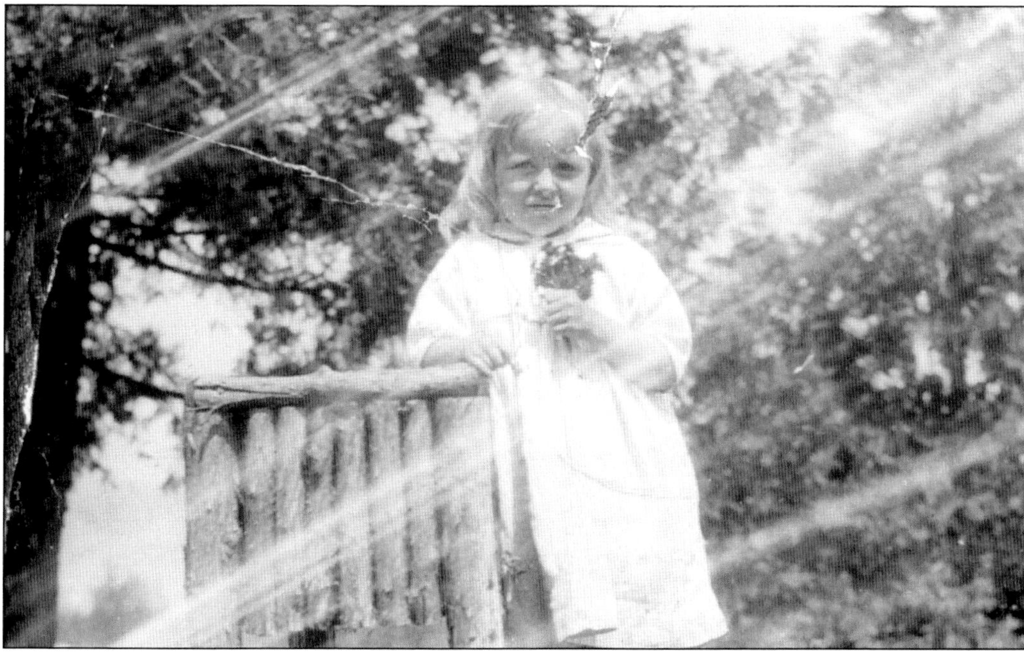

This early photograph of Janet was taken around 1925. She is standing next to the "twig" flower pot. Several of these were located around the lighthouse site during the tenure of keeper James McCormick. It is unknown if he made these flower pots or if they were on site prior to his family's arrival. (Courtesy Grand Traverse Lighthouse Museum Collection.)

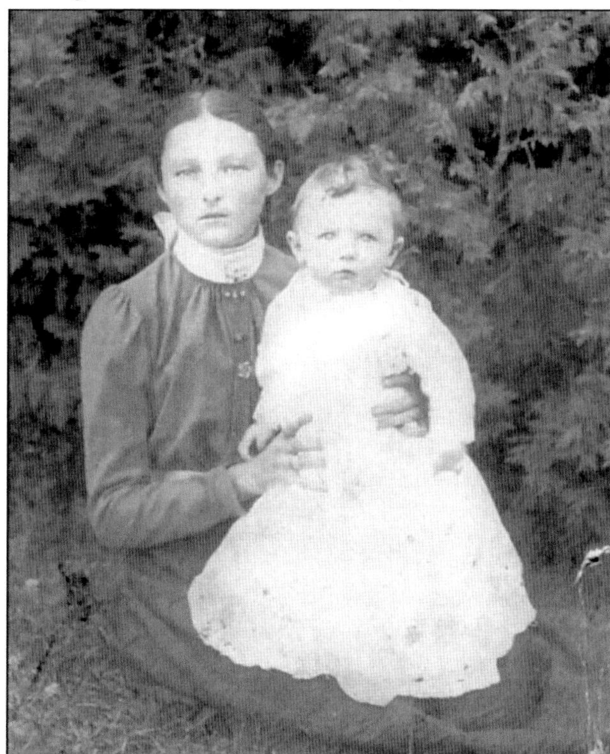

Mary E. (Watcher) McCormick, wife of keeper James McCormick, is shown here with their son Willy John McCormick. She was born in 1880 in Cheboygan to James and Mary Watcher. James Watcher was a lighthouse keeper at Green Island Light in Wisconsin and in Michigan at Squaw Island and Grand Traverse Light. Willy John died in infancy in 1901. Mary E. died in 1959. (Courtesy Grand Traverse Lighthouse Museum Collection.)

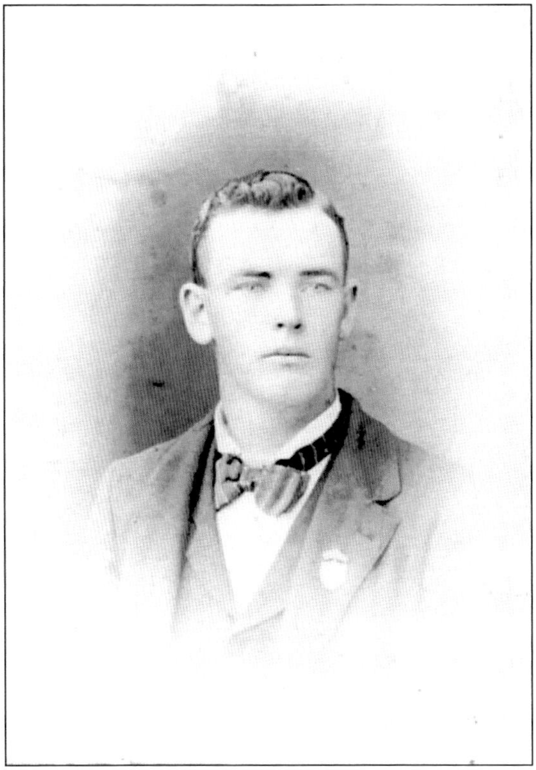

Here is a very early photograph of keeper James McCormick. He was born in Cross Village in 1872 to David and Grace McCormick, who were Scotch-Irish immigrants. He spent 34 years as a lighthouse keeper, retiring at age 65. He died in 1953 and is buried in Muskegon. (Courtesy Grand Traverse Lighthouse Museum Collection.)

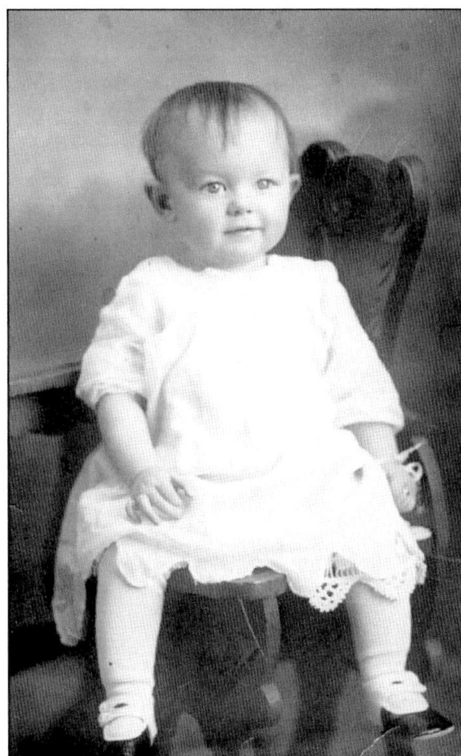

Pictured is Rosalie (Carlson) Stengal as a baby. She was the daughter of Violet (McCormick) and Irving Carlson and was the granddaughter of keeper James. Rosalie was the third baby born at the Grand Traverse Lighthouse. She was born in the southwest bedroom of the lighthouse, which was the bedroom of keeper James and his wife, Mary. Rosalie passed away December 21, 1999, and is buried in Lansing, Illinois. (Courtesy Grand Traverse Lighthouse Museum Collection.)

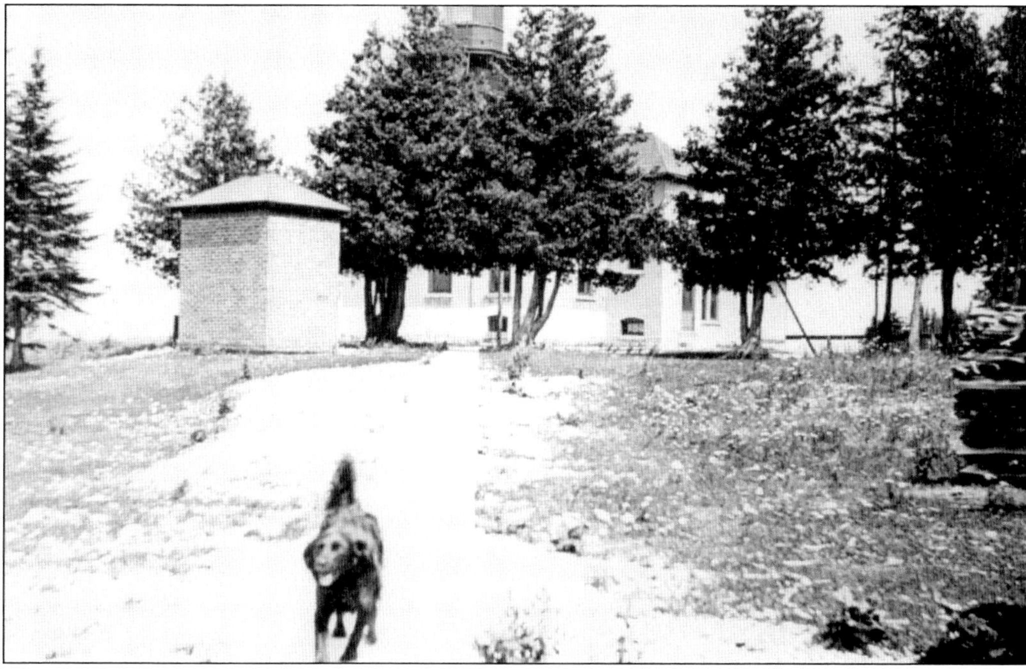

This is keeper James's dog Laddie, running toward the Fog Signal Building just southwest of the lighthouse (in the background). Laddie is buried in the keeper's lighthouse uniform in Stronack. (Courtesy Grand Traverse Lighthouse Museum Collection.)

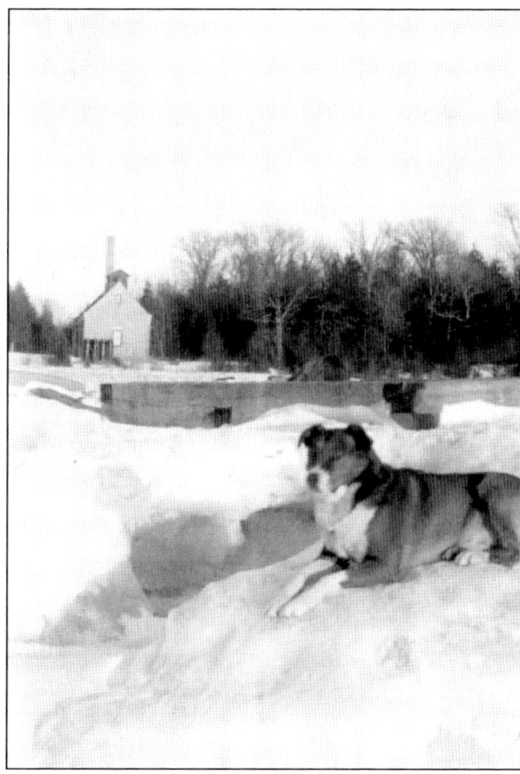

Dogs were common mascots of lighthouse stations. Here is Jack out on the ice caves that formed along the lake's shoreline each winter. The Fog Signal Building in the background means Jack was on a big westerly adventure. (Courtesy Grand Traverse Lighthouse Museum Collection.)

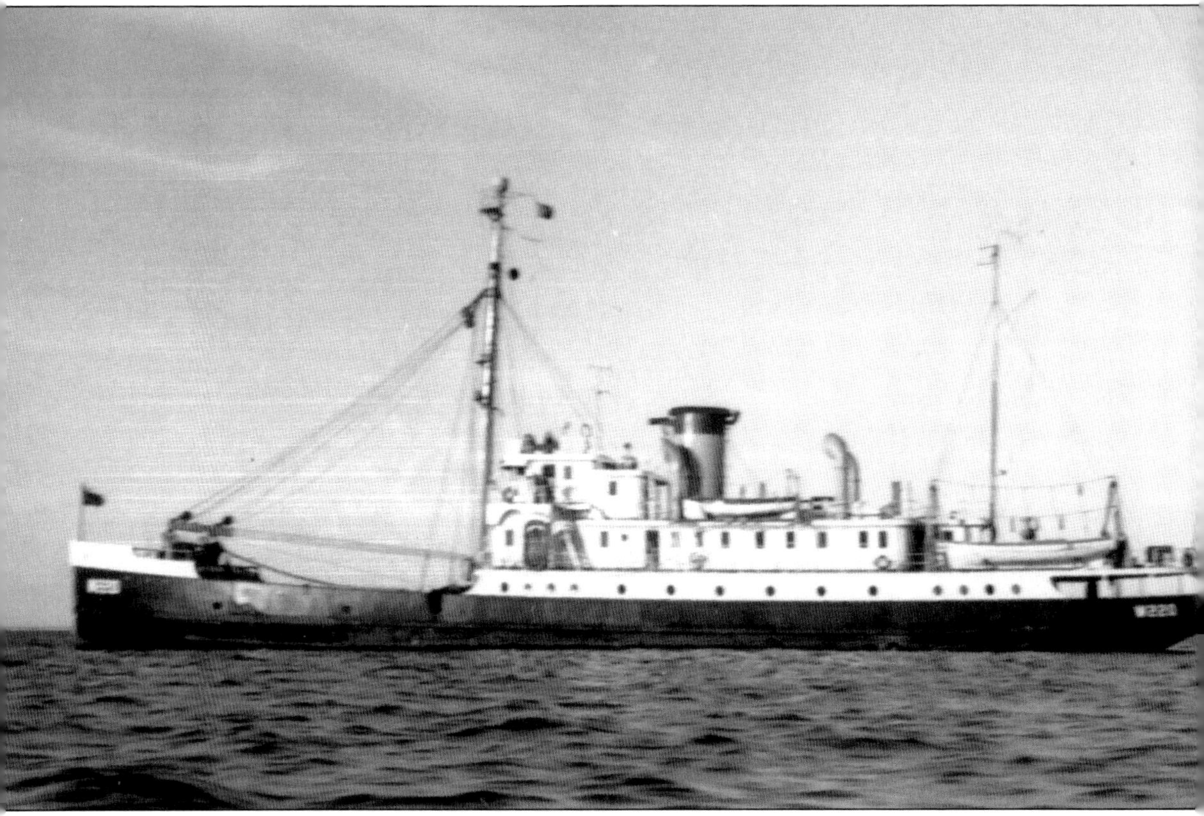

The U.S. Lighthouse Service tender *Hollyhock* is at anchor in Milwaukee. The *Hollyhock* was part of the Hollyhock class of 1937. It was originally constructed by Defoe Boat and Motor Works of Bay City and launched on March 24, 1937. The cost was $347,800. The vessel had a complement of 74 men. (Courtesy Grand Traverse Lighthouse Museum Collection.)

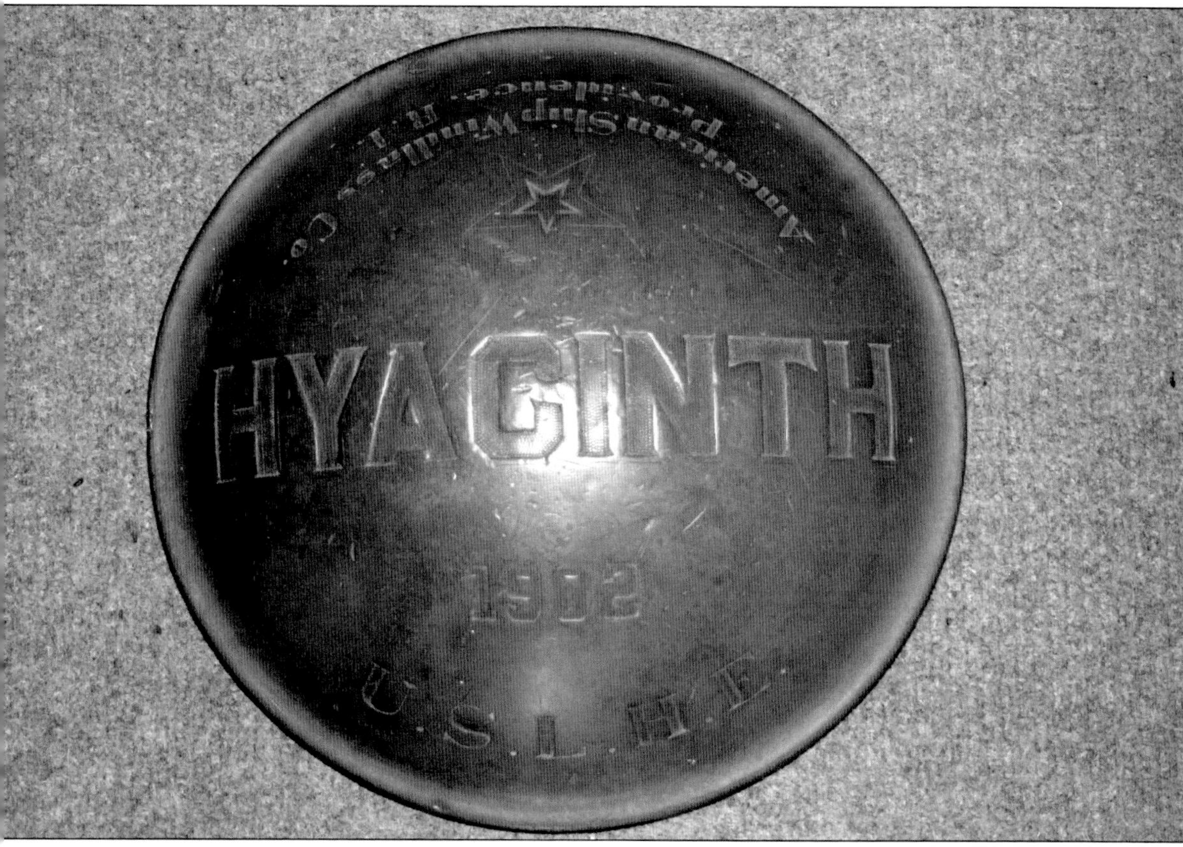

Here is the lighthouse tender *Hyacinth* capstan cover. The *Hyacinth*, *Hollyhock*, and *Sumac* were some of the lighthouse tenders that frequented Grand Traverse Light every three months, bringing supplies and materials needed to maintain the light station. Items might include coal, tools, paint, brushes, and brooms. Food was obtained from Northport or Suttons Bay to the south as well as grown in gardens, hunted, or caught in the lake.

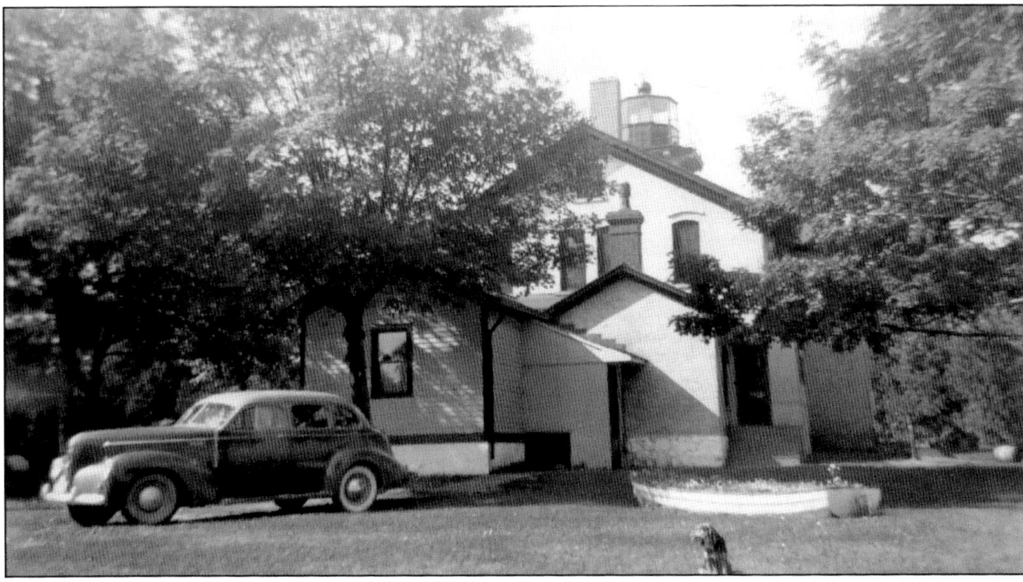

This photograph of the east side of Grand Traverse Light shows the flower boat and a dog in the foreground. The car is keeper James McCormick's Plymouth. Very few pictures show the detail of the additions to the building on the east side like this one. (Courtesy Grand Traverse Lighthouse Museum Collection.)

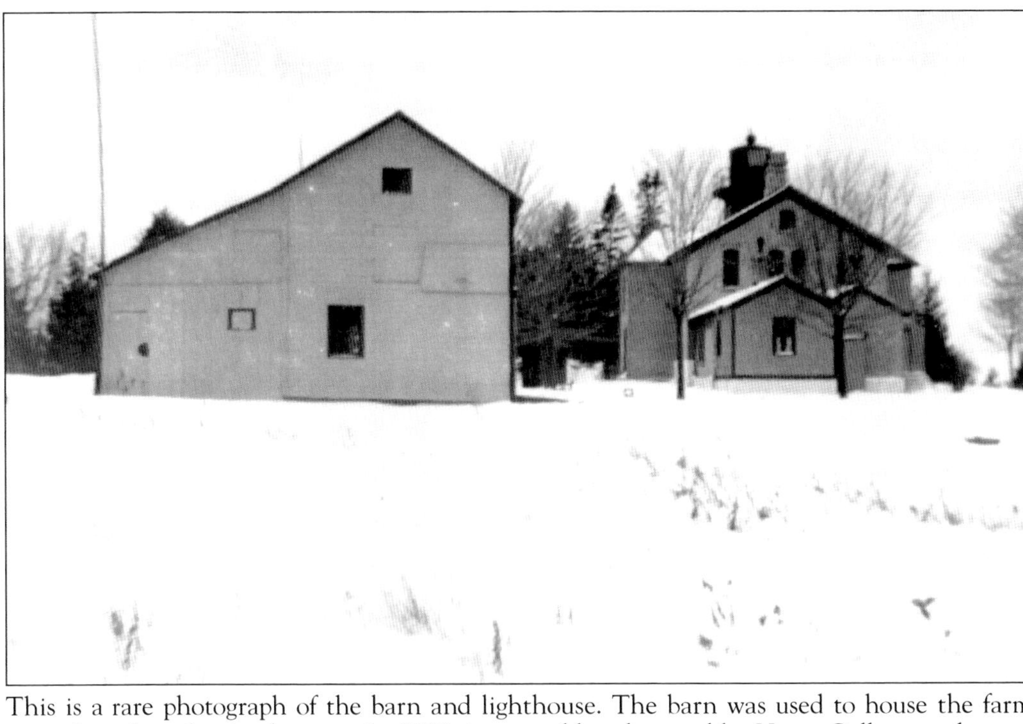

This is a rare photograph of the barn and lighthouse. The barn was used to house the farm animals and garden implements. In 1960, it was sold and moved by Harry Calhoun, who was contracted to build a four-bay garage for the U.S. Coast Guard. The garage still exists today and is used as a gift store and education center for the lighthouse museum.

Four

U.S. Coast Guard 1939–1950

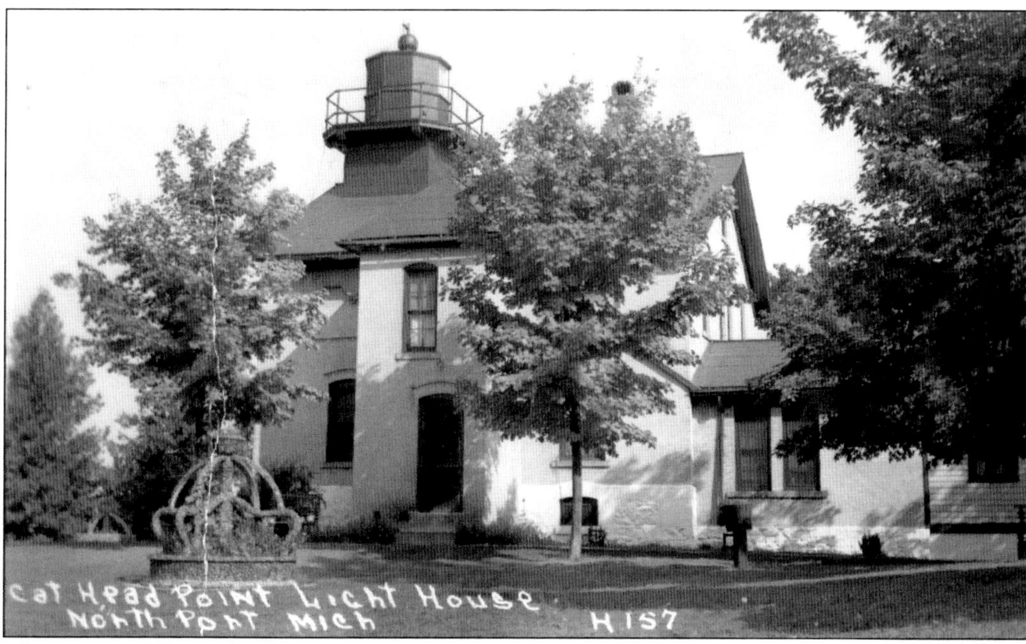

This postcard from about 1940 shows the south side of the lighthouse. The card is postmarked May 28, 1941, and is addressed to Willis Cain of Levering. The message reads, "We will see you May 29 early or on evening of May 28," signed Allen. It then says, "Picture of our light." Willis was the brother of Allen Cain who was a keeper of the Grand Traverse Lighthouse from 1938 to 1946. (Courtesy Grand Traverse Lighthouse Museum Collection.)

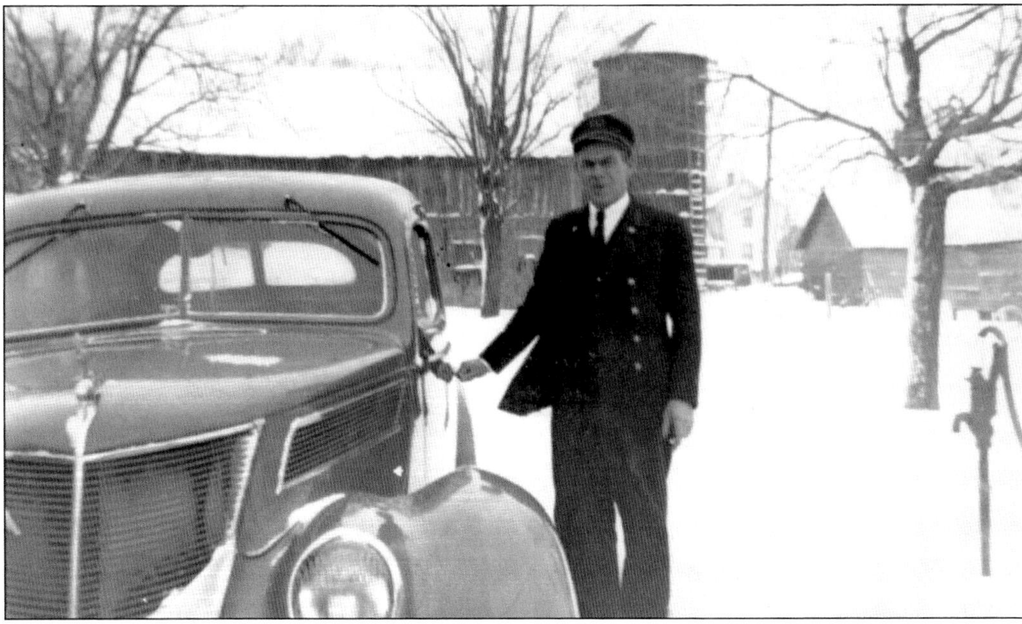

This photograph of assistant keeper Allen Cain from about 1940 was taken at the Baumberger Farm in Northport. He is dressed in full lighthouse keeper uniform. The lighthouse keeper's uniform includes a "bell top" cap with basic insignia, eight button double-breasted jumper with basic insignia, white cotton shirt, black tie, and black leather belt. (Courtesy Grand Traverse Lighthouse Museum Collection.)

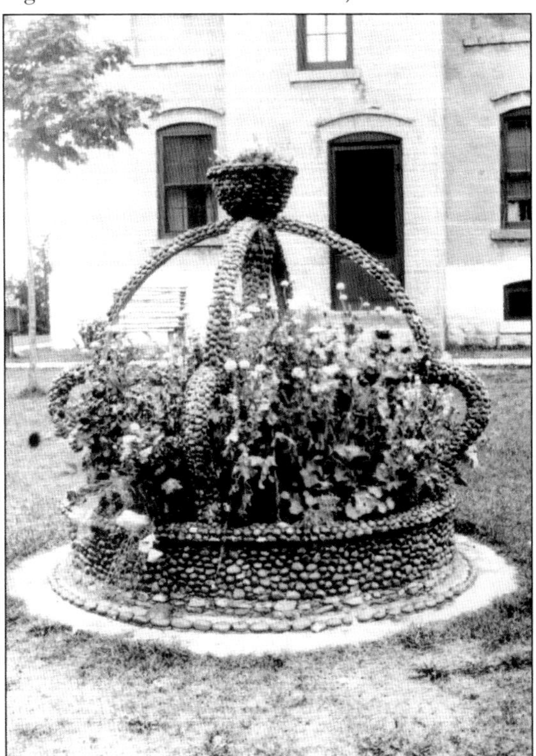

Here is a photograph of the stone crown planter, located on the south side of the lighthouse. The planters were filled with beautiful flowers such as roses, dahlias, and poppies. During her time at the lighthouse, Mary McCormick took great pride in planting and caring for the flowers and gardens of the site. (Courtesy Archives of Michigan, Negative 18800.)

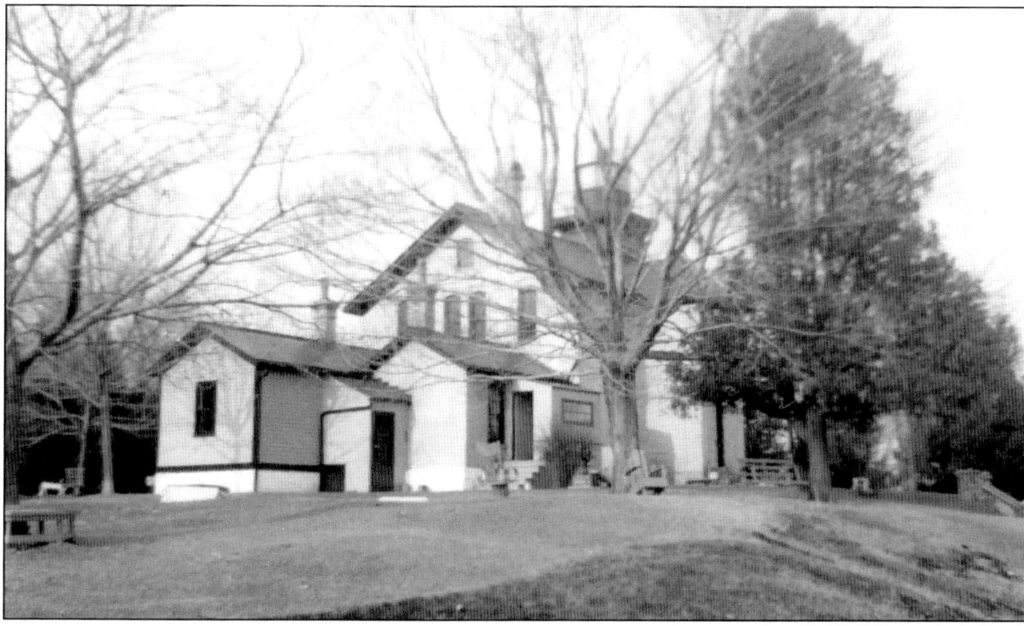

Taken in the spring of 1942, this photograph shows the northeast lawn. Keepers of the light during this time were Ernest Hutzler and assistant Cain. Hutzler was stationed in Michigan at Grand Traverse Lighthouse, North Manitou Light, Seul Choix Point Light, South Manitou Island Light, St. Martin Light, and at Tail Point Light in Wisconsin. (Courtesy Grand Traverse Lighthouse Museum Collection.)

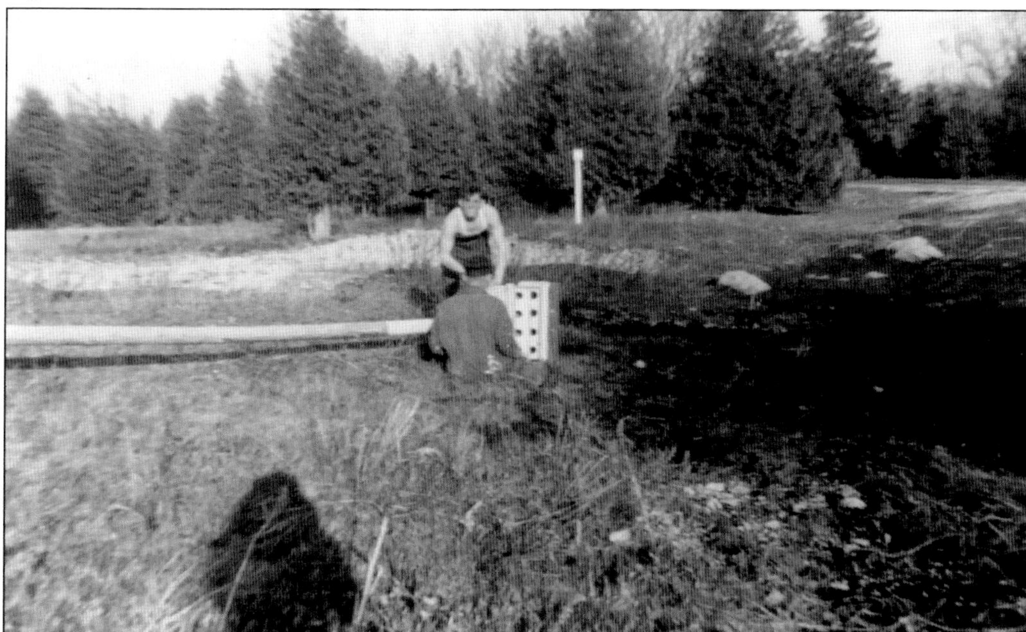

Putting up the wren house are Hutzler (facing the camera) and assistant keeper Cain (back to camera) around 1940. This birdhouse was made by Cain. It was placed on the lawn on the western side of the lighthouse where the garage, now a gift shop, is located today. (Courtesy Grand Traverse Lighthouse Museum Collection.)

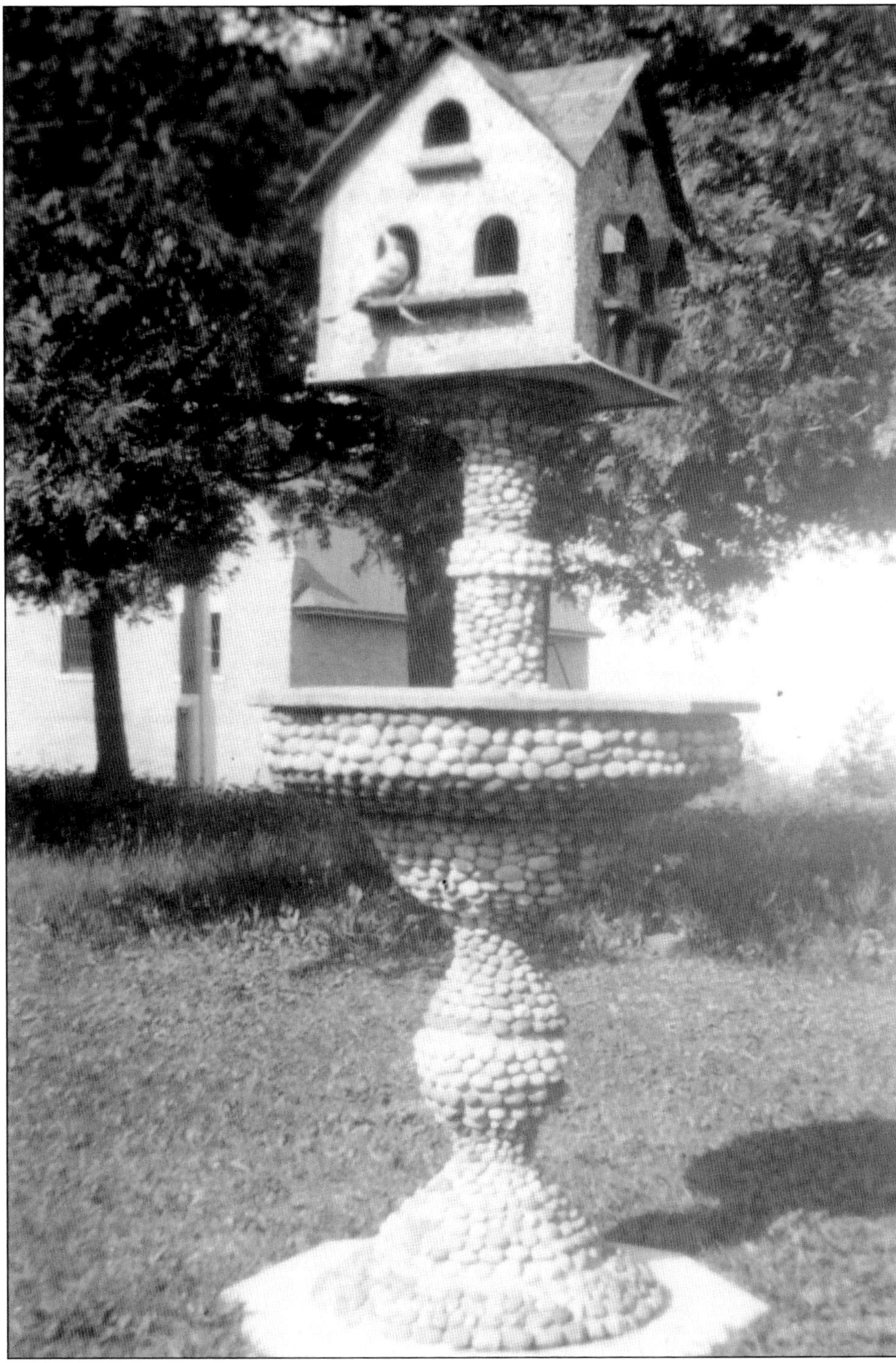

A stone birdhouse with birdbath is pictured around 1934. Notice the cardinal in the window taking in a little sun. The structure is built of rocks and stones gathered from along the beach and built by keeper James McCormick. His son Doug McCormick rebuilt it in 1983. It still stands today, but is in need of restoration. (Courtesy Grand Traverse Lighthouse Museum Collection.)

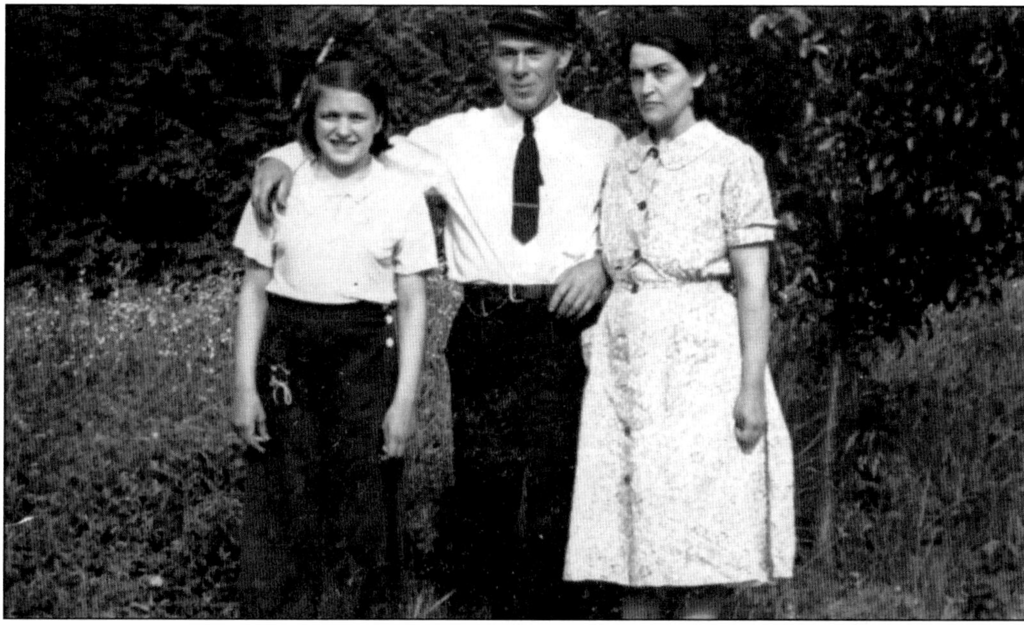

Assistant keeper Allen Cain poses here with daughters Marie and Lillian just after arriving at his new post at Grand Traverse Lighthouse. On October 17, 1938, Cain received a letter from T. S. Thompson, chief clerk of the U.S. Lighthouse Service, requesting him to report as the first assistant keeper at Grand Traverse Light Station on November 1, 1938. (Courtesy Grand Traverse Lighthouse Museum Collection.)

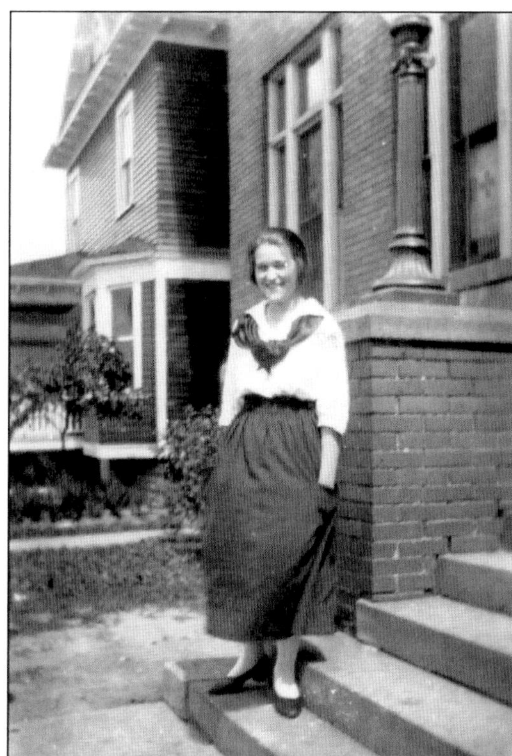

This photograph from about 1918 is of Ruth E. (Huyette) Cain, the first wife of first assistant keeper Cain. They had three children, Marie (Cain) Baumberger, Lillian (Cain) Howarth, and Albert Leroy Cain. Ruth died of cancer 30 days after the Cain family moved to the Grand Traverse Lighthouse in 1938. (Courtesy Grand Traverse Lighthouse Museum Collection.)

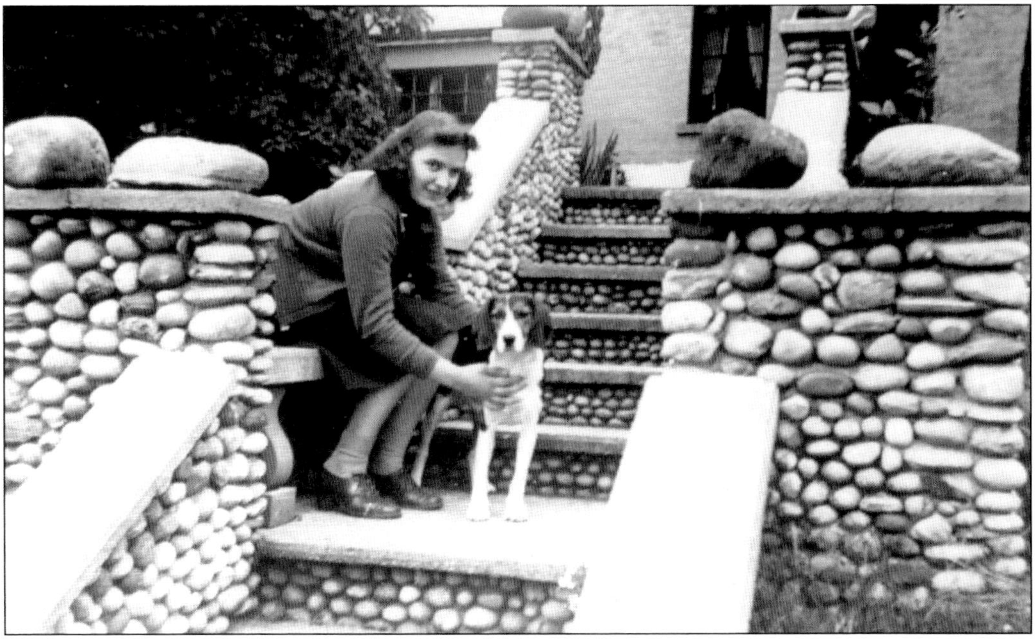

Marie (Cain) Baumberger, daughter of first assistant keeper Allen Cain is pictured around 1940 on the stone steps located on the north side of the lighthouse. She is seated with their dog Stub. The stone steps over the years became a popular stop for photographs of keeper's families and visitors to the Grand Traverse Light Station. (Courtesy Grand Traverse Lighthouse Museum Collection.)

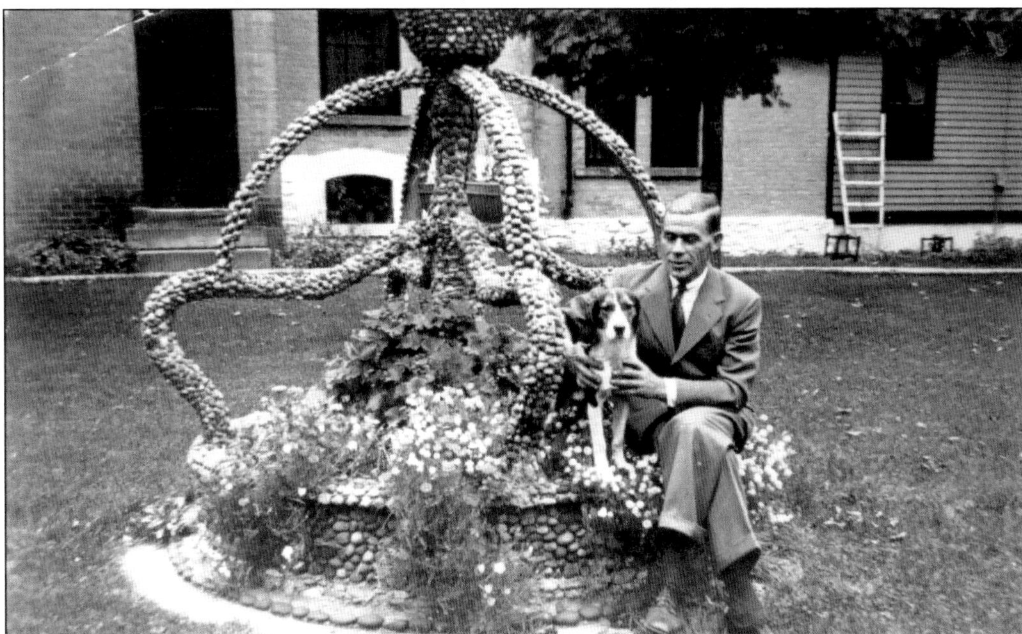

Cain poses with his dog Stub on the stone crown planter around 1940. There was great pride in all of the stonework on the property, as evidenced in the many photographs taken with it as a backdrop. Cain was one of three assigned to the lighthouse during this time; he was the only civilian stationed there. (Courtesy Grand Traverse Lighthouse Museum Collection.)

Here is Cain and his second wife, Anna (Dolwick) Cain. This was taken on the Baumberger farm in Northport. On May 20, 1946, Cain received an official very good efficiency rating based on his performance during the period of April 1, 1945, to March 31, 1946, from the U.S. Coast Guard. (Courtesy Grand Traverse Lighthouse Museum Collection.)

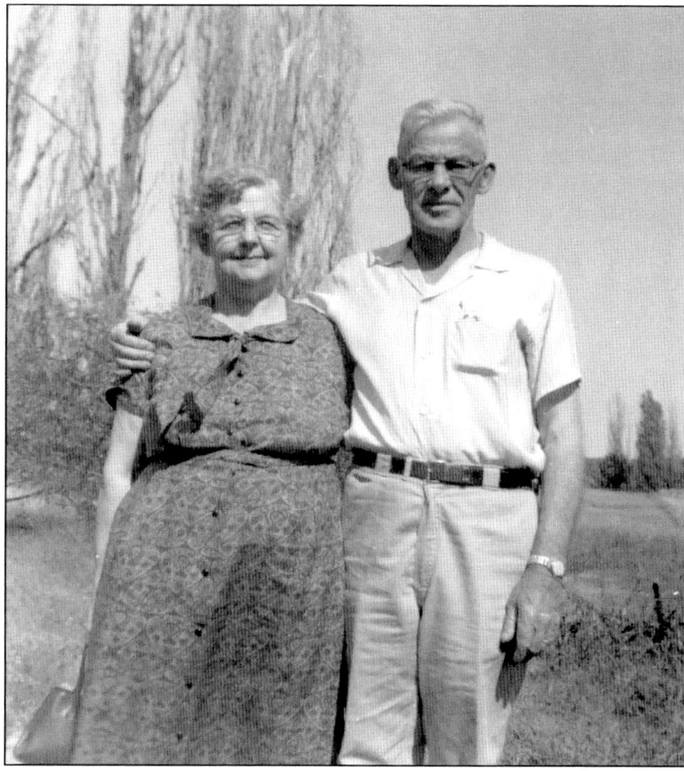

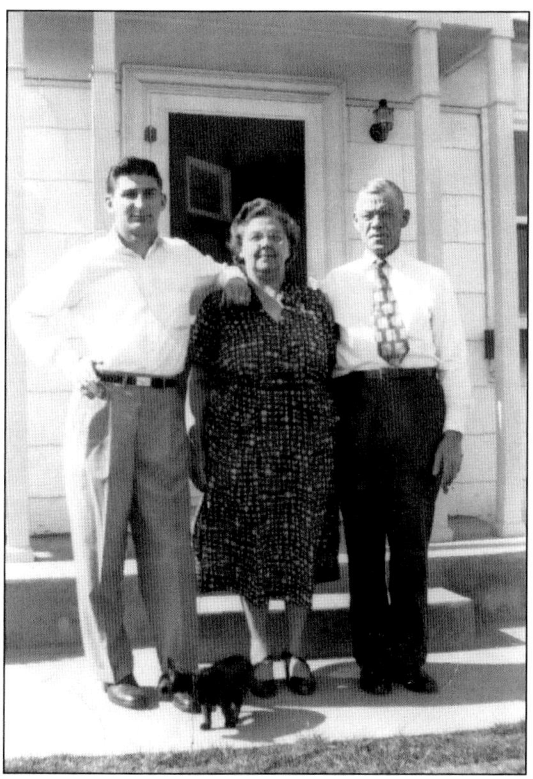

From left to right are Anna's son Frank Dolwick, Anna, and Cain. In August 1946, Cain received notice that as the only civilian keeper at the Grand Traverse Light Station, the hours of duty could not be increased as they could for enlisted personnel. Therefore it became necessary to transfer him to another station. (Courtesy Grand Traverse Lighthouse Museum Collection.)

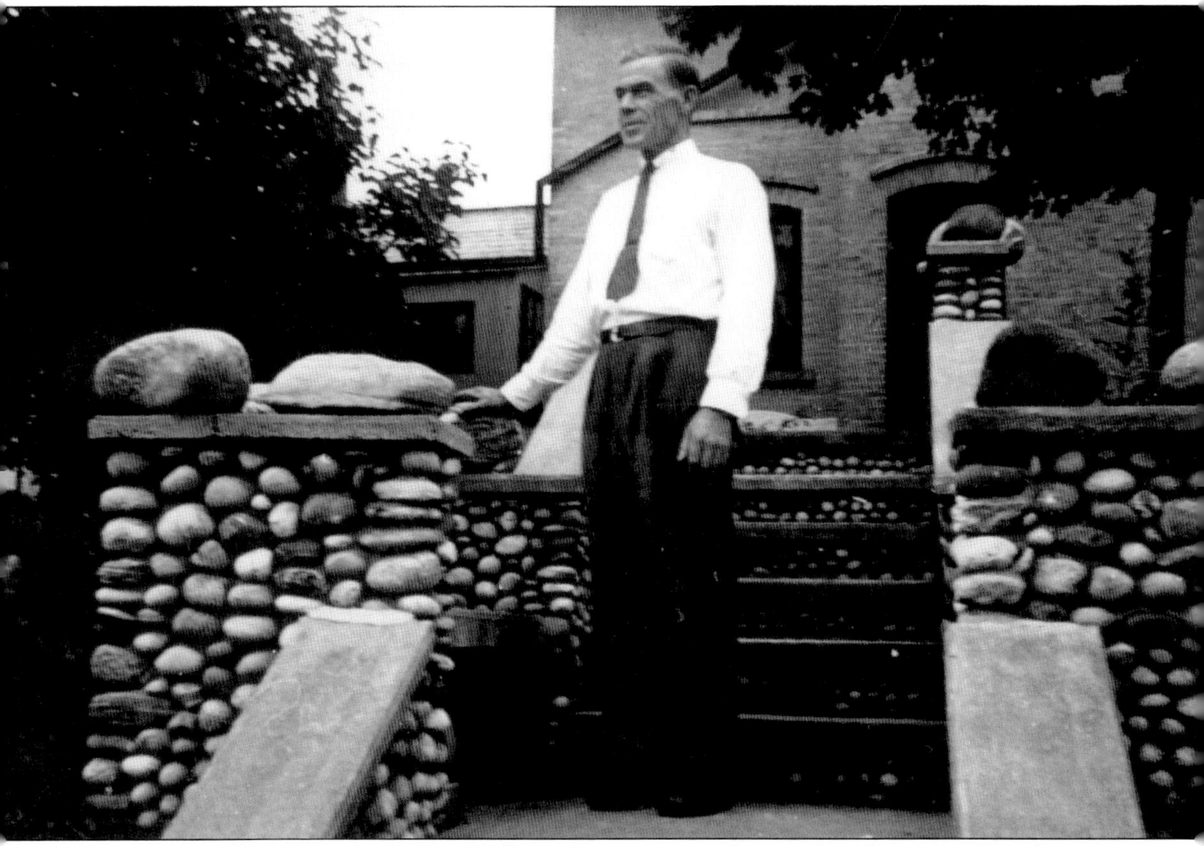

Here is Allen Cain standing on the stone steps on the north side of the lighthouse. In September 1946, Cain accepted a transfer, without a change in current pay, to the position of second assistant keeper at the South Fox Island Light Station, 17 miles northwest of his present station assignment. Cain remained on South Fox Island until it was automated in 1958, and he was transferred to the Alpena Light Station. (Courtesy Grand Traverse Lighthouse Museum Collection.)

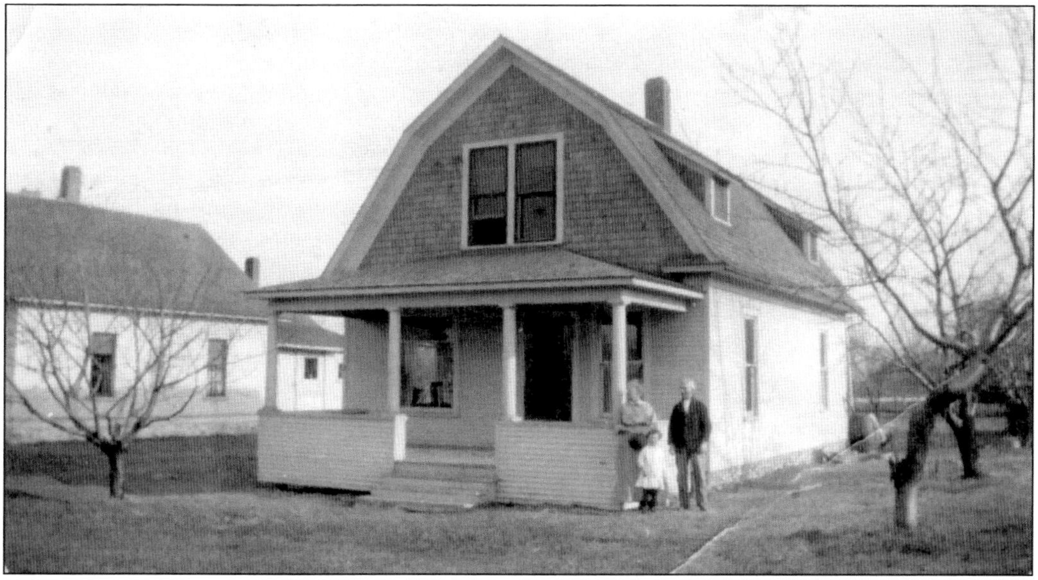

The Dame family is shown here at their home in Northport. Pictured are Ella Dame, her husband, assistant keeper Oscar Dame, and their daughter, Vivian (in front). Vivian, their only child, died at age 15 from a heart condition. (Courtesy Grand Traverse Lighthouse Museum Collection.)

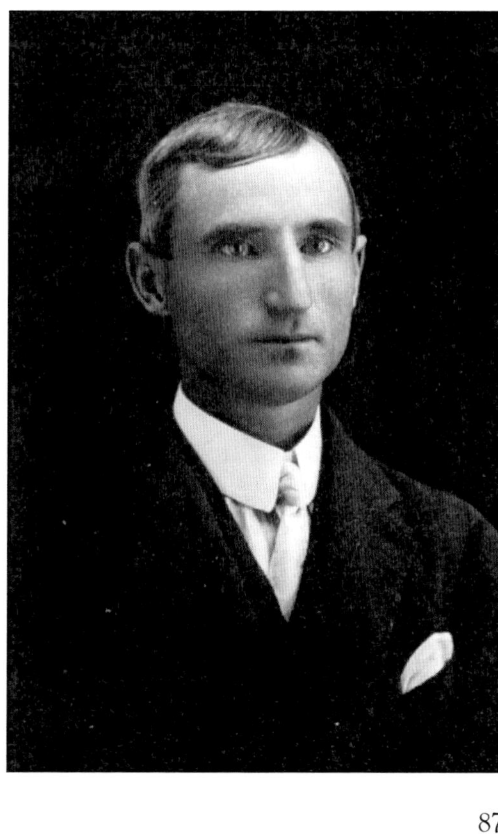

This is a portrait of Oscar from about 1916. He was a 25-year veteran in the U.S. Lighthouse Service and retired in 1939 after 11 years of service at South Fox Island Light, 11 years at Grand Traverse Light, and three years in Kenosha, Wisconsin. (Courtesy Grand Traverse Lighthouse Museum Collection.)

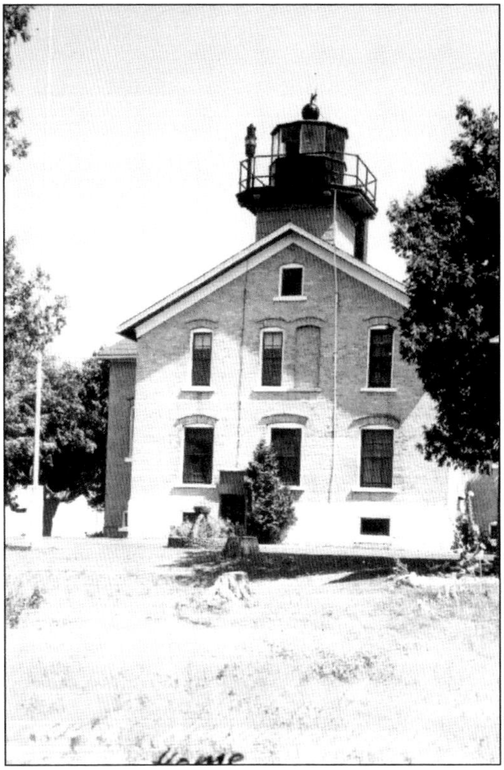

The western face of the lighthouse shows the winter light in place on the tower's catwalk. This light was used during the winter months when the light station was closed, yet some vessel traffic continued. Winter lights were initiated during World War II. Two gauged, acetylene gas tanks were attached to the building under a lean-to and powered the light that was fastened to the deck and railing. It could be seen about 10 miles away. There is also a lightning rod on the right-hand side of the tower. (Courtesy Grand Traverse Lighthouse Museum Collection.)

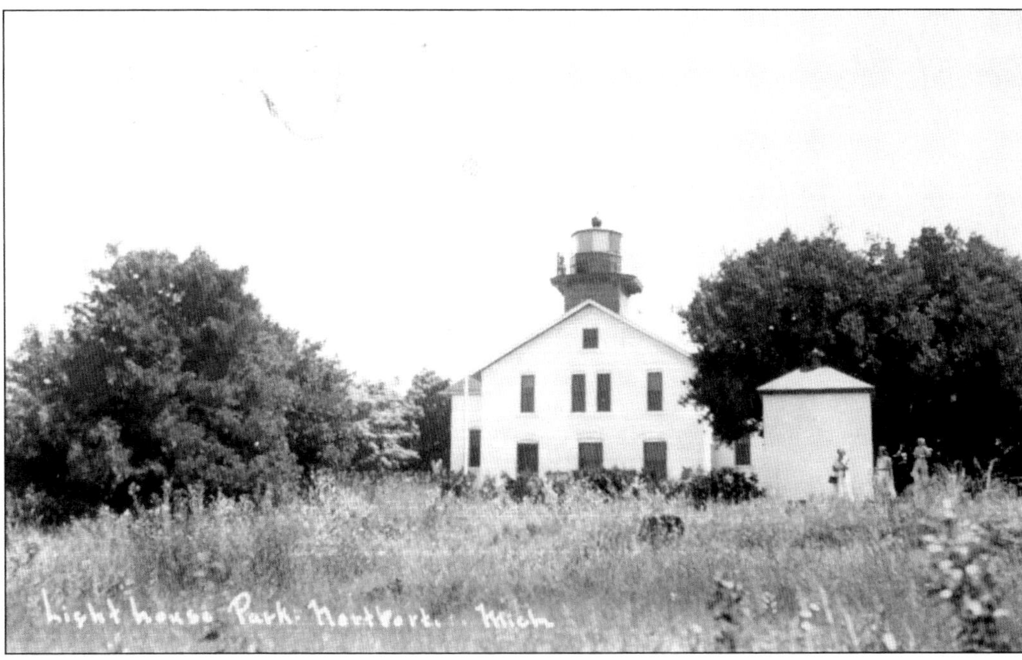

Approaching the mid-1940s, more and more shrub growth sprang up around the light station. The oil house is to the right in the photograph and appears to be painted white at this time. Whitewash was used on the stone section below the bricks to seal the stone and mortar. (Courtesy Grand Traverse Lighthouse Museum Collection.)

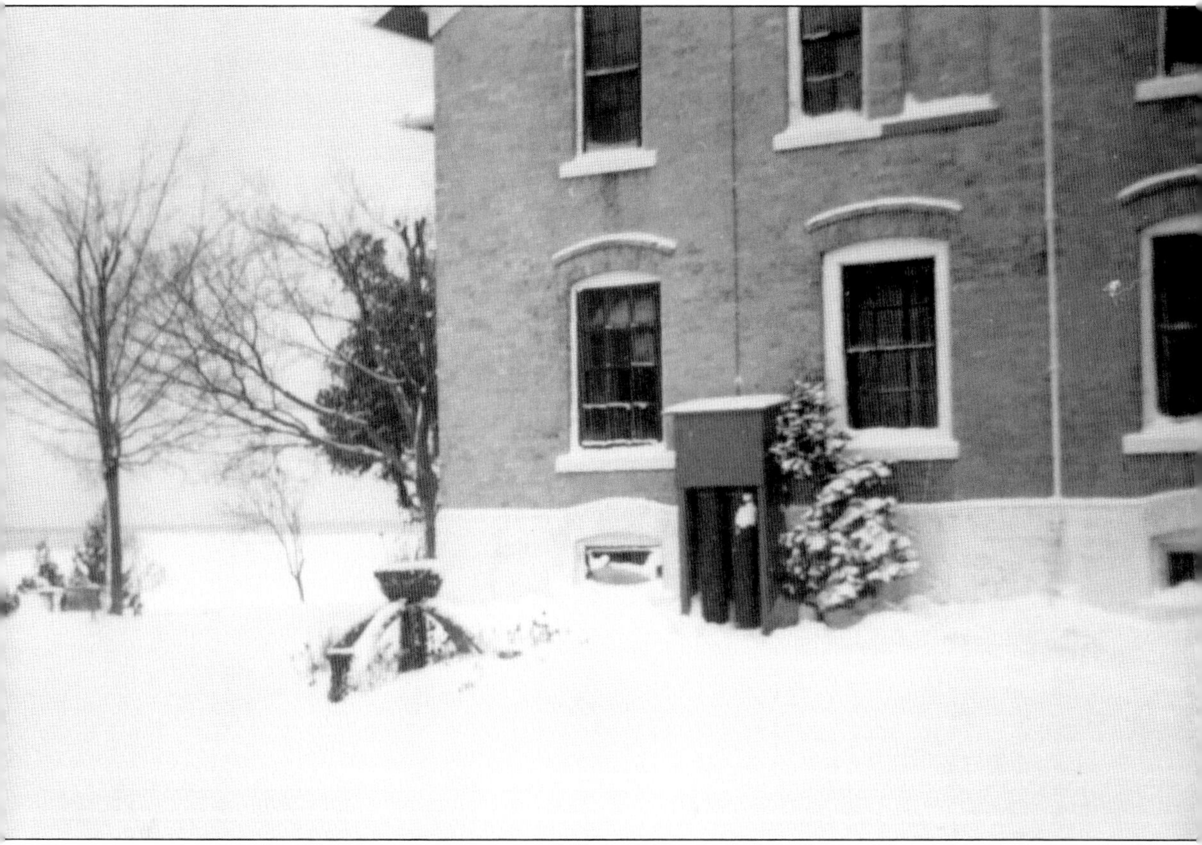

This winter photograph shows a close-up of the lean-to that housed the acetylene tanks for the winter light. Keepers and families vacated the lighthouse from December 15 to April 1, at which time the shipping industry reopened on the lakes. (Courtesy Grand Traverse Lighthouse Museum Collection.)

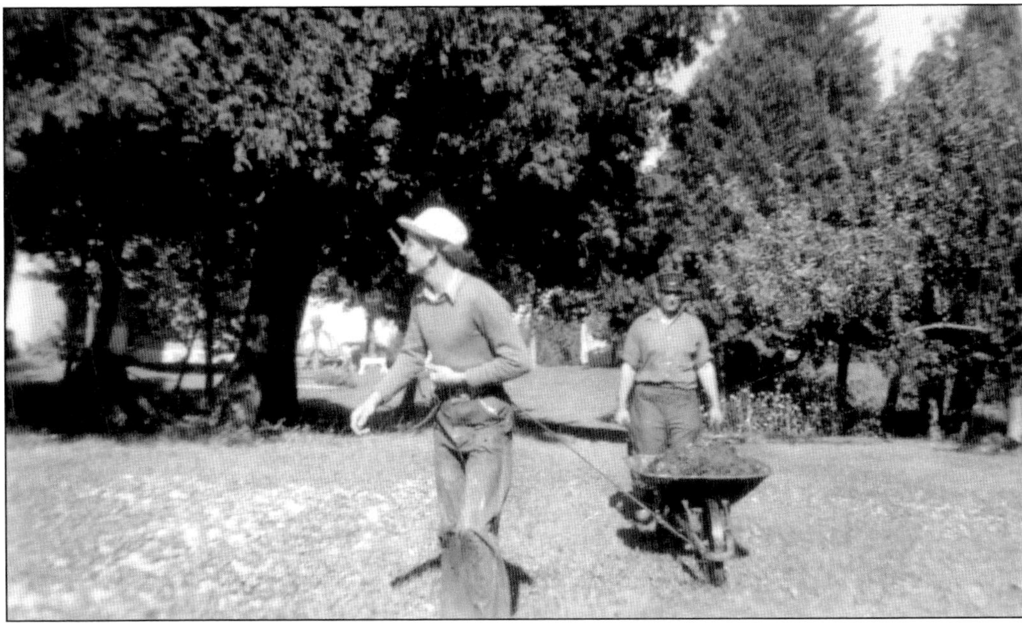

This photograph from about 1941 shows keeper Ernest Hutzler and his son Dale doing the annual cleaning out of the privy. Dale found that putting a clothespin on his nose made the work more bearable. The privy was located on the south side of the lighthouse. The assistant keeper's family had the "two-holer" to the left and the keeper and his family had the "two-holer" with a smaller one for the kids on the right. (Courtesy Grand Traverse Lighthouse Museum Collection.)

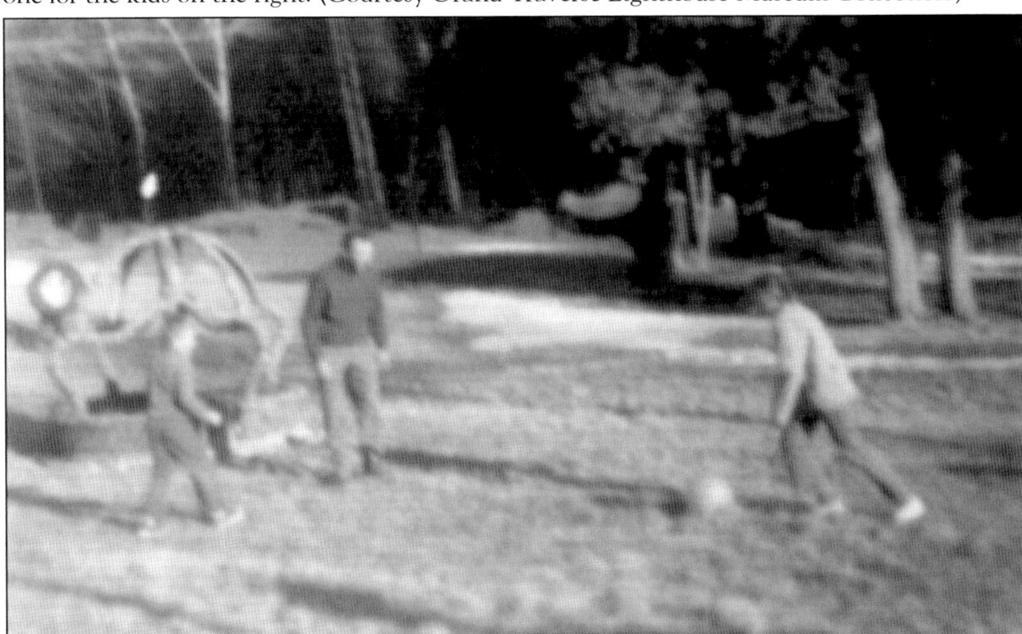

Children of keepers often had to find ways to entertain themselves. Around the dawn of the 20th century, children played board games, cards, or took up a musical instrument. In this photograph, the children are enjoying a game of kick ball, which, over the years, has remained a very popular game around the playground or backyard.

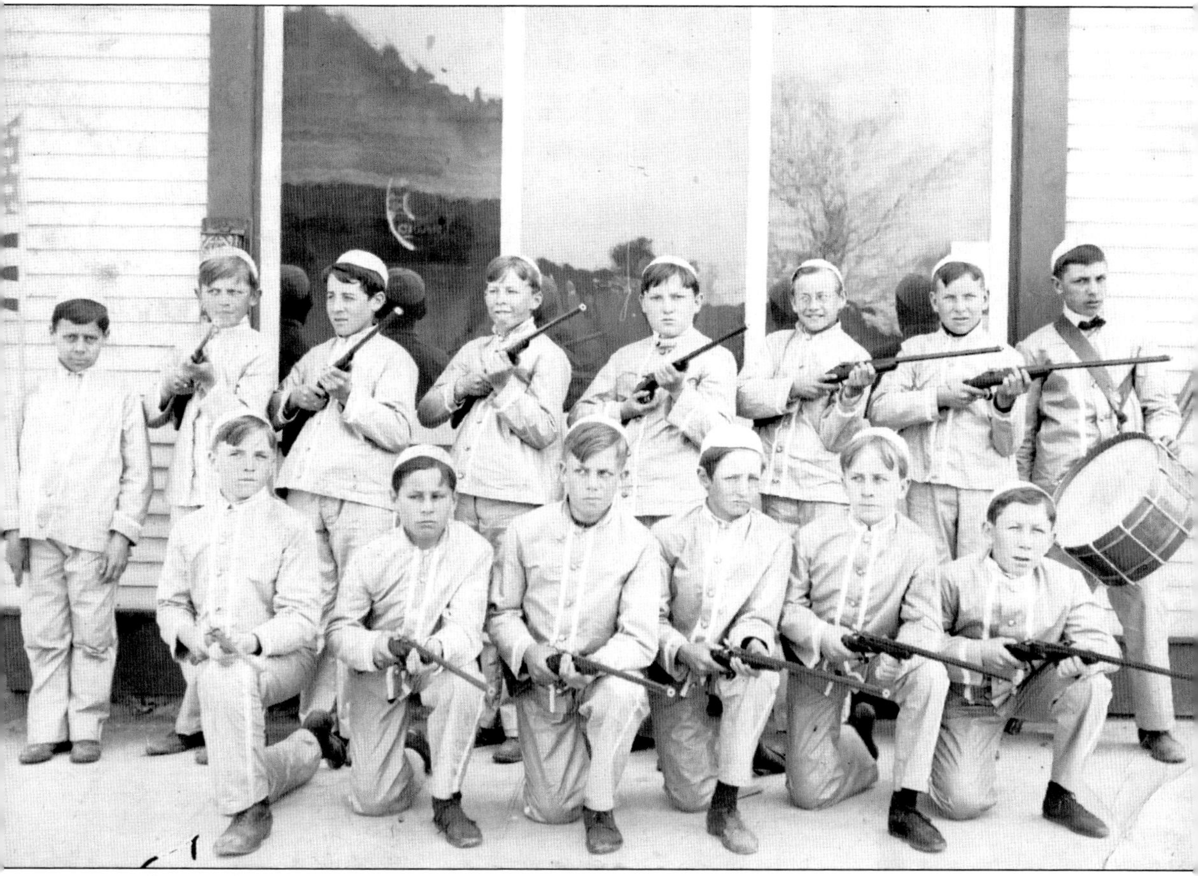

Here is the Northport marching group with boys holding the flag, a drum, and guns. The young man standing third from the left is Northport resident Fred Leslie at about age 12. Leslie became the officer in charge at the Grand Traverse Light Station from 1946 to 1950. (Courtesy Grand Traverse Lighthouse Museum Collection.)

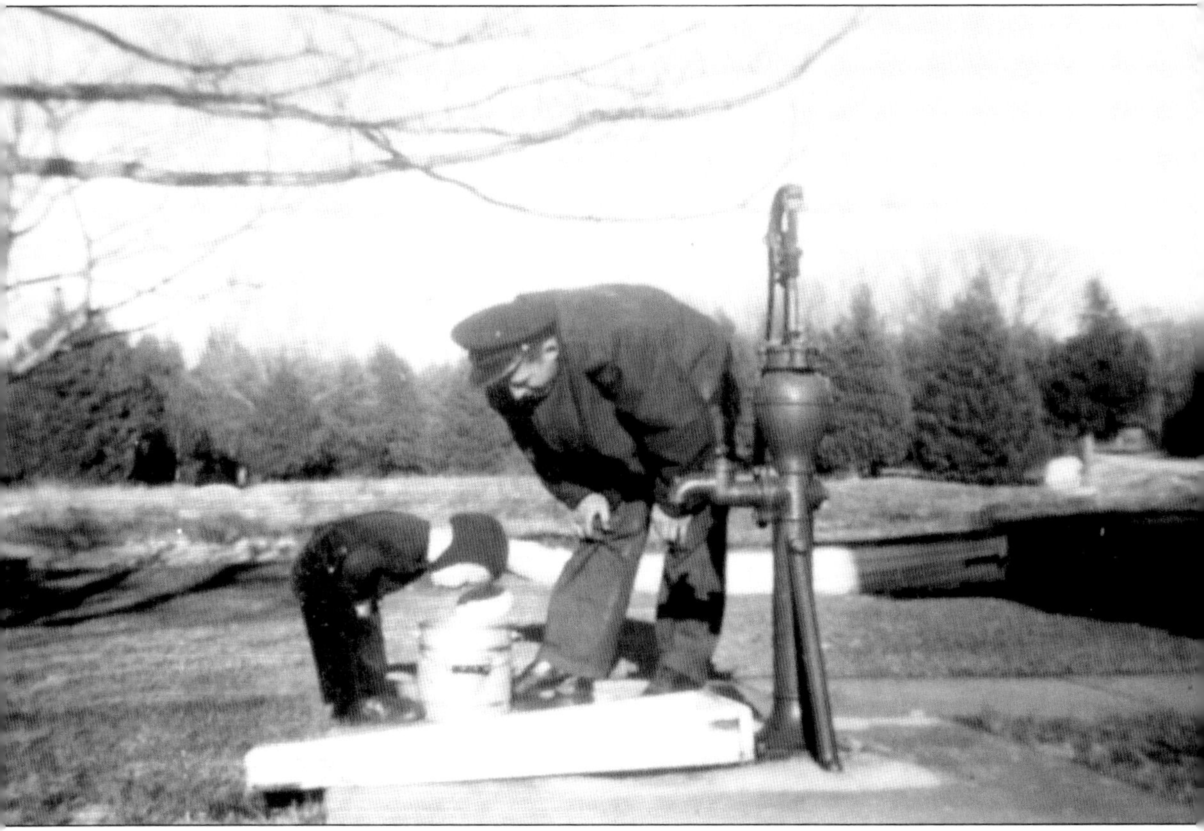

Coastguardman Carl Oleson was stationed at the lighthouse from 1940 to 1945. He is pictured here with his son Carl Jr., who is looking down into a bucket next to the water pump located to the north of the dwelling. (Courtesy Grand Traverse Lighthouse Museum Collection.)

Five

U.S. Coast Guard 1950–1972

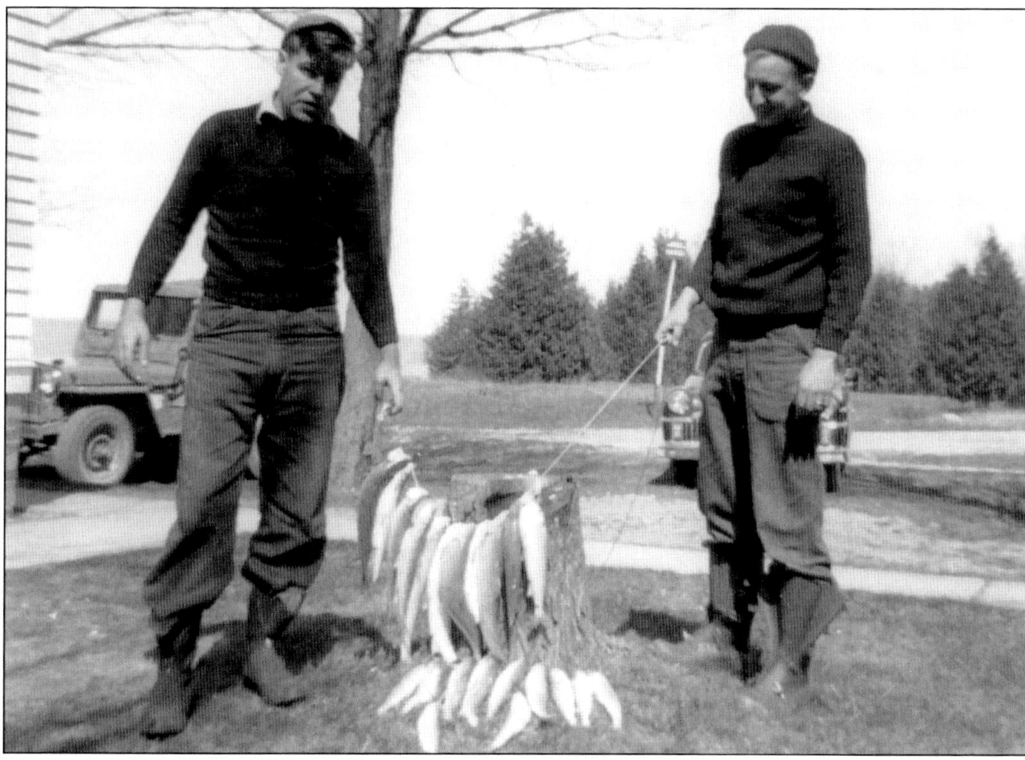

Coastguardman Edwin I. "Johnny" Johnson (right) and Bill Kelly (left) are pictured with an early-spring herring catch. Fishing was an integral part of living at a lighthouse. Many earlier keepers and their families supplemented food supplies from the U.S. Lighthouse Service with whatever they could catch from the lake, hunt in the woods, or grow in their gardens. (Courtesy Grand Traverse Lighthouse Museum Collection.)

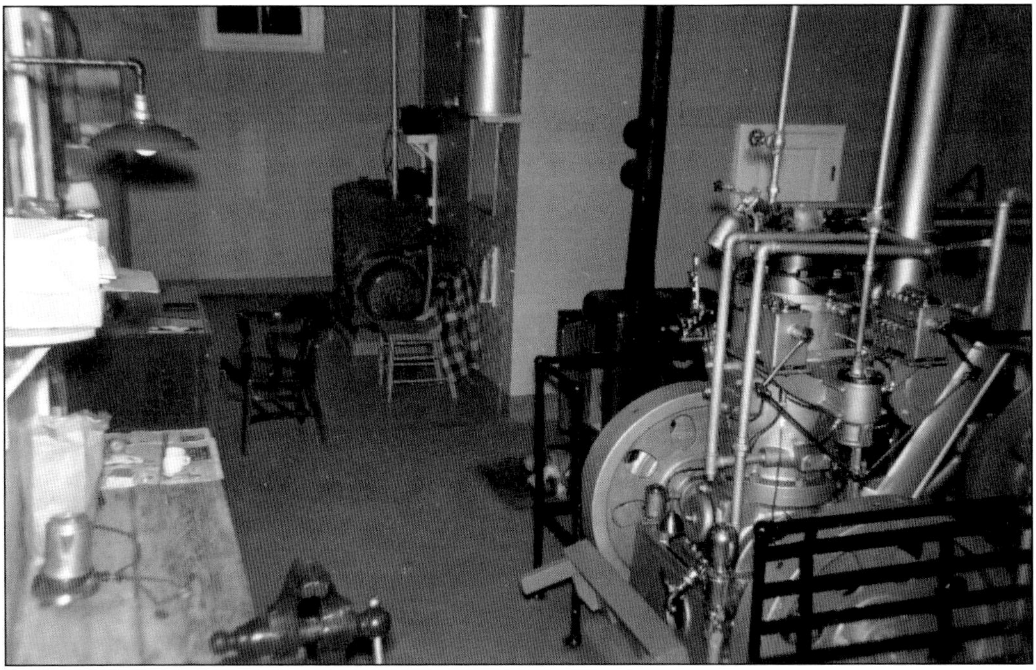

These photographs were taken in December 1952 by coastguardman Al Tarsa. In the background is the Kahlenberg engine and the diesel generator used for emergency electric power. This equipment was used to blow the Type F air diaphone fog signal located in the cupola atop the building. In 1966, it is believed the Kahlenberg engine was dismantled and buried on the east side of the Fog Signal Building. In 2004, University of Michigan students, using metal detecting devices, had many metal hits around this area. (Courtesy Grand Traverse Lighthouse Museum Collection.)

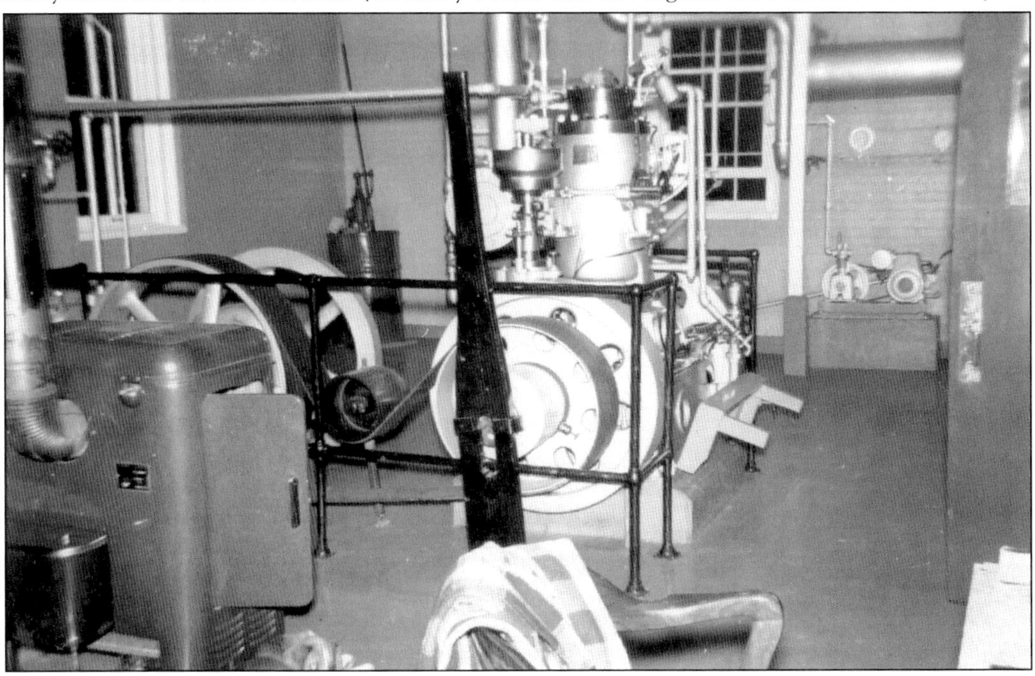

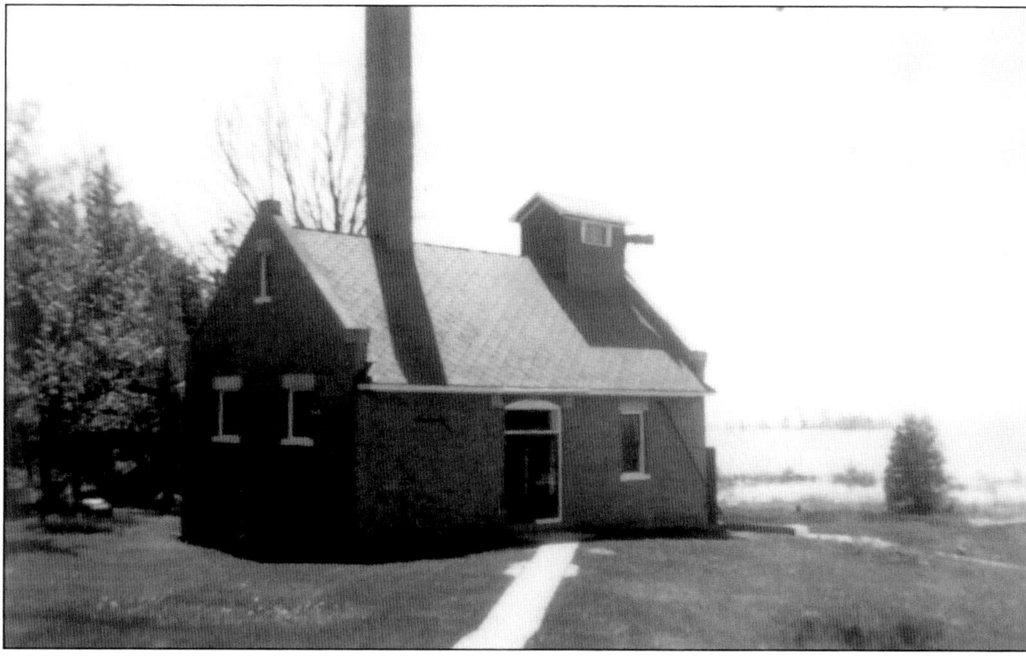

This photograph of the Fog Signal Building was taken by coastguardman Al Tarsa in 1952. The building remained unchanged from 1933 when the Type F air diaphone fog signal was installed until the time of this photograph. The fog signal was so loud that it could be heard nine miles away in Northport. (Courtesy Grand Traverse Lighthouse Museum Collection.)

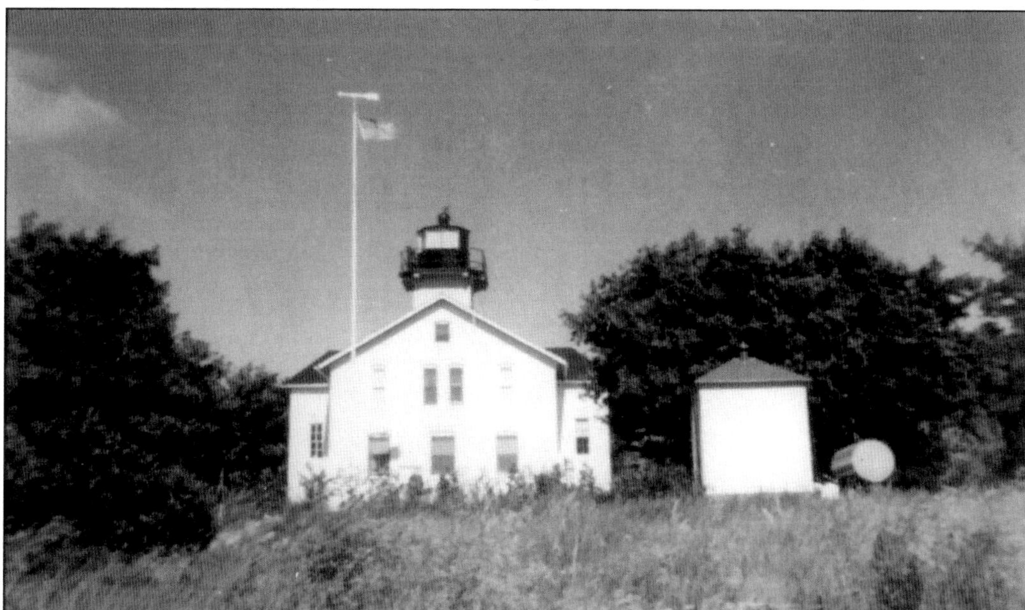

Sometime between 1940 and 1952, the Lighthouse was painted completely white. The lighthouse, built of Milwaukee Cream City bricks, went from its original yellow-brick color to white. Also in the 1952 photograph, all second-floor openings have functioning windows. This took place in 1950 when the U.S. Coast Guard officially took over the station. All the windows were replaced and the building was completely updated and painted.

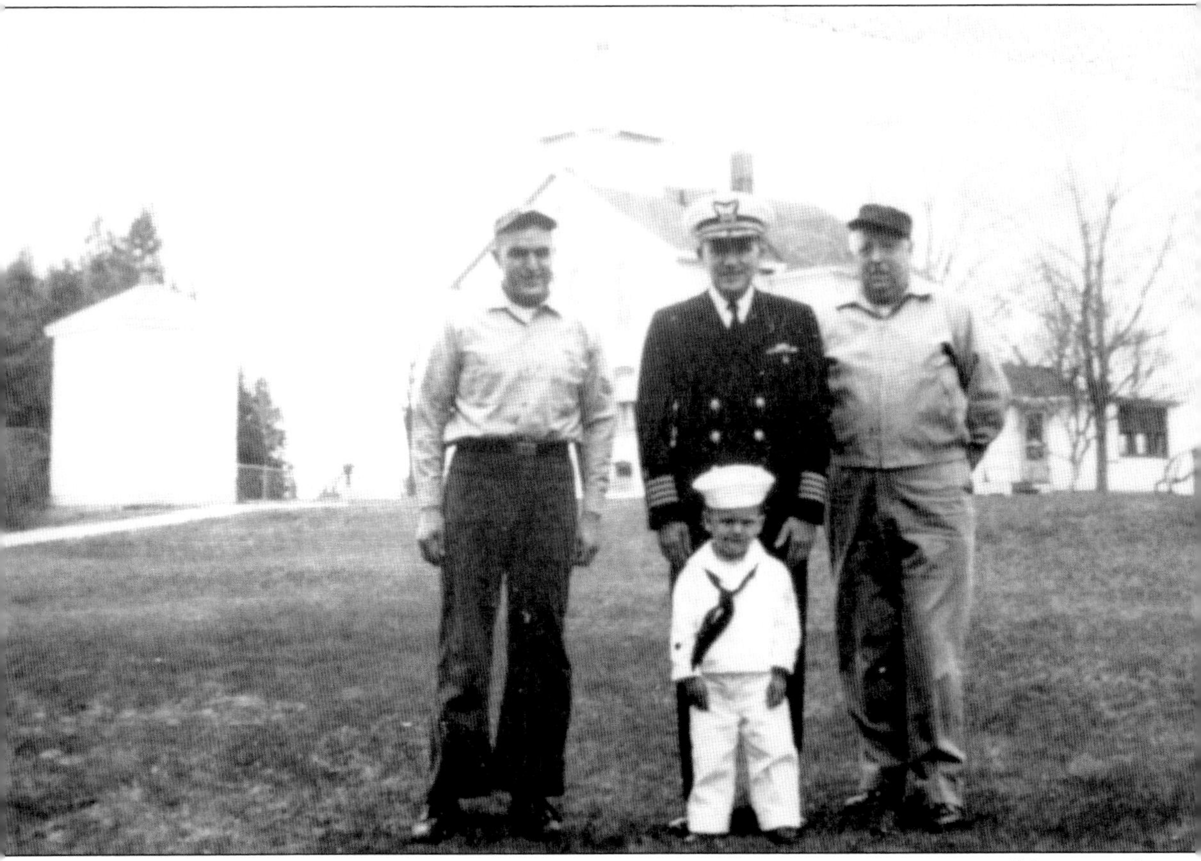

When the U.S. Coast Guard absorbed the U.S. Lighthouse Service in 1939, it gave all keepers of the lighthouse service a choice to remain a civilian lighthouse keeper or officially become part of the U.S. Coast Guard. The last civilian lighthouse keeper of the Grand Traverse Lighthouse was John Marken. From left to right, this photograph shows Marken, unidentified gentleman, and Anthony Tombolillo with his son in front of them. Marken was stationed at Grand Traverse from 1955 to 1967. He and his wife, Beatrice, were killed in a car accident during a blizzard on December 24, 1967, when coming home from a Christmas party in Northport. Upon entering the light station property (where the Leelanau State Park entrance sign stands today), they missed the corner, and their car slid off the road and hit a tree.

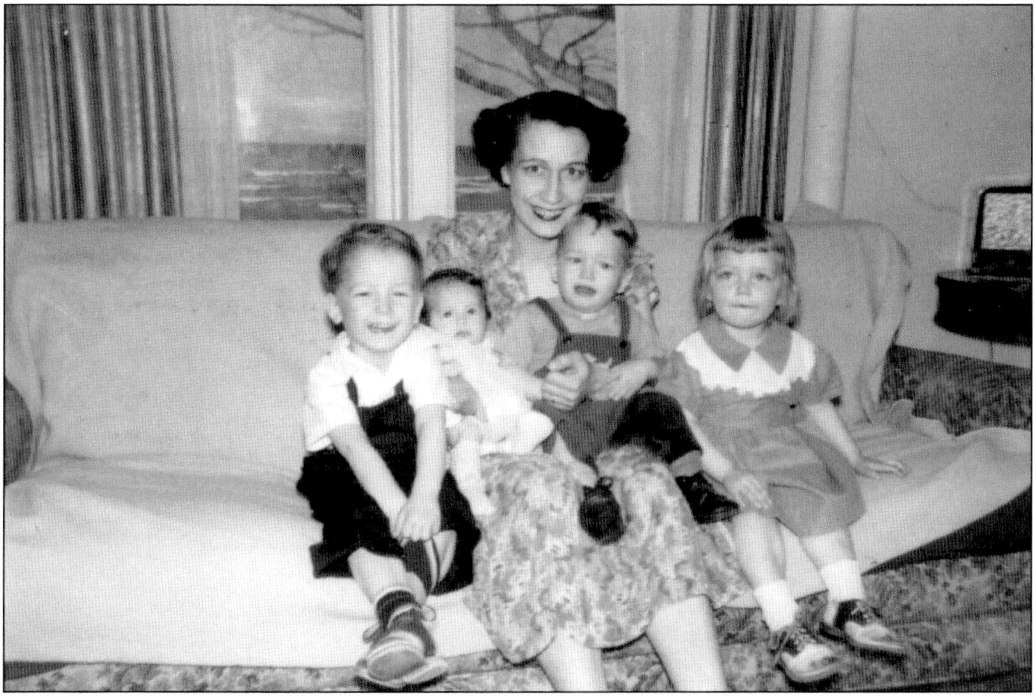

Mrs. Bill Kelly, wife of coastguardman Bill Kelly, is photographed here with her children. This was taken in June 1953 in the northern apartment of the lighthouse with Lake Michigan visible through the window. The children seated from left to right are Eddie, Sarah, John, and Peggy. (Courtesy Grand Traverse Lighthouse Museum Collection.)

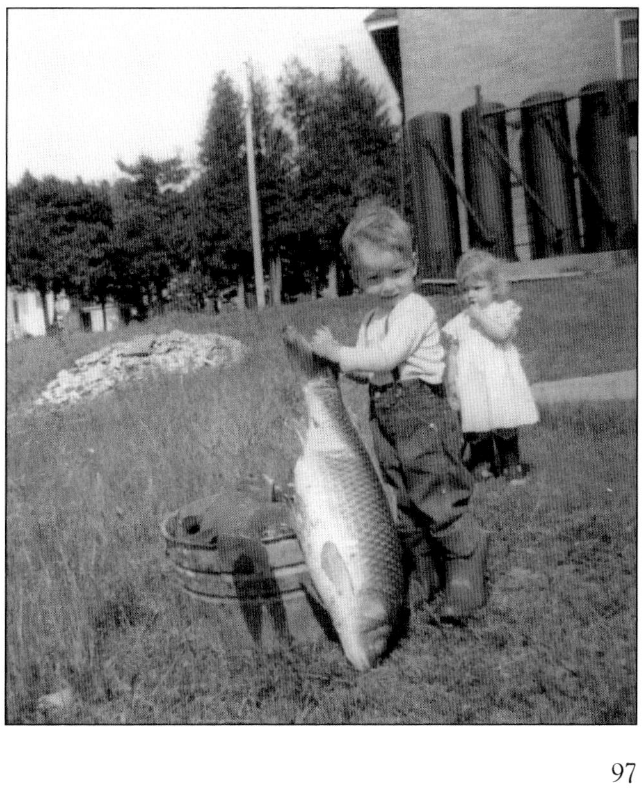

Here is Eddie Kelly Jr. holding a large carp almost the same size as him. His younger sister is standing right behind him. Their father was machinist Bill Kelly, stationed at the Grand Traverse Lighthouse in the early 1950s. According to coastguardsman Al Tara, who donated this photograph, carp came into a temporary pond and Bill and John Johnson (officer in charge) shot them with a .22 rifle and gave them to the local mink farmer for food. (Courtesy of Al Tarsa.)

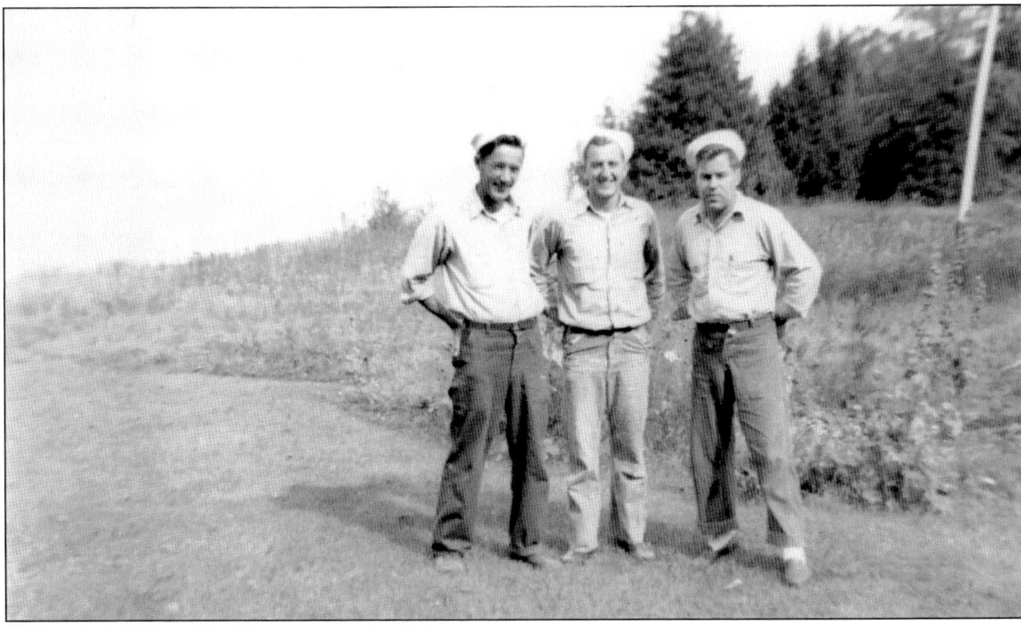

From left to right are seaman Al Tarsa, engineer first class Bill Kelly, and boatswain mate first class Edwin I. "Johnny" Johnson around 1952. Kelly was stationed at Grand Traverse Light from March 1951 to November 1953. During 19 years in the service, he was awarded the World War II Victory Medal, National Defense Service Medal with one star, and the U.S. Coast Guard Good Conduct Metal with four stars. (Courtesy Grand Traverse Lighthouse Museum Collection.)

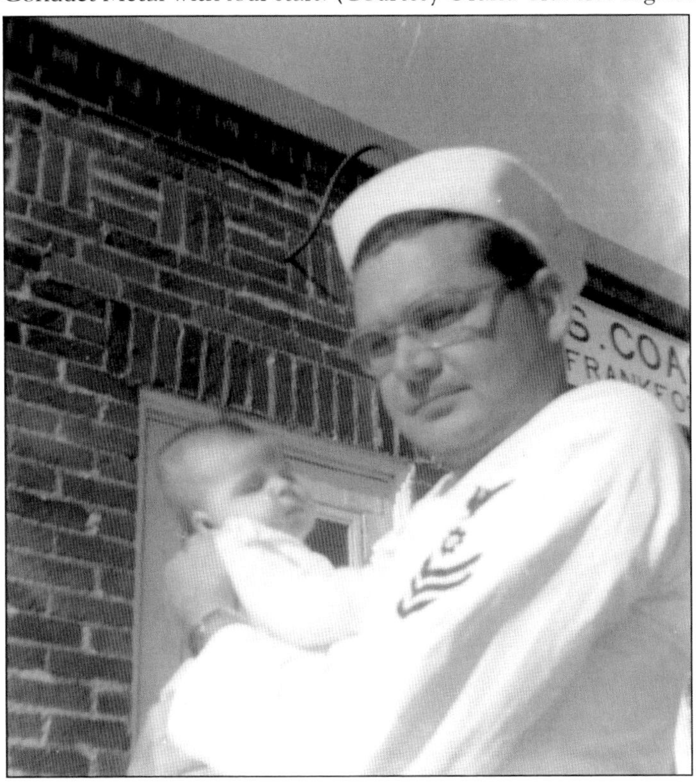

Pictured are coastguardman John Kester and his new son in front of the Frankfort station. Kester was stationed at Grand Traverse from December 1953 to February 1955. For three months in 1954, he was acting officer in charge until a replacement for Edwin I. "Johnny" Johnson could be found. Kester spent six years in the service, receiving the Good Conduct Medal and the National Defense Service Medal. (Courtesy Grand Traverse Lighthouse Museum Collection.)

Johnson and his Jeep are pictured on the beach with fellow coastguardsmen. Most of the shoreline surrounding Grand Traverse Light consists of many stones and rocks, including Petoskey stones. A Petoskey stone is fossilized coral with a hexagonal pattern throughout. It was named the Michigan state stone in 1965. (Courtesy Grand Traverse Lighthouse Museum Collection.)

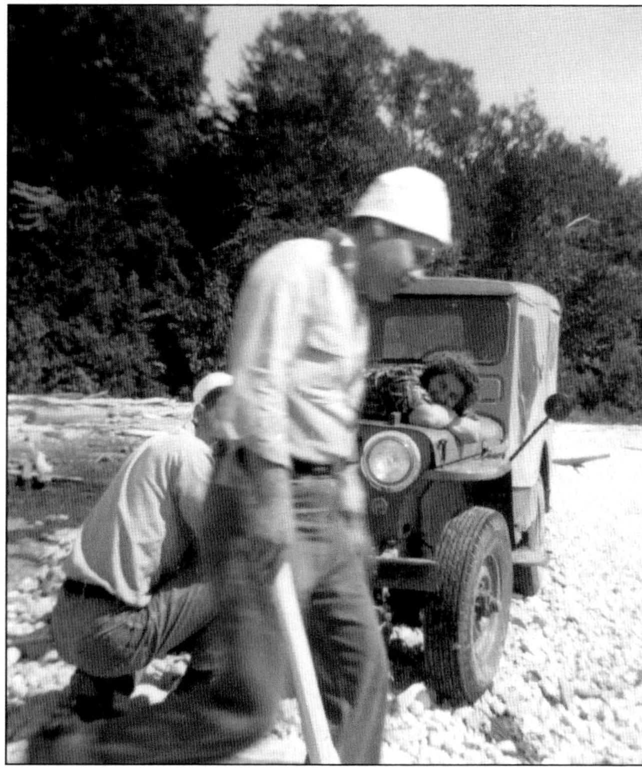

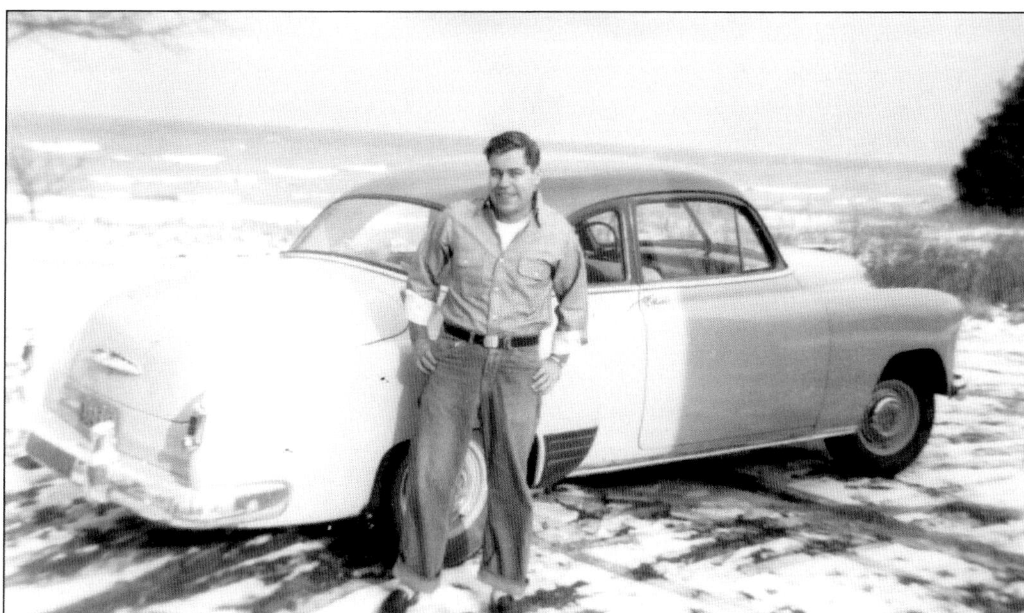

Johnson poses with his Studebaker on the shore of Lake Michigan. On a clear day, one can see Beaver Island 25 miles to the north. Beaver Island is the next point on the navigational course toward the Mackinac Straits. Each year, hundreds of yachtsmen participate in the race on Lake Michigan from Chicago to Mackinaw. The 100th race for the Chicago Yacht Club is in 2008. (Courtesy Grand Traverse Lighthouse Museum Collection.)

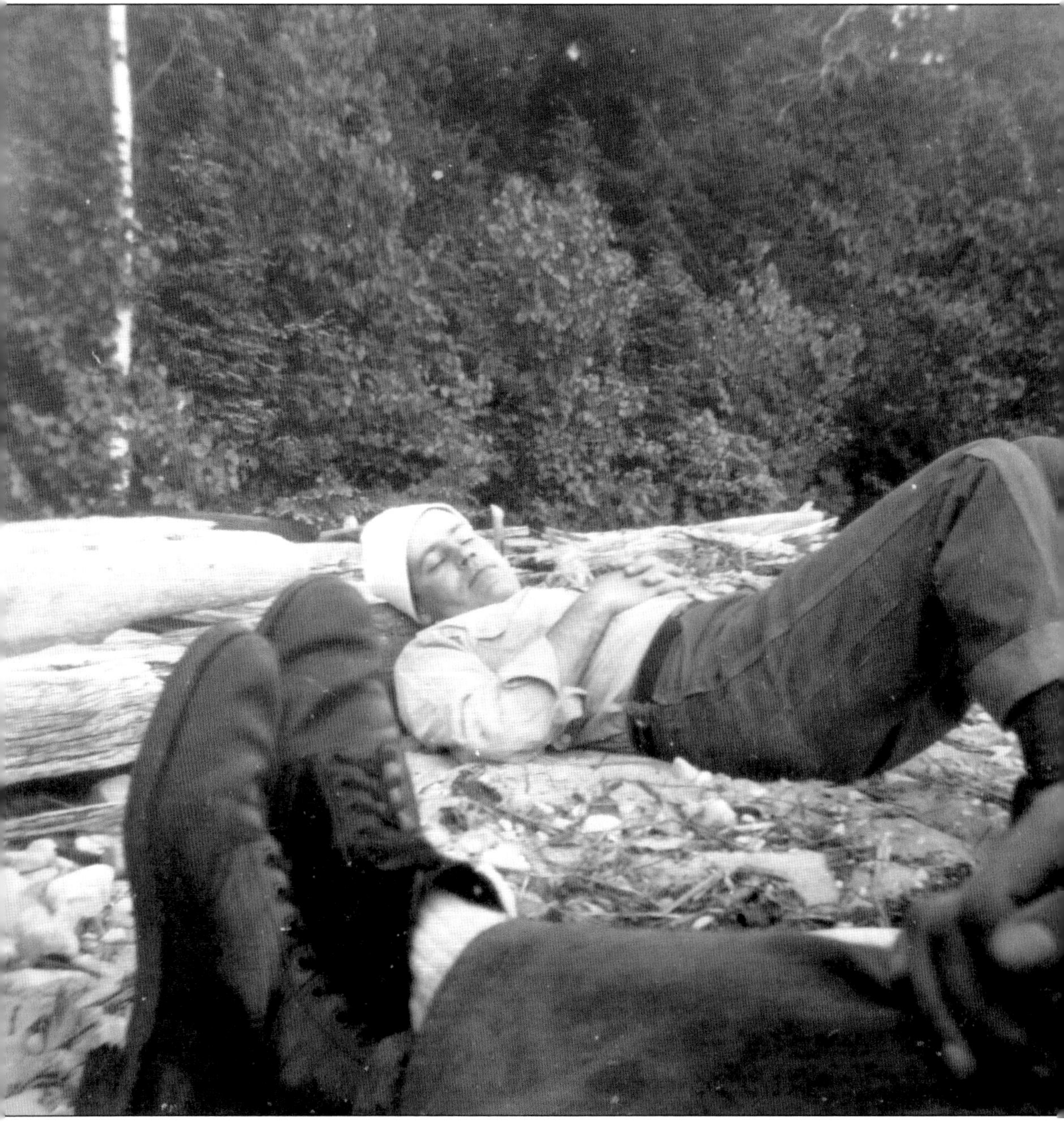

Edwin I. "Johnny" Johnson takes a nap on the shoreline of lighthouse point. Johnson began his assignment as the officer in charge at Grand Traverse Light Station on February 1, 1952, and continued until June 22, 1954. Prior to his service at Grand Traverse, he was stationed in St. Augustine, Florida, San Juan, Puerto Rico, and aboard the lighthouse tender *Hollyhock*. (Courtesy Grand Traverse Lighthouse Museum Collection.)

THE GUARDIAN OF LIGHT

(For John and Evelyn Johnson)

Out on the 'little finger'
    The stalwart lighthouse stands,
One, somehow, loves to linger
    Among the rock and sands
And watch the waters churning.....
    The deep expanse of blue,
To feel the sudden yearning
    As all the coast guards do.....
A wish to be a 'tender'
    A watcher in the night;
Throughout the storms - to render
    A soft and mellow light
That casts a steady gleaming
    Across the wavy foam .....
And with its yellow beaming
    To guide the sailor home.

When all the world is quiet
    There's one who stands on shore
To aid the vessel's pilot.
    It seems a little chore.....
But 'way out on the waters,
    Far more than lips can tell
There's many sons and daughters
    Rejoicing "All is well".
The light, in all its glory
    Is guiding them afar;
And like the ancient story
    They follow, like the star.
So to the men who 'tend' her
    Give honor evermore.....
With courage they defend her....
    The lighthouse on the shore.

Myra Hawkins
August 20, 1952

The poem "Guardian of Light" was written by Northport resident Myra Hawkins on August 20, 1952, for her friends, John and Evelyn Johnson. (Courtesy Grand Traverse Lighthouse Museum Collection.)

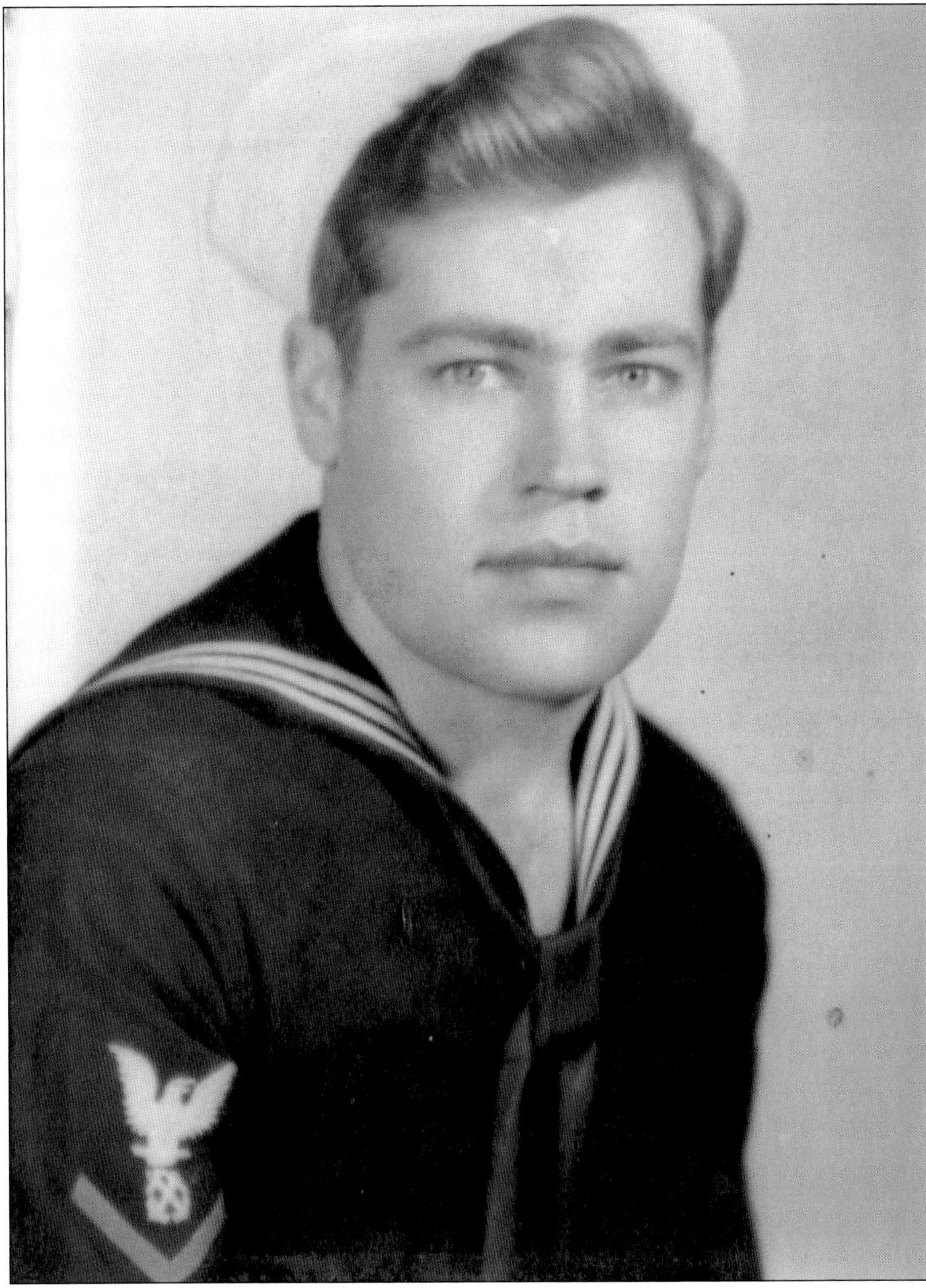

Here is a photograph of Edwin I. "Johnny" Johnson just after he entered the U.S. Coast Guard on October 20, 1942. Over the next 32 years, he was appointed to seven different stations and awarded the Good Conduct Medal, American Campaign Medal, and the World War II Victory Medal. (Courtesy Grand Traverse Lighthouse Museum Collection.)

Johnson is pictured here around 1960. After retiring from the Coast Guard, he moved to Northport to spend the remainder of his days. He passed away in 1997. When cleaning his house, his family threw away all of his military papers, uniforms, and photographs. A local Northport resident found this material and brought it all to the Grand Traverse Lighthouse Museum for safe keeping. The material chronicled Johnson's entire military life.

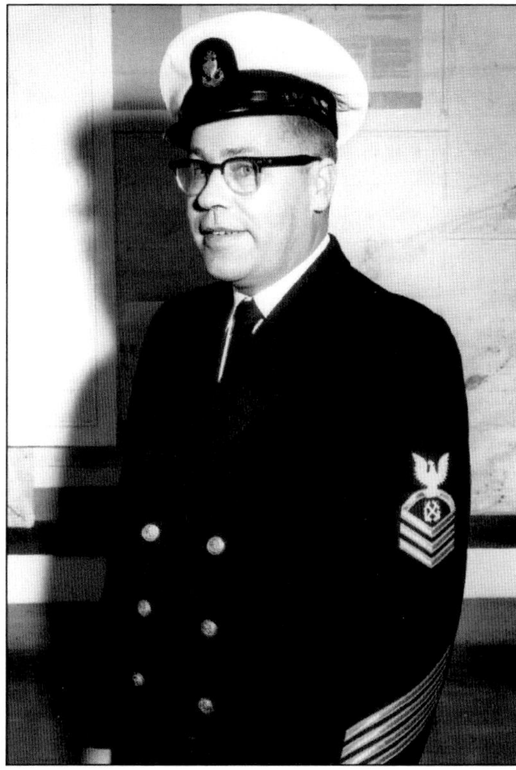

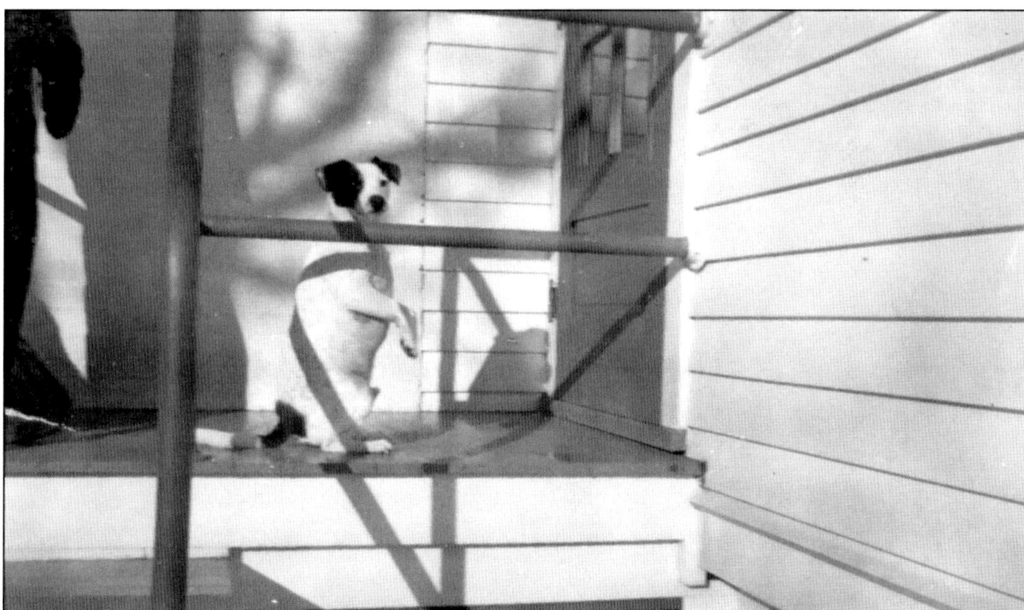

Johnson's dog is pictured here sitting on the south steps of the Lighthouse porch. Lighthouse dogs have been prevalent in the U.S. Lighthouse Service from the very beginning. The porches, one on the north side and the other on the south side, were designated as separate entrances for the Coast Guard personnel who resided at the light. (Courtesy Grand Traverse Lighthouse Museum Collection.)

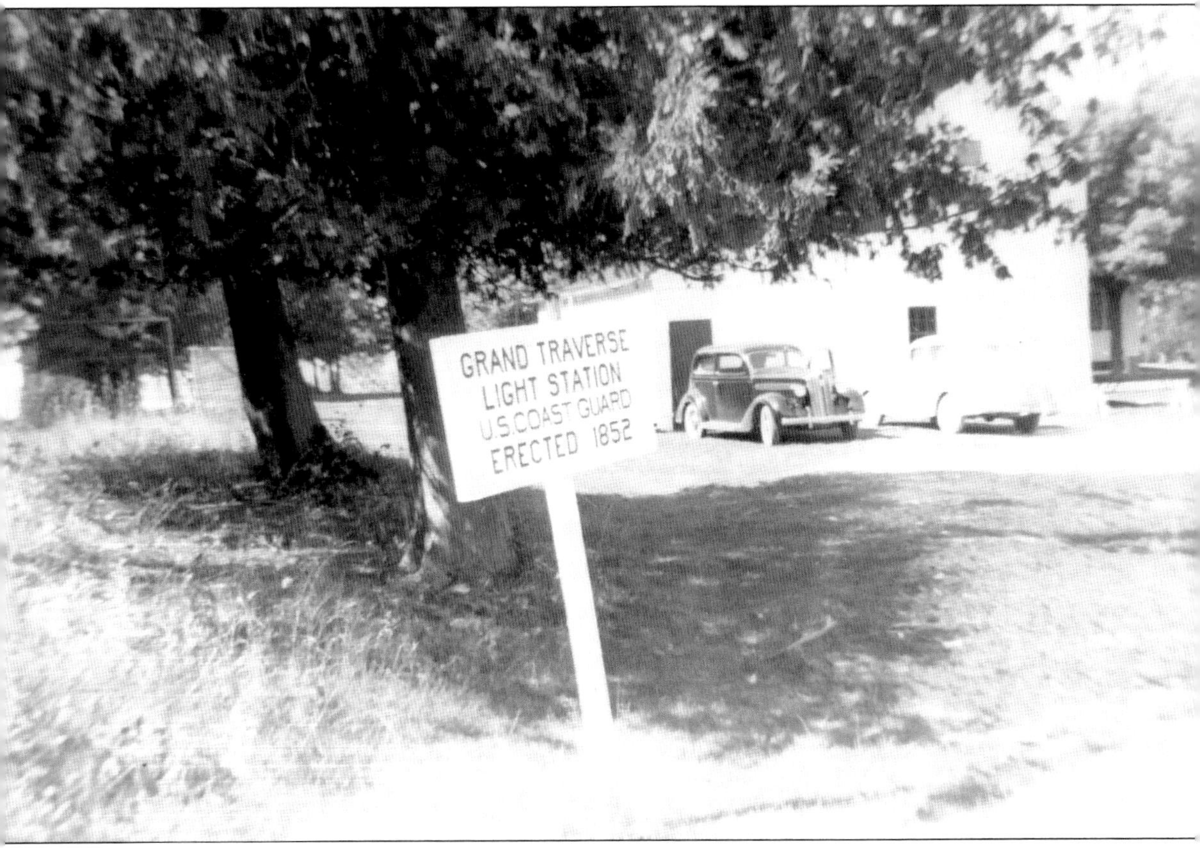

The sign says, "Grand Traverse Light Station, U.S. Coast Guard, Erected 1852." In a 1999 letter, coastguardman Al Tarsa speaks of arriving at the lighthouse in the spring of 1952 and was greeted with a sign that indicated, to his surprise, the station was established in 1852. It was one of many unexpected discoveries that were a bit shocking for this inexperienced traveler. He was surprised and a bit concerned that he had to drive so far north to find his new assignment. His concern soon disappeared when, "I became aware of the beauty of Leelanau County and Lake Michigan." (Courtesy Grand Traverse Lighthouse Museum Collection.)

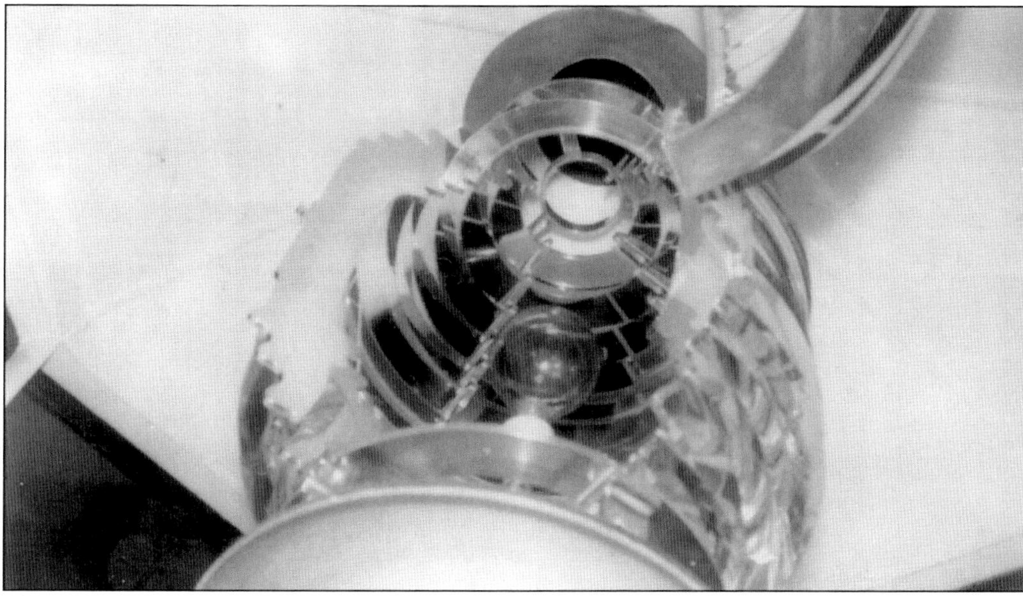

This is the only known photograph of the fourth-order Fresnel lens at the Grand Traverse Light Station. It was taken in 1953. A fourth-order lens could be seen up to 17 nautical miles. Frenchman Augustin Fresnel invented the lens using prisms that magnified and projected the light more powerfully than any other light developed to date. By the beginning of the Civil War, all American lighthouses were outfitted with this new technological advancement. (Courtesy Grand Traverse Lighthouse Museum Collection.)

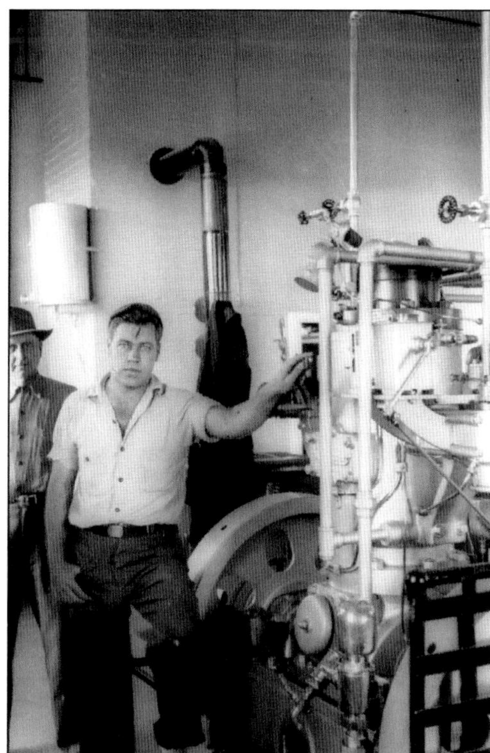

Edwin I. "Johnny" Johnson is pictured here in the Fog Signal Building at the Grand Traverse Light Station. To his left is a man named Bud. All the equipment needed to run the fog signal was located in this building, in which electricity was not installed for another several years. (Courtesy Grand Traverse Lighthouse Museum Collection.)

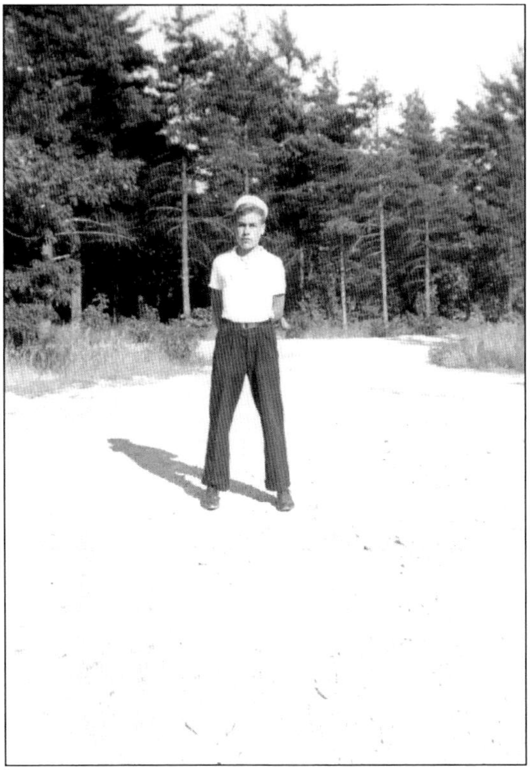

Edwin I. "Johnny" Johnson is pictured here on the shore of Lake Michigan. Five miles to the west is Cathead Bay. It is believed there are two shipwrecks in Cathead Bay, schooners *Sardinia* and *Tribune*. The *Sardinia*, built in 1860 in Detroit, was lost in a storm on November 4, 1874, with no loss of life. The *Tribune*, a 102-foot schooner with two masts, disappeared in April 1848 while en route from Chicago to New York with a load of wheat. (Courtesy Grand Traverse Lighthouse Museum Collection.)

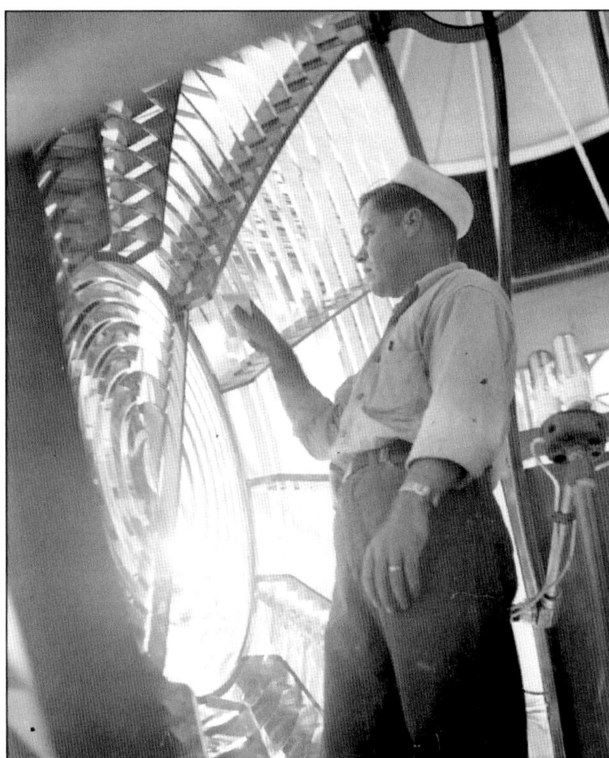

Pictured here, Johnson is cleaning the clamshell lens at the White Shoal light station, which is located in the western end of the Straits of Mackinac. This candy cane–striped light tower was erected in 1910, replacing the lightship No. 56, which was assigned to the station since 1891. The light still remains operational today. The early lens was removed and is on display at the Whitefish Point Lighthouse near Paradise. (Courtesy Grand Traverse Lighthouse Museum Collection.)

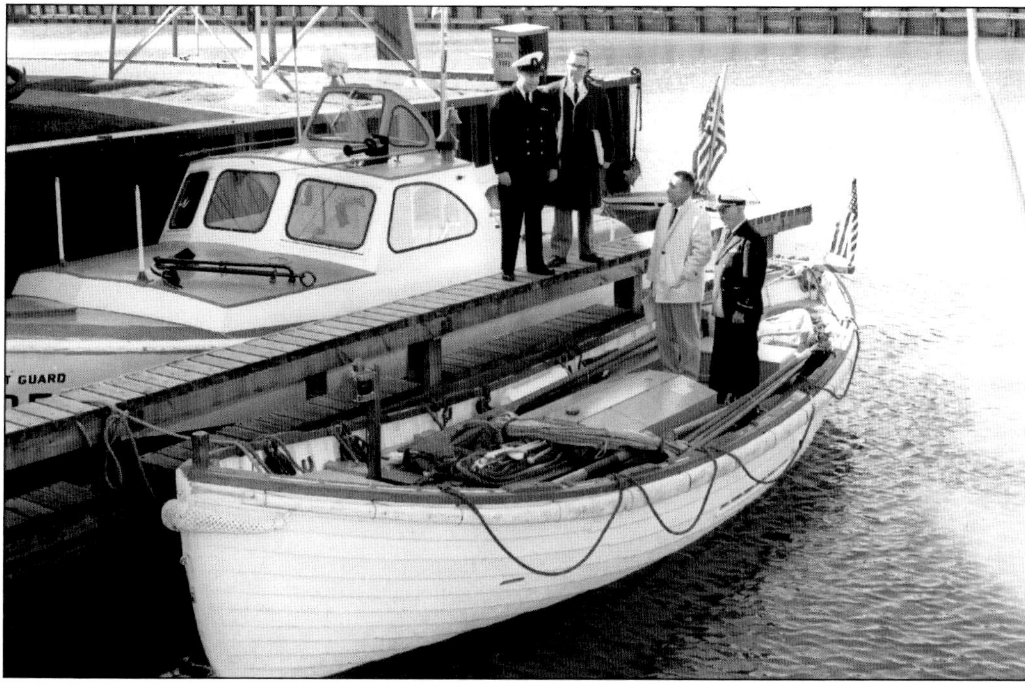

In the background is a U.S. Coast Guard 40-foot motor launch from about 1954. These types of boats were used at many stations around the Great Lakes in addition to the larger Coast Guard cutters, buoy tenders, and ice breakers. (Courtesy Grand Traverse Lighthouse Museum Collection.)

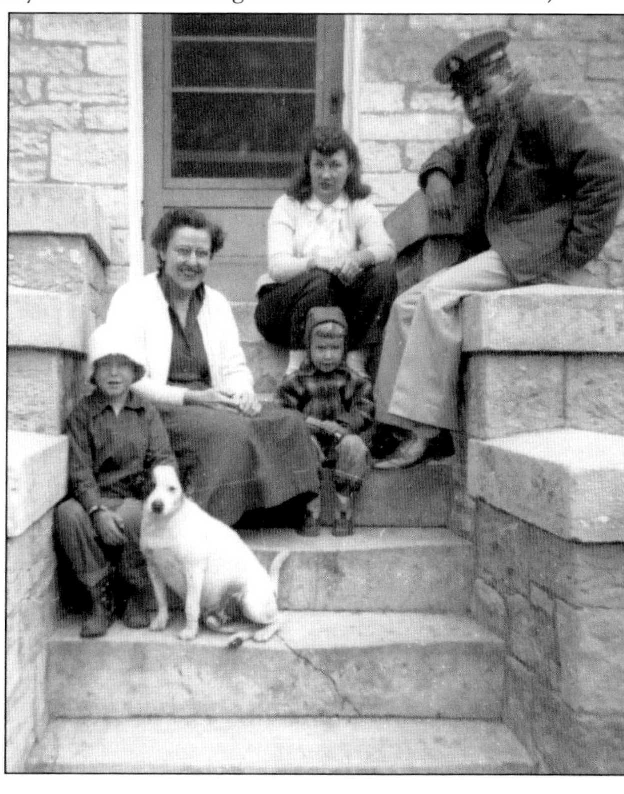

Johnson is pictured here with his wife, Evelyn (Ninnimen) Johnson, his sister Evelyn (Johnson) Brady, niece Sue Brady, and nephew Jack Brady. The location of this photograph is unknown but is suggested to be at one of the stations Johnson was appointed. He married Evelyn on October 12, 1948. She passed away in 1972. (Courtesy Grand Traverse Lighthouse Museum Collection.)

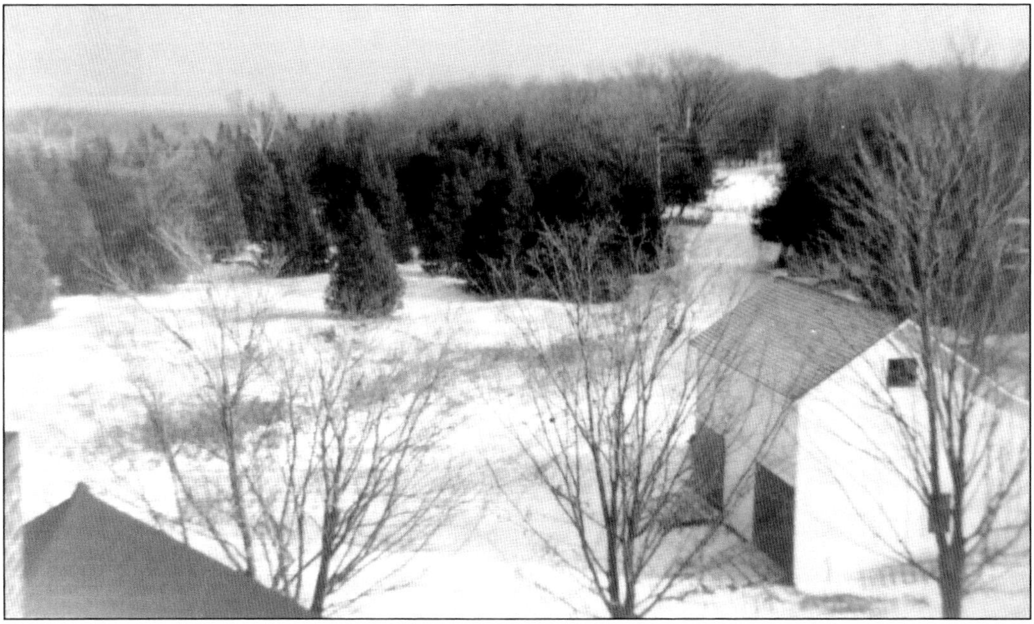

This photograph, taken from the lighthouse tower's catwalk, is dated November 30, 1952, and shows the light station looking to the east. The barn is on the right and the county road from Northport (nine miles away) is in the background. Northport was an important shipping port during the mid-1800s, exporting a variety of agricultural goods. (Courtesy Grand Traverse Lighthouse Museum Collection.)

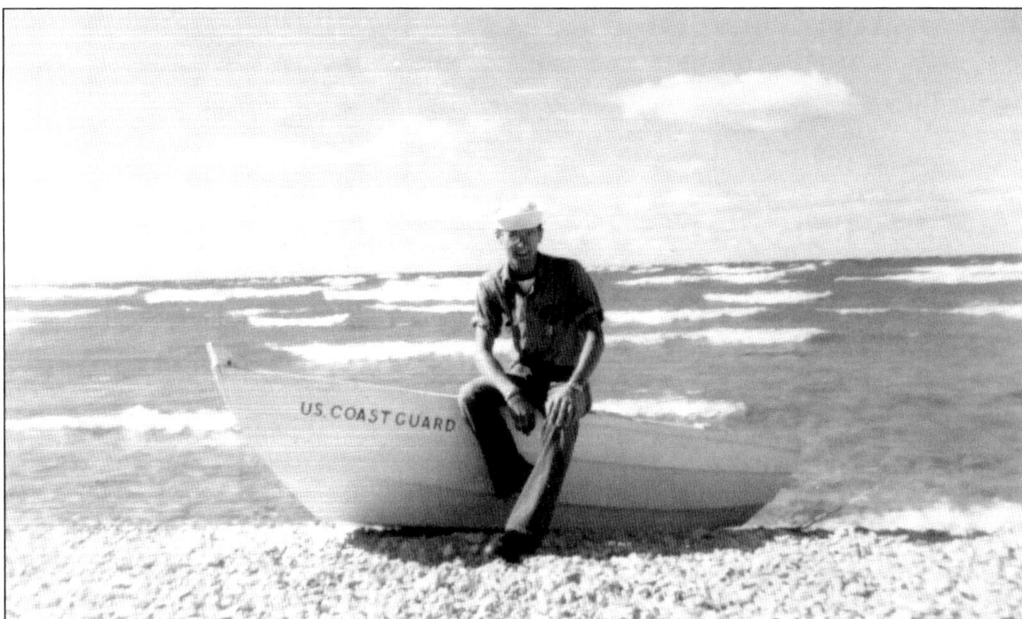

Here a coastguardman is sitting on the U.S. Coast Guard 10-foot dinghy. The station had only a small rowboat that was used for maintaining the aids to navigation under their charge. South Fox Island is in the far distance. Many lighthouse keepers rotated between Grand Traverse and South Fox Island Light Stations. (Courtesy Grand Traverse Lighthouse Museum Collection.)

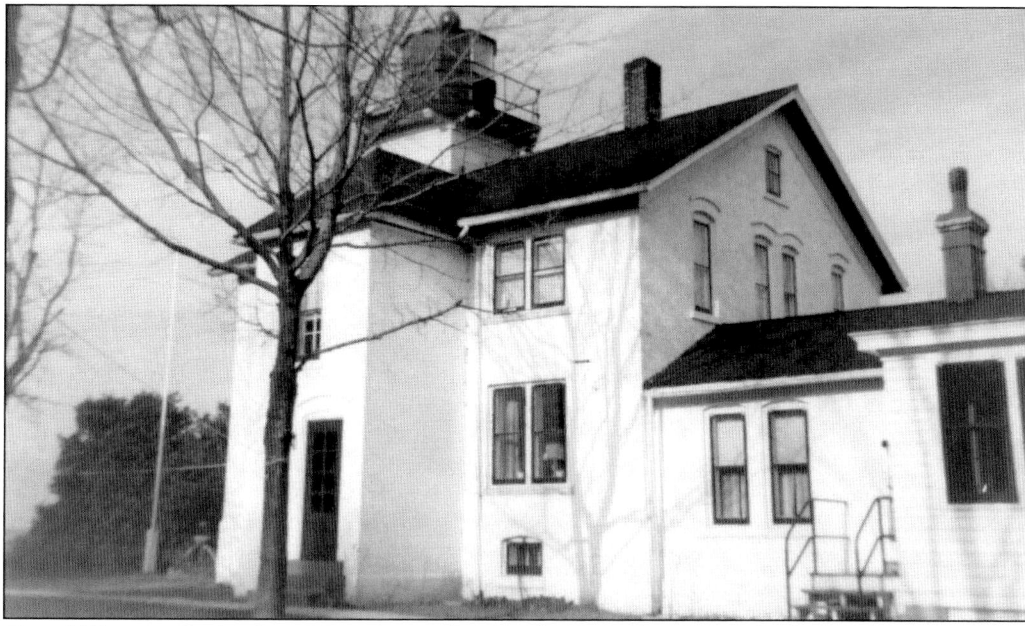

Grand Traverse Light Station is pictured around 1952. The entire dwelling is painted white, including the tower. Enclosed porches were added to the east elevation on both the south and north sides just two years prior to this photograph. The gutters around the roof were also removed and many modern updates took place, including the installation of electricity and plumbing for the first time. (Courtesy Grand Traverse Lighthouse Museum Collection.)

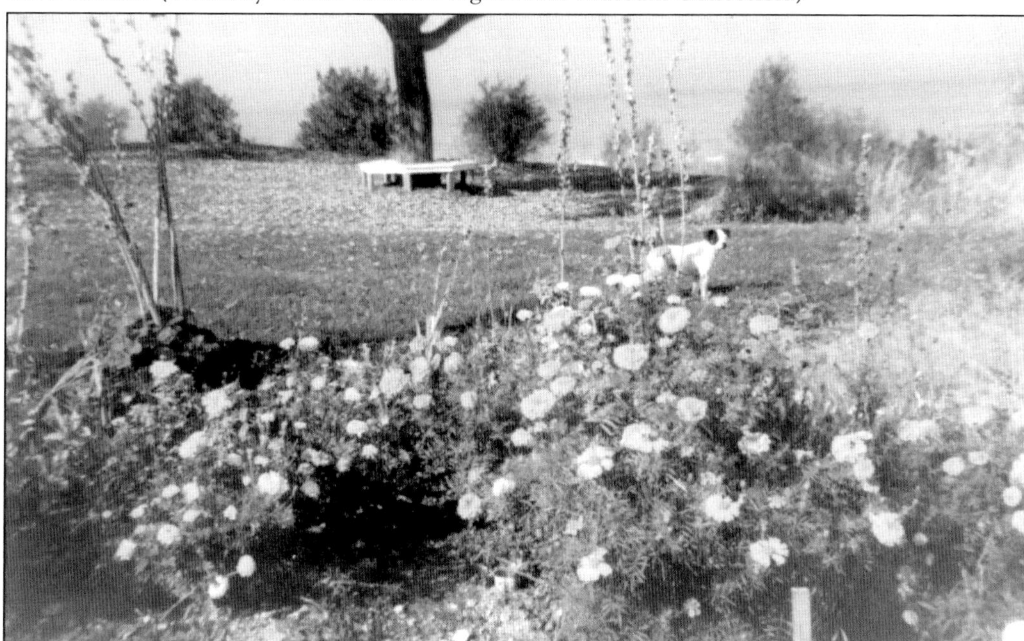

This garden, located where the Coast Guard garage is today, shows beautiful flowers in the foreground, Edwin I. "Johnny" Johnson's dog, and the eight-sided bench around the maple tree in the background. The eight-sided bench disappeared in the 1960s but was rebuilt around the same maple tree in 2007.

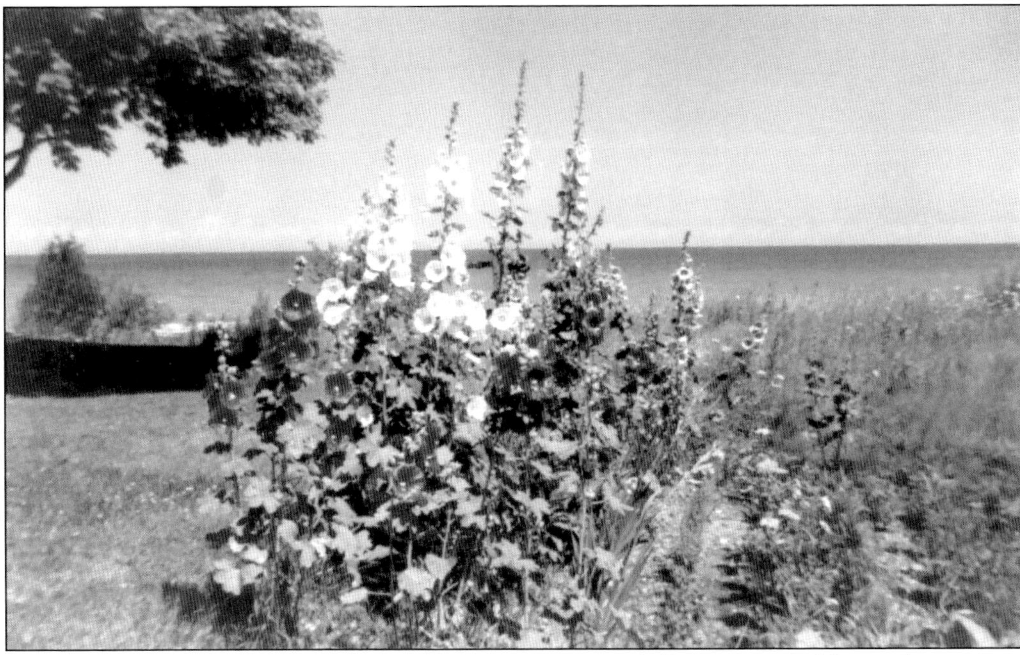

This is the flower boat around 1952. Over the years, many different types of flowers have graced the boat. In this particular year, beautiful hollyhocks are adding color and elegance to the site. There were at least five other gardens around the station used for growing vegetables, herbs, and flowers. (Courtesy Grand Traverse Lighthouse Museum Collection.)

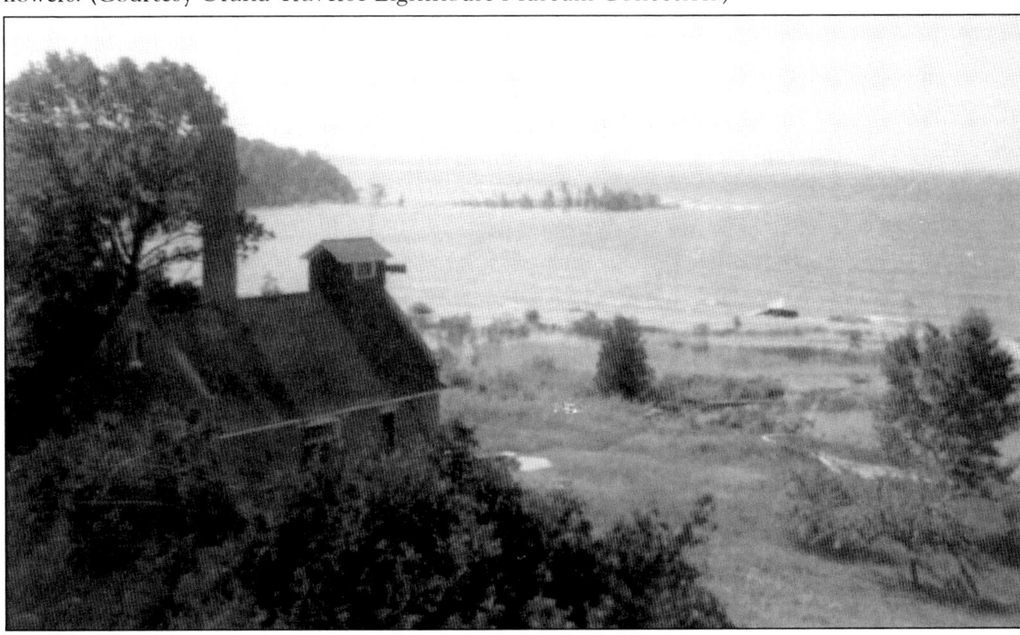

Here is a southwest view from the tower catwalk. The Fog Signal Building can be seen in the foreground while Cathead Bay is in the distance. Just past Cathead Bay is the Manitou Passage that leads to Chicago. There are many shipwrecks in the passage, including the 1911 wreck of the *Three Brothers*, a wooden steamer. It was beached on South Manitou Island. (Courtesy Grand Traverse Lighthouse Museum Collection.)

Looking northwest toward Lake Michigan, the grounds of the Grand Traverse Light Station are pictured. A maple tree with an eight-sided bench is to the left. From this vantage point on a clear day, one can see North and South Fox Islands, which are only 17 miles out in Lake Michigan. A webcam shows the South Fox Island Light Station. (Courtesy Grand Traverse Lighthouse Museum Collection.)

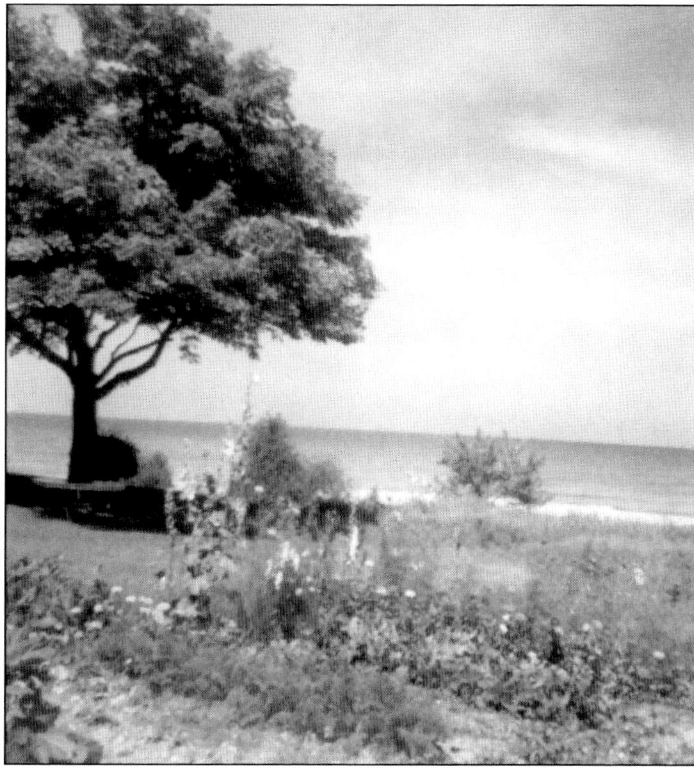

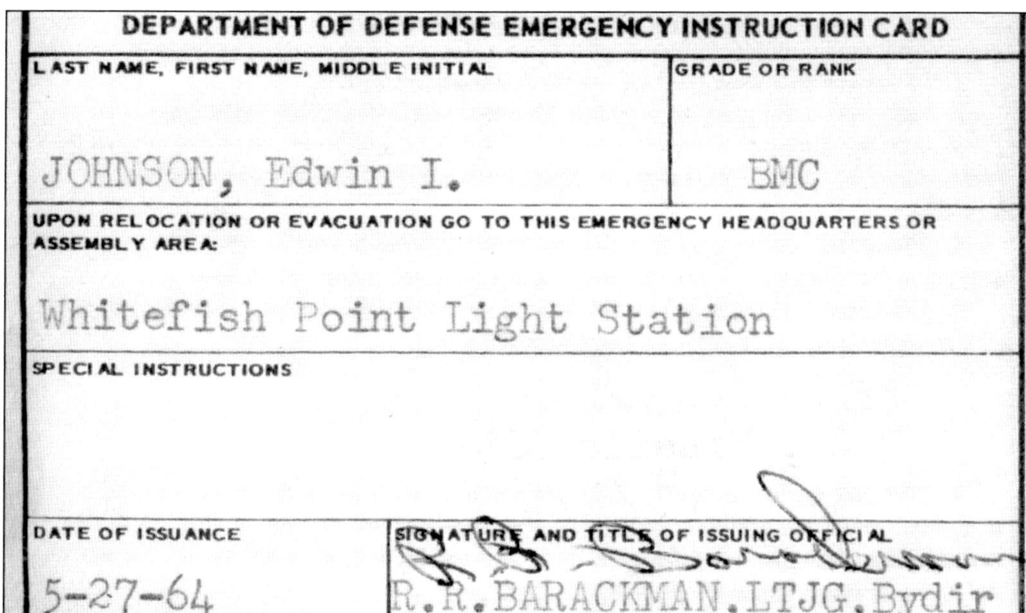

DEPARTMENT OF DEFENSE EMERGENCY INSTRUCTION CARD

LAST NAME, FIRST NAME, MIDDLE INITIAL	GRADE OR RANK
JOHNSON, Edwin I.	BMC

UPON RELOCATION OR EVACUATION GO TO THIS EMERGENCY HEADQUARTERS OR ASSEMBLY AREA:

Whitefish Point Light Station

SPECIAL INSTRUCTIONS

DATE OF ISSUANCE	SIGNATURE AND TITLE OF ISSUING OFFICIAL
5-27-64	R.R.BARACKMAN,LTJG,Bydir

This is a Department of Defense emergency instruction card for Edwin I. "Johnny" Johnson. He was issued this card while serving the Whitefish Point Light Station on May 27, 1964. This is one of approximately 100 military documents that were discovered in a dumpster and donated to the Grand Traverse Lighthouse Museum. (Courtesy Grand Traverse Lighthouse Museum Collection.)

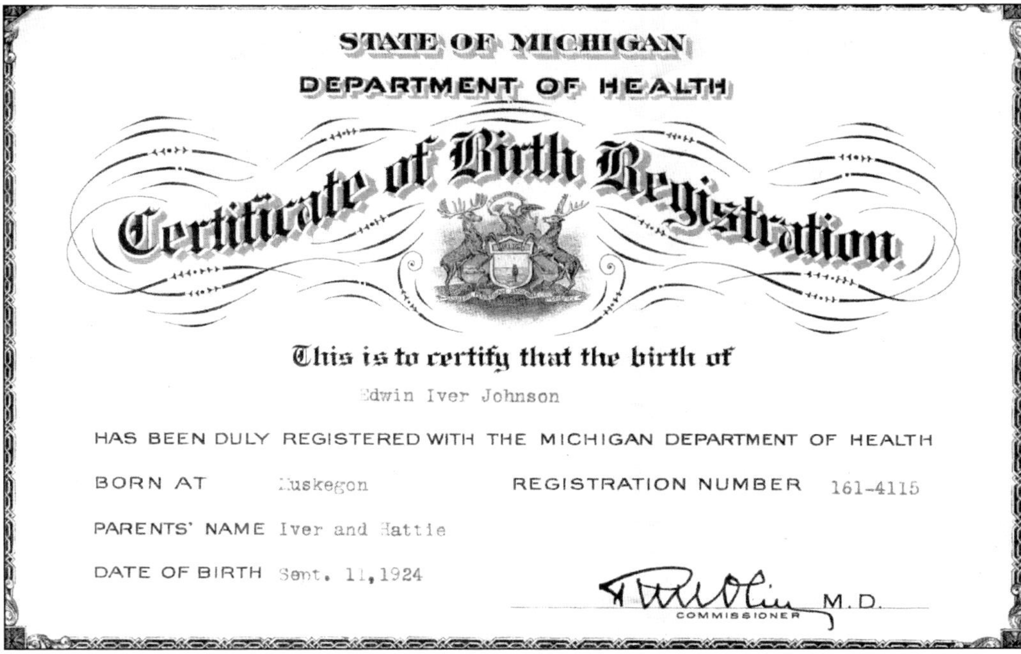

STATE OF MICHIGAN

DEPARTMENT OF HEALTH

Certificate of Birth Registration

This is to certify that the birth of

Edwin Iver Johnson

HAS BEEN DULY REGISTERED WITH THE MICHIGAN DEPARTMENT OF HEALTH

BORN AT Muskegon REGISTRATION NUMBER 161-4115

PARENTS' NAME Iver and Hattie

DATE OF BIRTH Sept. 11,1924

M.D.
COMMISSIONER

Edwin I. "Johnny" Johnson was born to Iver and Hattie Johnson on September 11, 1924, in Muskegon. Johnson spent 22 years in the Coast Guard, and after retiring, he worked for Kal Excavating of Omena for 21 years. He was also a 40-year member of the Masonic Lodge. (Courtesy Grand Traverse Lighthouse Museum Collection.)

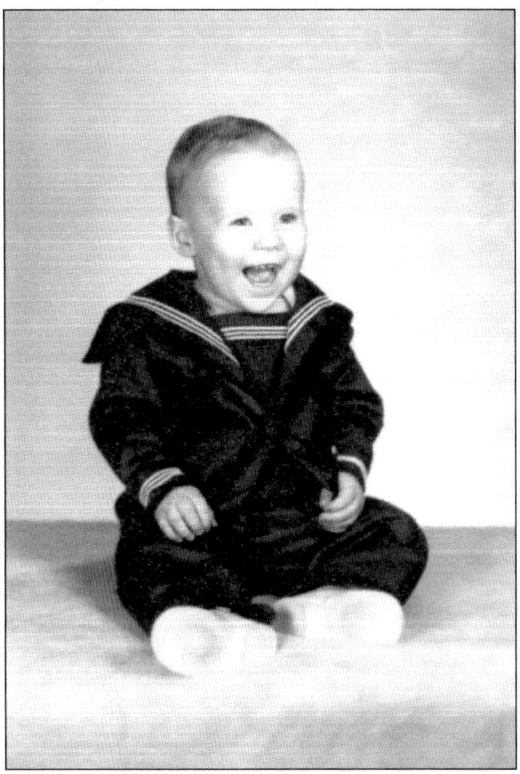

Michael Briggs, son of coastguardman David D. Briggs, was born on February 2, 1967. He was the last child to be born during the time the Coast Guard occupied this station. This was his first home. Michael was one of five children over the past 150 years either born at Grand Traverse Light Station or born during the time their father's were stationed there. (Courtesy Dave Briggs.)

David D. Briggs is pictured here around 1965. He was stationed at Grand Traverse Light Station from 1966 to 1967. Others stationed with him were civilian keeper John Marken and coastguardman Sterling Nickerson. Nickerson entered the Coast Guard on May 12, 1964, spending most of his time at the Grand Traverse Light Station before being discharged in 1968. (Courtesy Dave Briggs.)

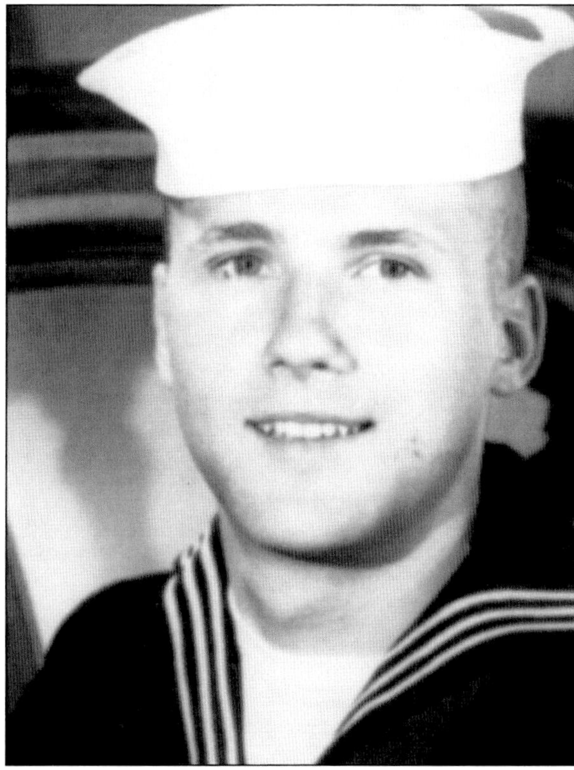

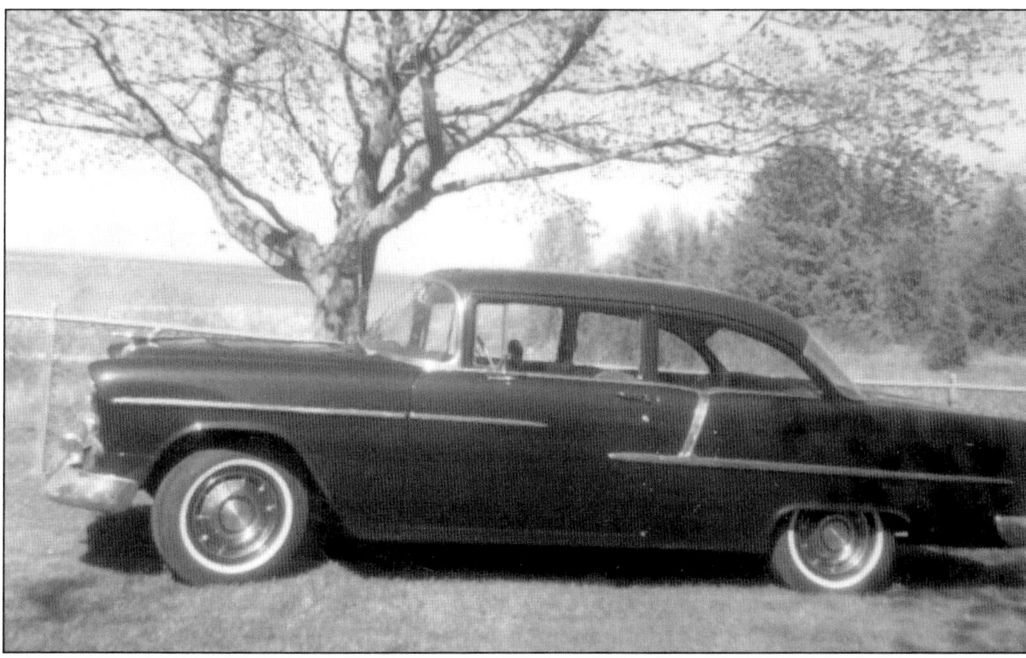

Here is a view from the lighthouse looking northwest toward Charlevoix with Dave Briggs's car in the foreground. Legend has it that Capt. Peter Nelson's ship, the *Venus*, is wrecked just north of the light station toward Charlevoix, and a mystery ship is sunk in that same area holding a treasure trove of gold. (Courtesy Dave Briggs.)

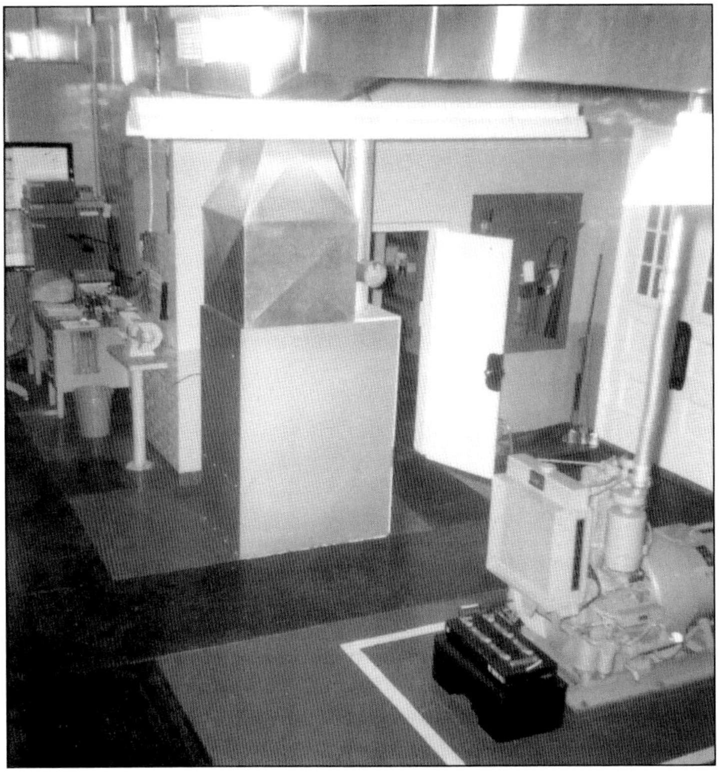

This is the interior of the Fog Signal Building, dated October 1967. Electricity was installed in this building in 1966 when the oscillating fog signal was installed on the exterior of the building. Blowing the foghorn became easier with just the switch of a button to turn it on and off. (Courtesy Dave Briggs.)

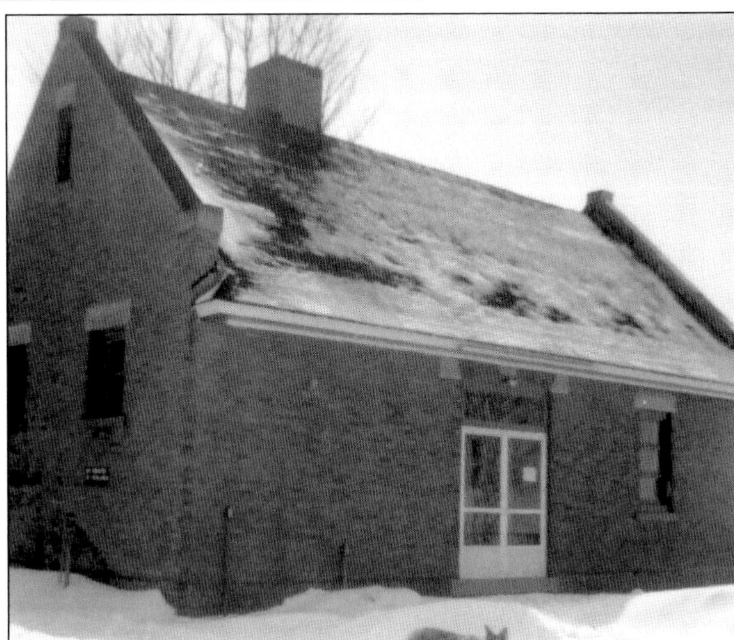

Pictured here is the exterior of the Fog Signal Building with the dog Sox in the foreground. The cupola is no longer on the roof. The electric oscillating horn was used until 1970 when it was deemed unnecessary as technological advances had progressed to the extent that most fog signals around the Great Lakes were no longer needed or useful. (Courtesy Dave Briggs.)

Dave Briggs and his dog Sox are in the front yard of the light station. Notice the station has a metal fence surrounding it. The photograph is dated October 1967. From the very beginning, the light station has had some kind of fencing. The original one was a white wooden-rail fence. (Courtesy Dave Briggs.)

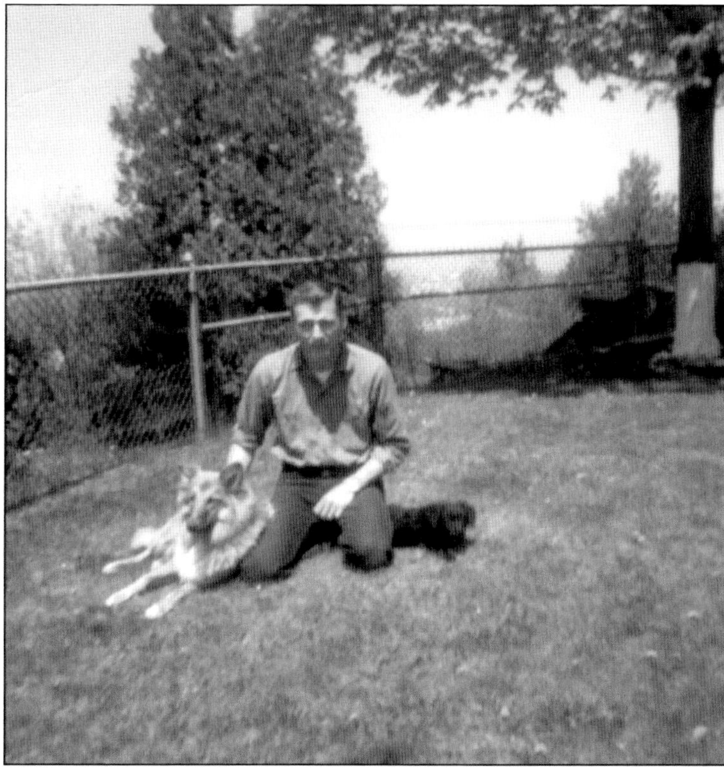

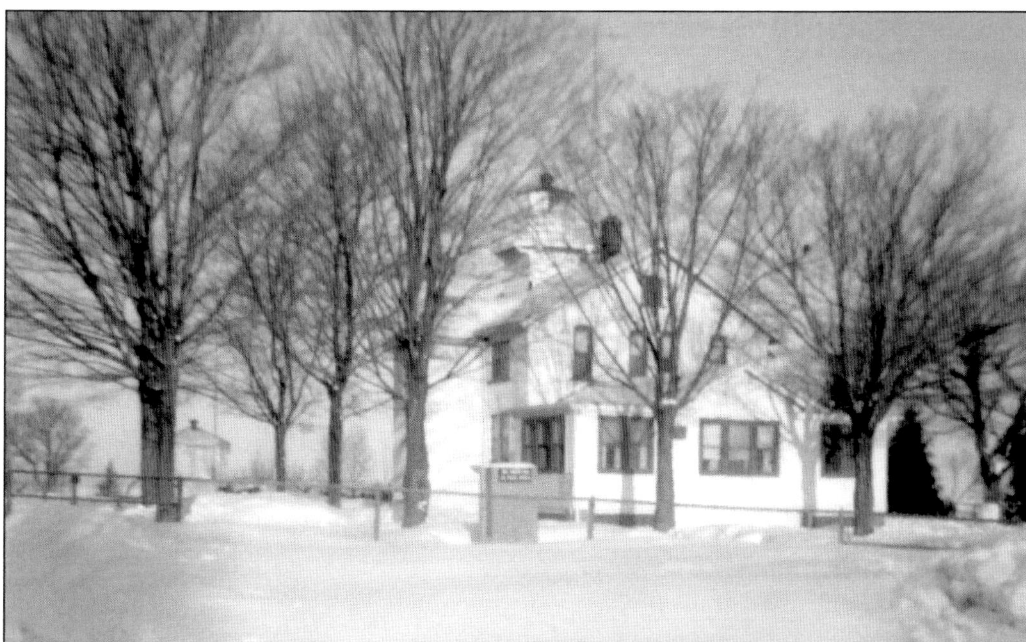

Here is a winter scene of the lighthouse, looking from the east. Several trees have grown in the immediate area surrounding the building. For the winter, the wooden screens were removed from the 49 windows and replaced with heavy-duty winter storms, sealing the interior from the fierce northeasterly winds. They attach from the outside of the building. (Courtesy Dave Briggs.)

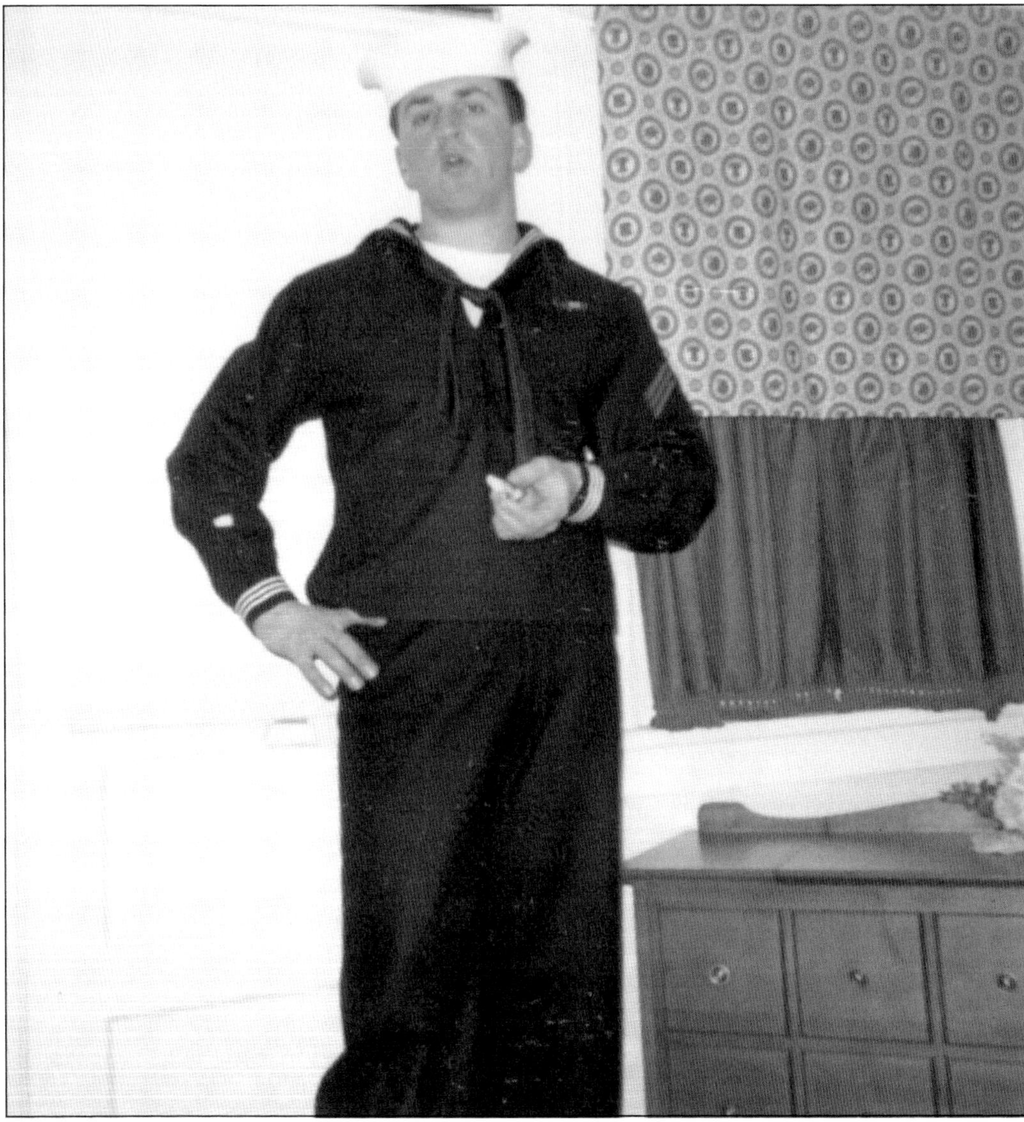

Coastguardman John J. Elias is pictured here around 1964. He was stationed at Grand Traverse with his wife, Karen, and six-week-old twins from March 1968 through May 15, 1971, at which time he left the Coast Guard. They remember the usual animals around the place, including skunks, raccoons, and a bobcat. (Courtesy Grand Traverse Lighthouse Museum Collection.)

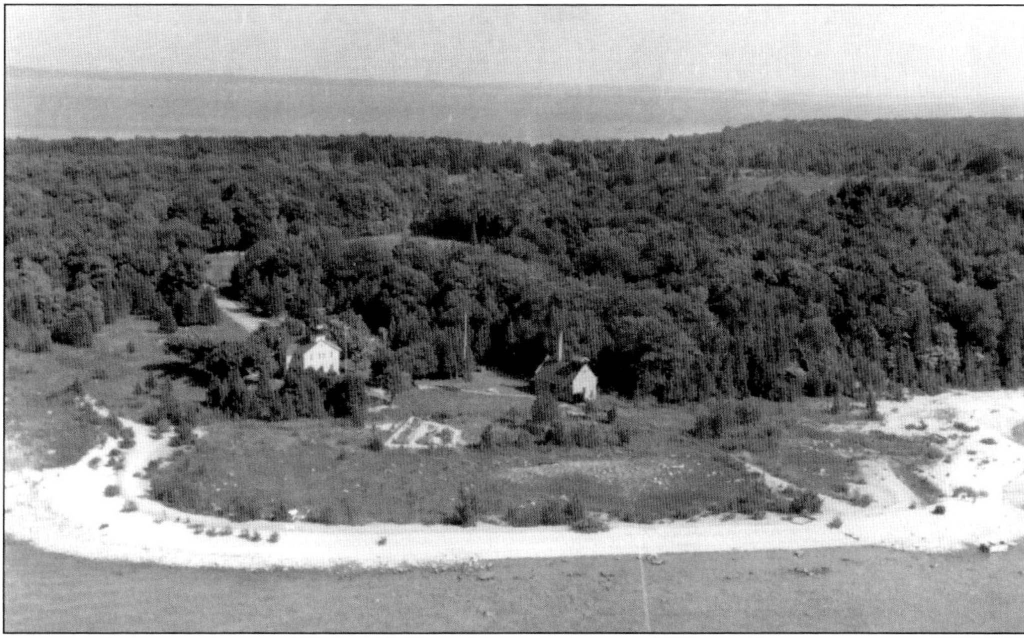

Here is another shot of Grand Traverse Light Station from the air. The fourth-order Fresnel lens was also removed at the time the lighthouse closed. The final disposition of this lens is unknown. Many times when a lens was removed, it was destroyed or put into storage. Often times, these lenses found their way into private ownership. (Courtesy Archives of Michigan, Negative 10378.)

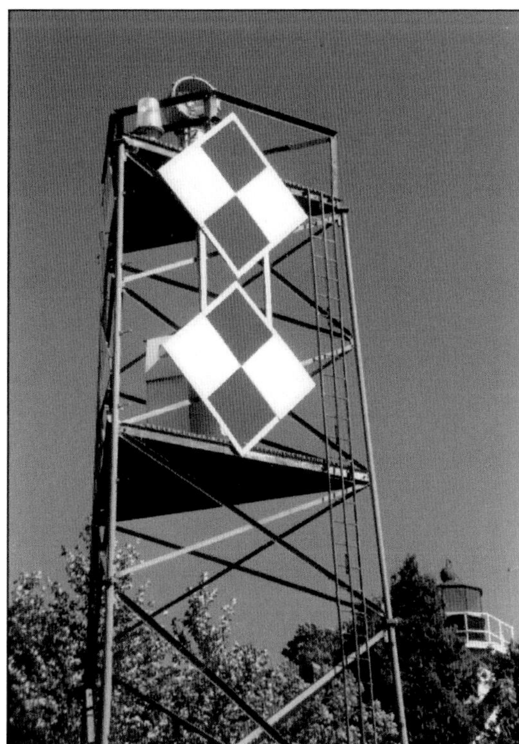

The 1972 steel tower, seen here with an automated revolving aero-beacon, was powered by electricity with a backup battery system. This system operated a small lamp when commercial power failed. This aero-beacon is similar to what might be found at an airport. It could be seen up to 17 nautical miles away. In 1996, the light began to fail and was replaced with a new light that could be seen for 24 nautical miles. (Courtesy Grand Traverse Lighthouse Museum Collection.)

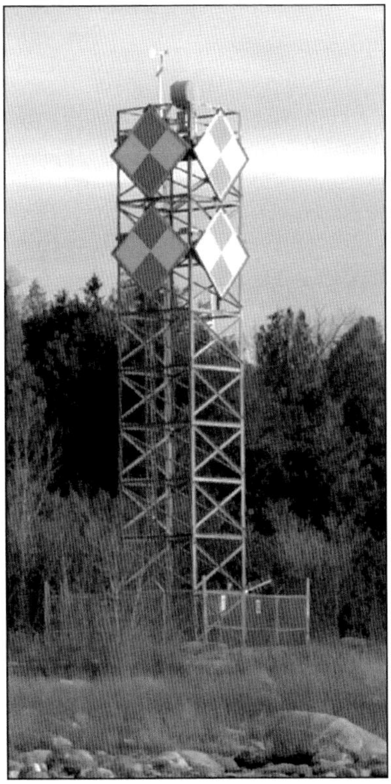

The new light continued to experience difficulties over the next four years, and in 2000, the entire tower was replaced, and a new light was placed atop the new 53-foot steel structure. Over the course of the last 150 years, the height of the light was always a challenge. When the first tower was built, it stood 30 feet tall; the second lighthouse was 49 feet tall. The first steel tower was 51 feet tall, and now the current tower is 53 feet tall. (Courtesy Mark Westmaas.)

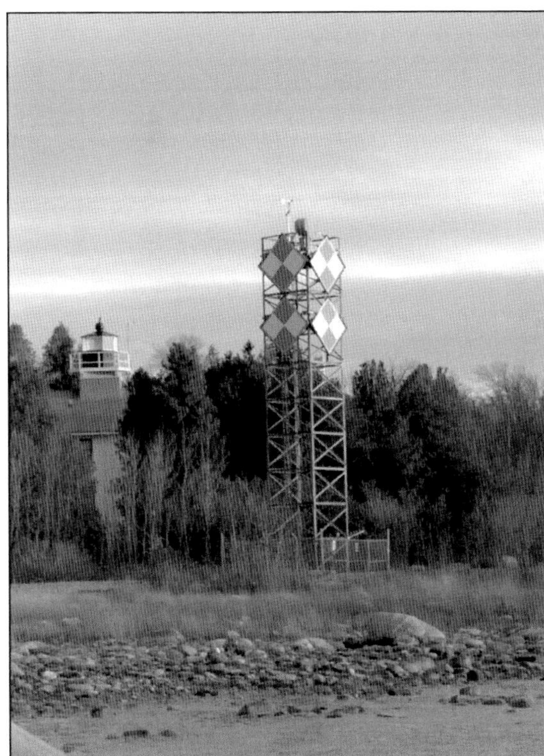

In 2007, the light once again began to falter; the motor burned up and the light would no longer rotate. The U.S. Coast Guard Air Station from Traverse City flew out in October to lift the aero-beacon from its post and replace it with a smaller, yet just as powerful light to guide the modern-day sailors. The old aero-beacon was given to the Grand Traverse Lighthouse Museum for display. (Courtesy Mark Westmaas.)

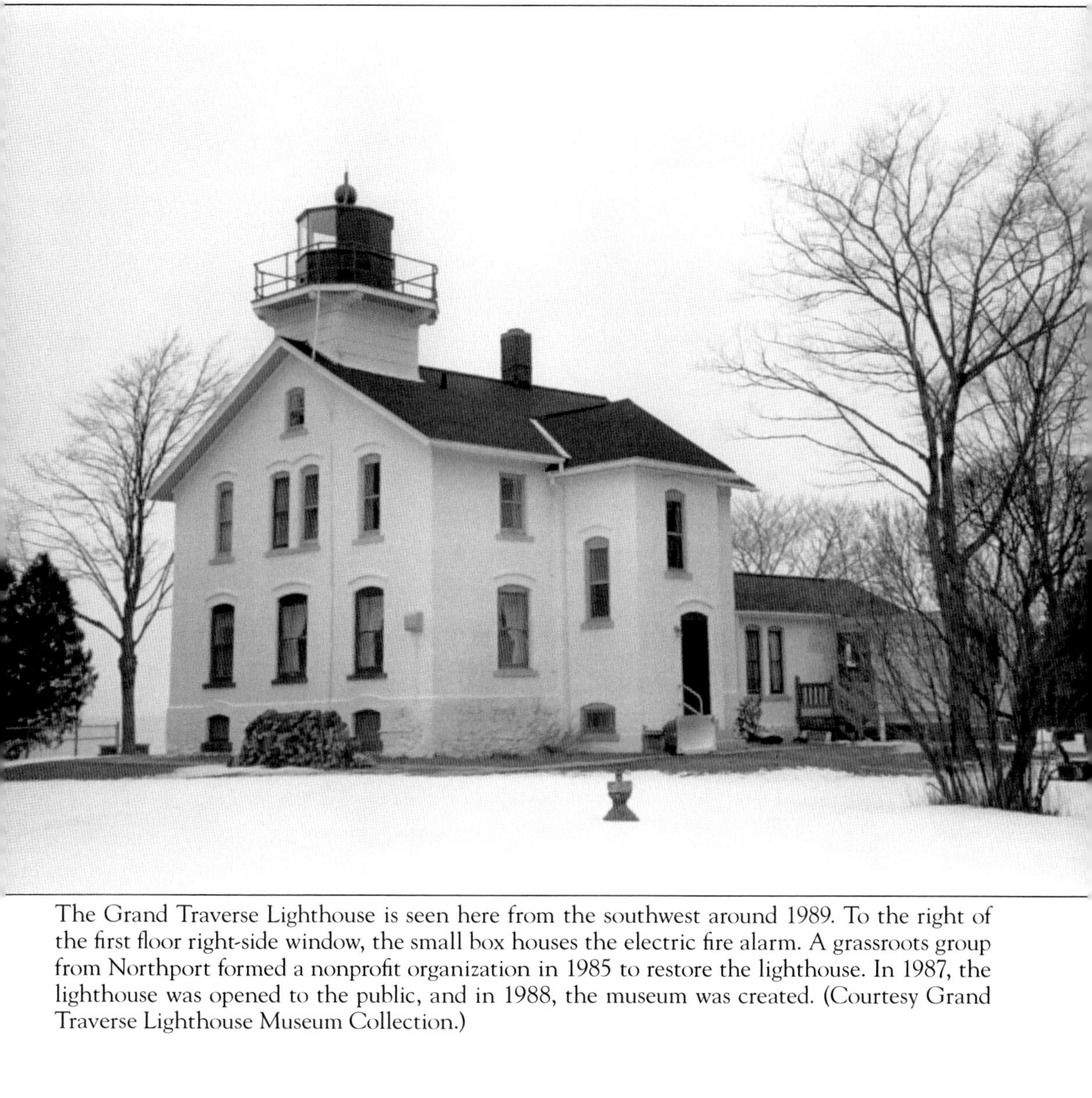

The Grand Traverse Lighthouse is seen here from the southwest around 1989. To the right of the first floor right-side window, the small box houses the electric fire alarm. A grassroots group from Northport formed a nonprofit organization in 1985 to restore the lighthouse. In 1987, the lighthouse was opened to the public, and in 1988, the museum was created. (Courtesy Grand Traverse Lighthouse Museum Collection.)

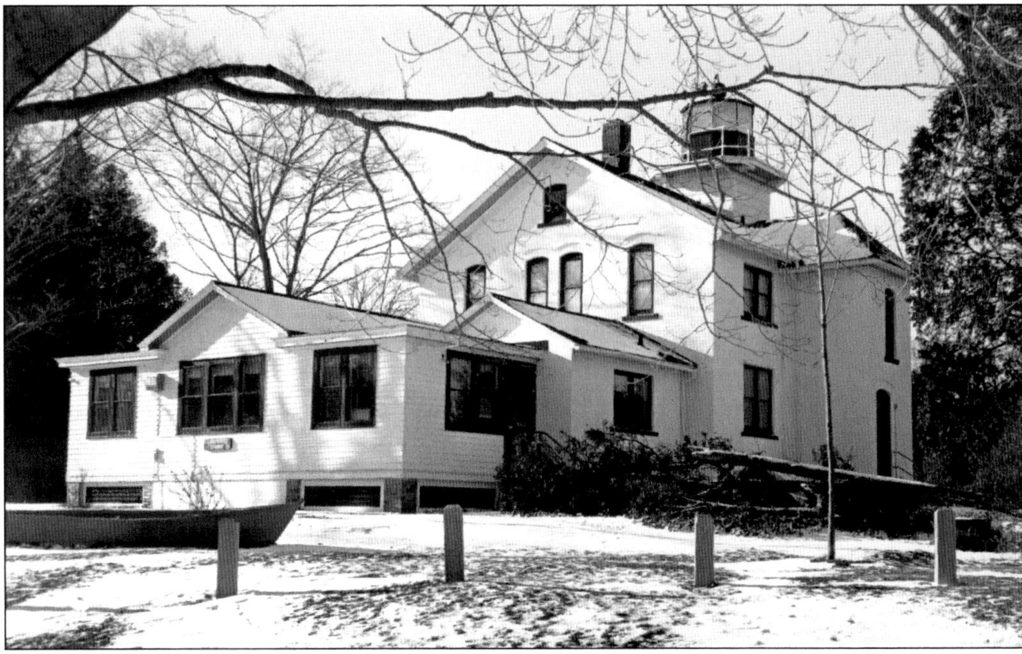

Today one can tour the restored Grand Traverse Light Station and embark on a journey of "days gone by." A climb to the tower offers a wonderful view of the surrounding area. Many people over the past 22 years have made this lighthouse museum what it is today. (Courtesy Grand Traverse Lighthouse Museum Collection.)

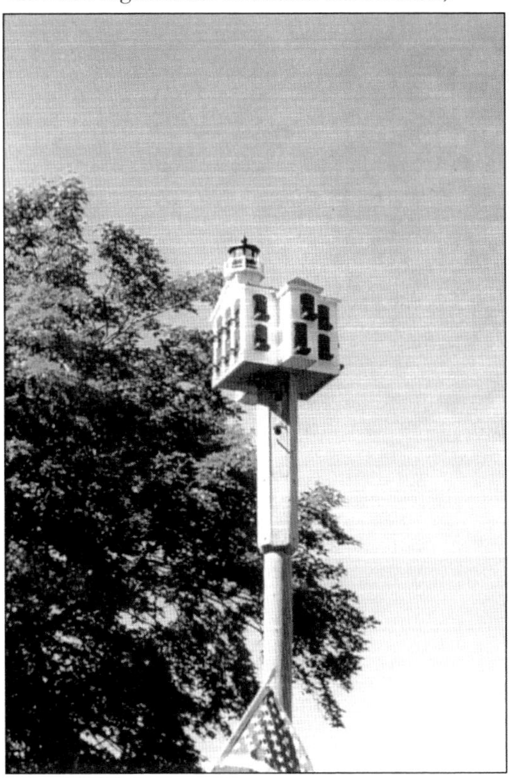

On top of a tall pole just west of the lighthouse is a birdhouse, in the shape of Grand Traverse Lighthouse, for purple martins or other birds to make their home. This unique miniature was made by Northport resident Trevor Jones. (Courtesy Doug McCormick.)

Six

Great Lakes Vessels
Historical Information

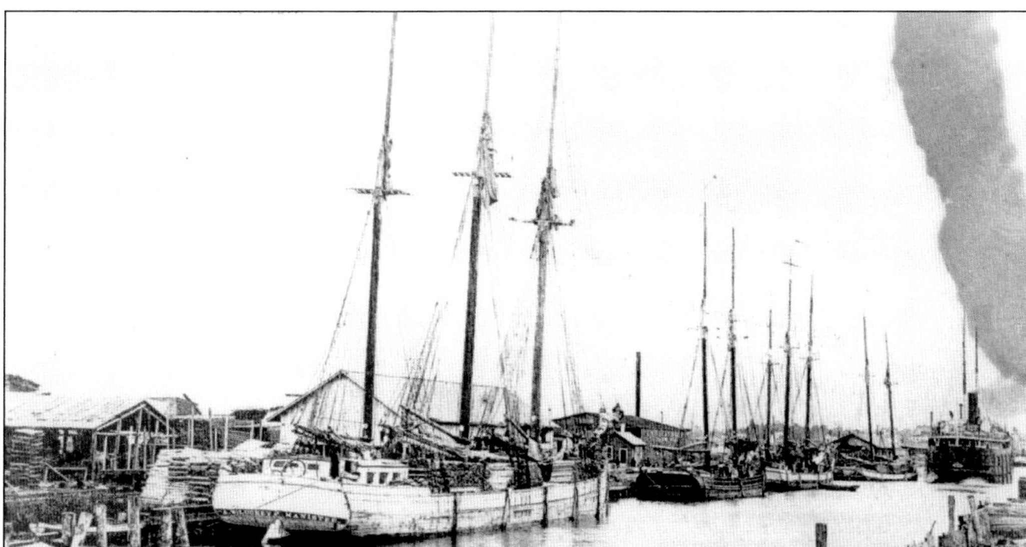

By the mid-1800s, shipping had increased on the Great Lakes as the primary and often only mode of transportation for goods and people. This photograph depicts what a typical shipping port around the Great Lakes might have looked like, filled with sailing vessels ready to load and begin their travel to other port cities. (Courtesy Grand Traverse Lighthouse Museum Collection.)

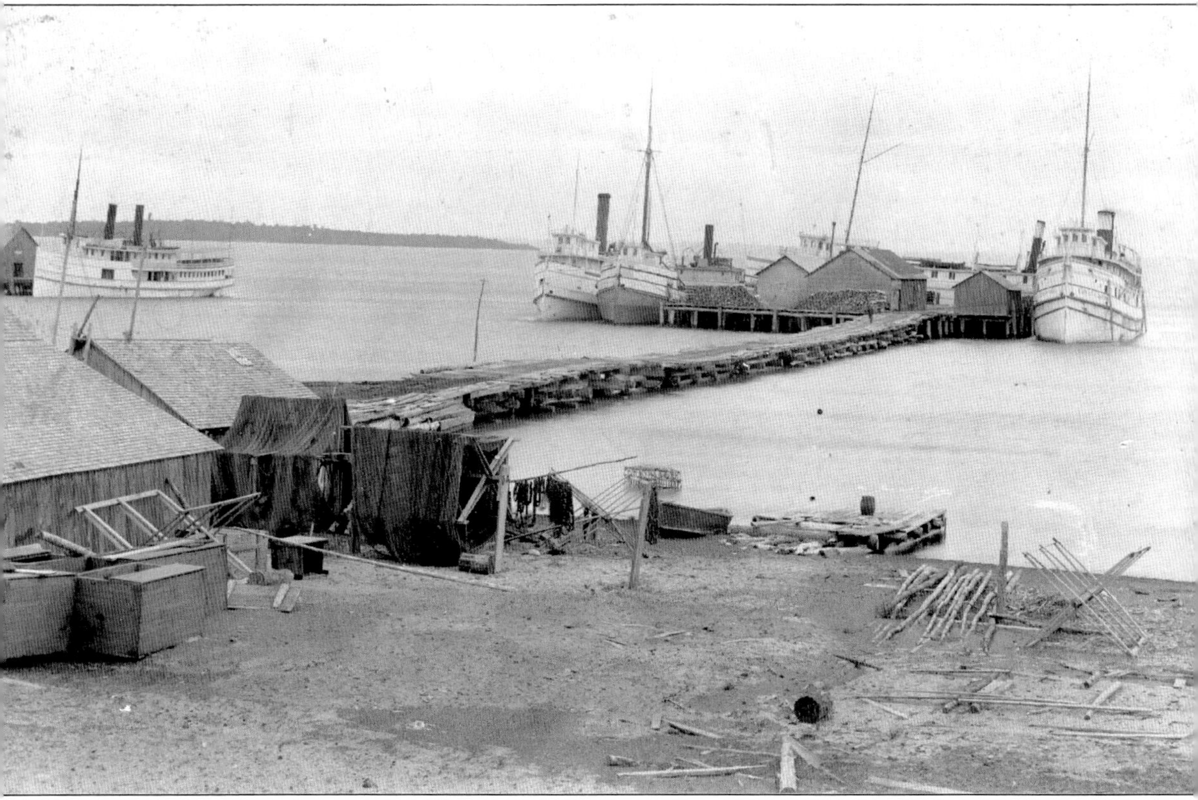

These are the docks of Northport. Grand Traverse Lighthouse was instrumental in the development of Northport as a major shipping port on the Great Lakes. Northport harbor was a natural safe harbor when vessels did not have to travel the expanse of Grand Traverse Bay south to Traverse City. Many agricultural goods were transported from Northport, including potatoes, apples, cherries, plums, and peaches. (Courtesy Grand Traverse Lighthouse Museum Collection.)

Here are two ships at dock in Northport. It was common, because of limited dock space, for two vessels to dock alongside each other while in port. The use of sailing vessels soon became extinct as the technology of steam-powered vessels became more efficient for moving goods and people. It was Deacon Joseph Dame who built the first dock in Northport, thus beginning a long run of shipping in and out of this area. (Courtesy Grand Traverse Lighthouse Museum Collection.)

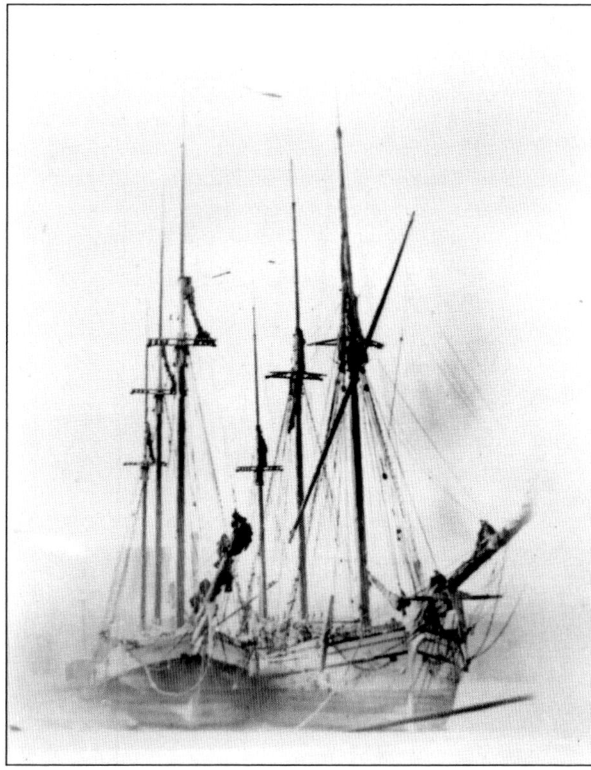

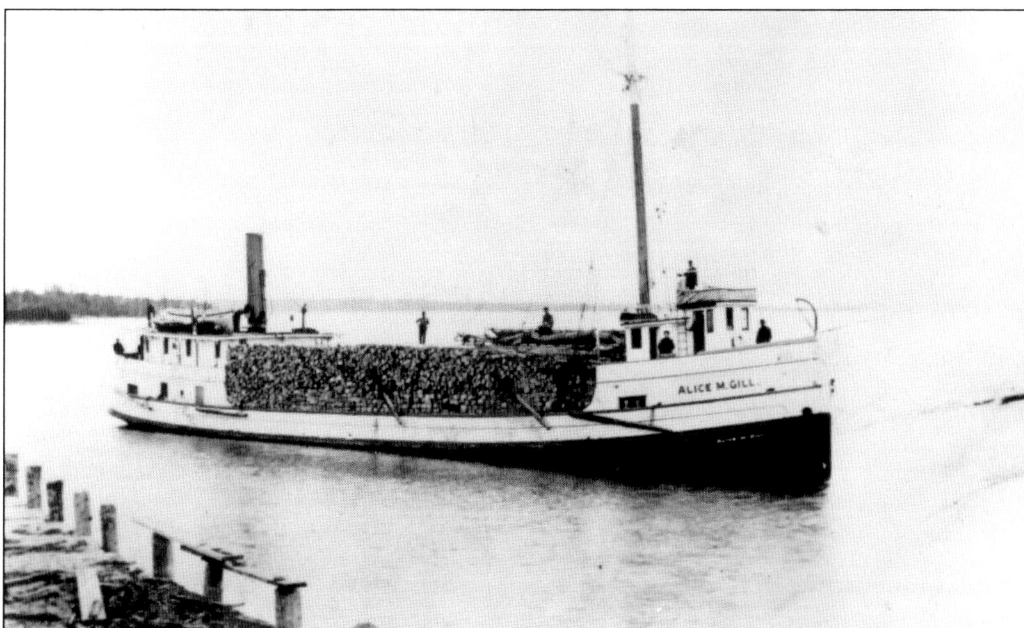

Pictured is the *Alice M. Gill* around 1899, with a load of lumber. As steam-powered vessels became more prevalent by the mid- to late 1800s, more than 15,000 cords of wood were sold as fuel for these steamers. Some of the other early vessels included the *Columbia*, *City of Grand Rapids*, *Lawrence*, and *Kimball*. (Courtesy Grand Traverse Lighthouse Museum Collection.)

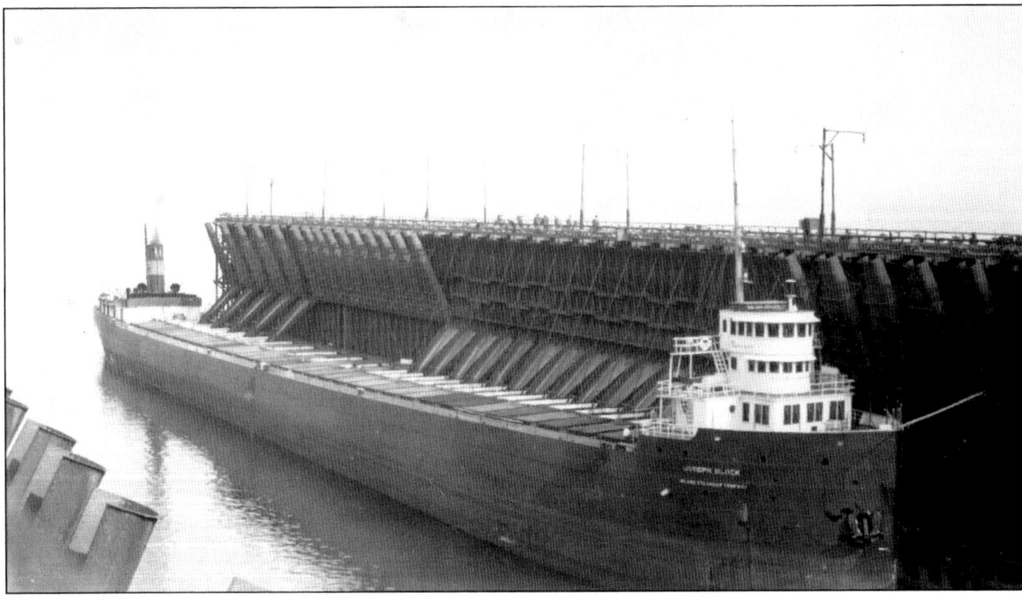

The freighter *Joseph Block*, seen at a loading dock, was originally launched as the *Arthur H. Hawgood* but was renamed *Joseph Block* in 1912. It was renamed again in 1969 as the *George M. Steinbrenner* after George Steinbrenner, who went into the shipping business with his father. The freighter was scrapped in 1978. (Courtesy Grand Traverse Lighthouse Museum Collection.)

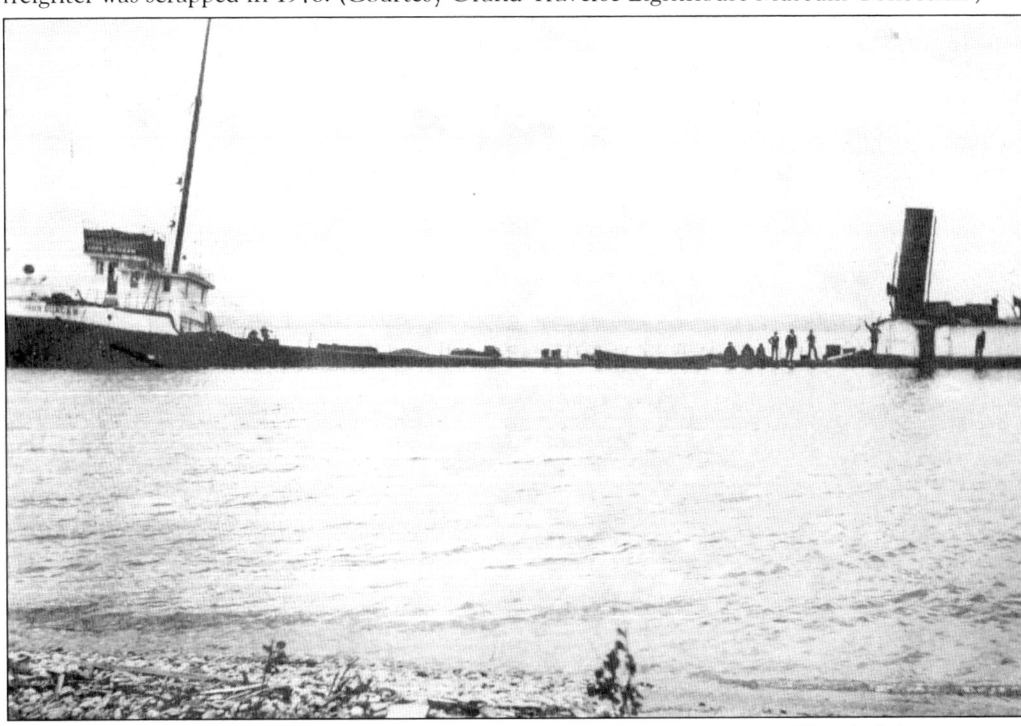

The freighter *John Duncan* sunk in Northport harbor during a storm. The 225-foot steamer, carrying a load of coal on Lake Michigan, sought shelter in Northport. The freighter was within 200 feet of the dock when it sank. The entire cargo was lost, but the crew was saved. (Courtesy Grand Traverse Lighthouse Museum Collection.)

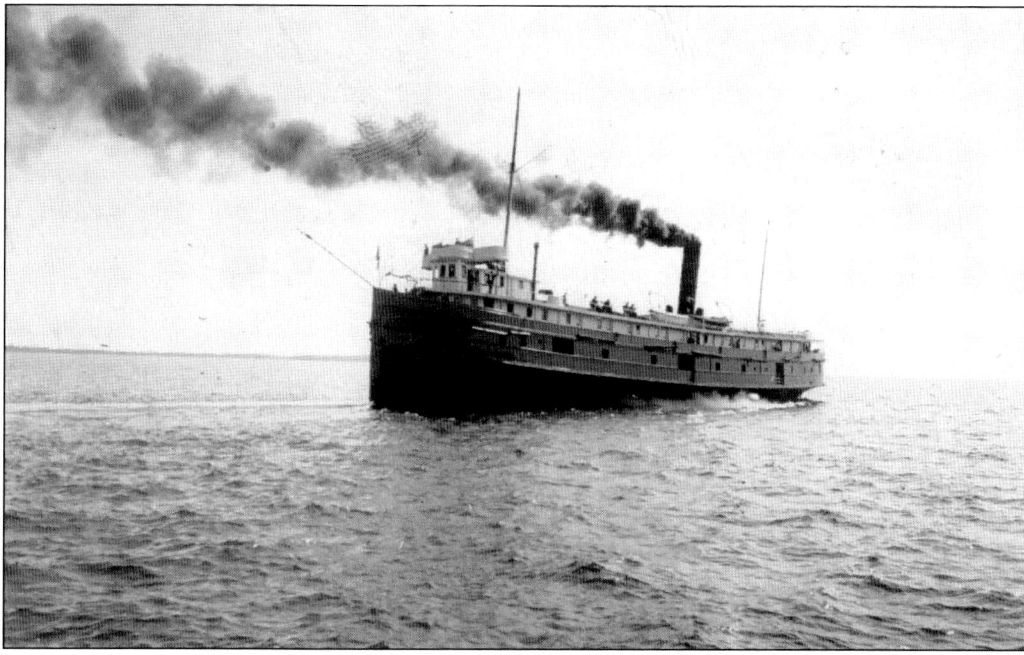

Here is the *City of Charlevoix* entering Northport Harbor. The photograph was taken by Northport resident Elden Dame. Passenger transportation on the Great Lakes was an important travel venue; it allowed people to move around to other parts of the state without the lengthy travel over land. (Courtesy Grand Traverse Lighthouse Museum Collection.)

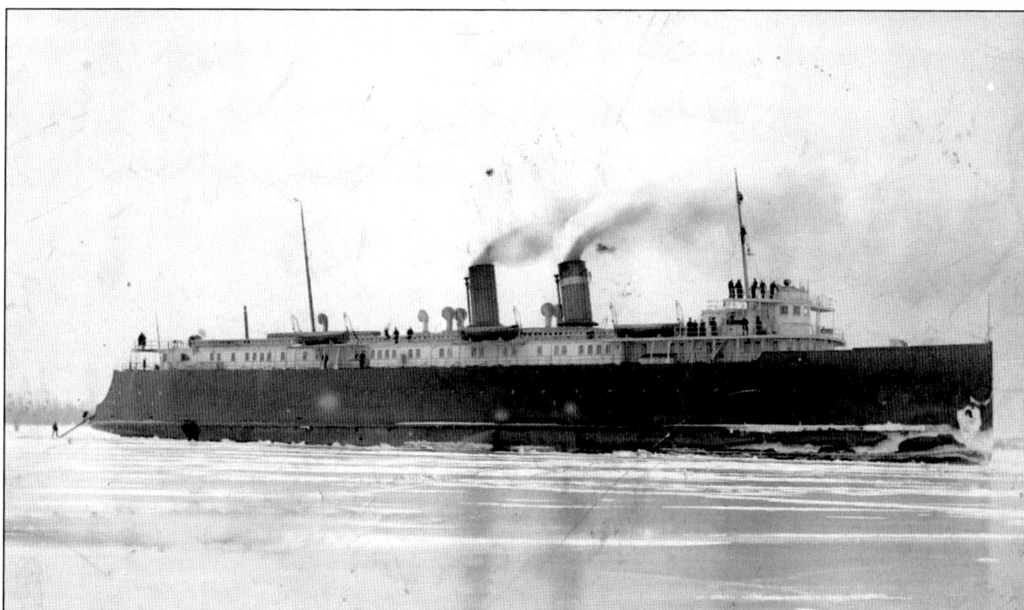

The *Manistique, Marquette, and Northern* car ferry is in the ice just off Grand Traverse Light Station around 1903. The winter ice around the shoreline often made it impossible for shipping to continue after December 1. The ferry service was discontinued in 1908 when the dock was sold to Haserot Canning Company, who shipped cherries on the *Gilman D.* (Courtesy Grand Traverse Lighthouse Museum Collection.)

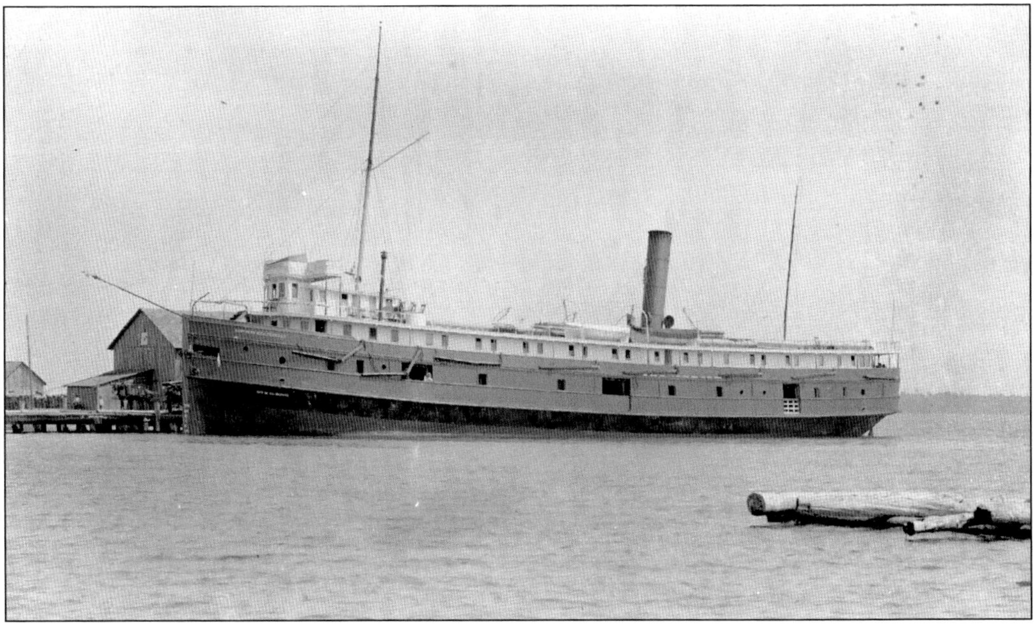

The *City of Charlevoix* is at the dock in Northport. Other smaller passenger boats like the *Crescent*, *Dorothy K*, and the *O-ne-ka-win* transported people around the Grand Traverse Bay area. The *O-ne-ka-win* and *Dorothy K* ferried visitors to Northport Point. The cost was 15¢ one way and 25¢ round-trip. The photograph was taken by Elden Dame. (Courtesy Grand Traverse Lighthouse Museum Collection.)

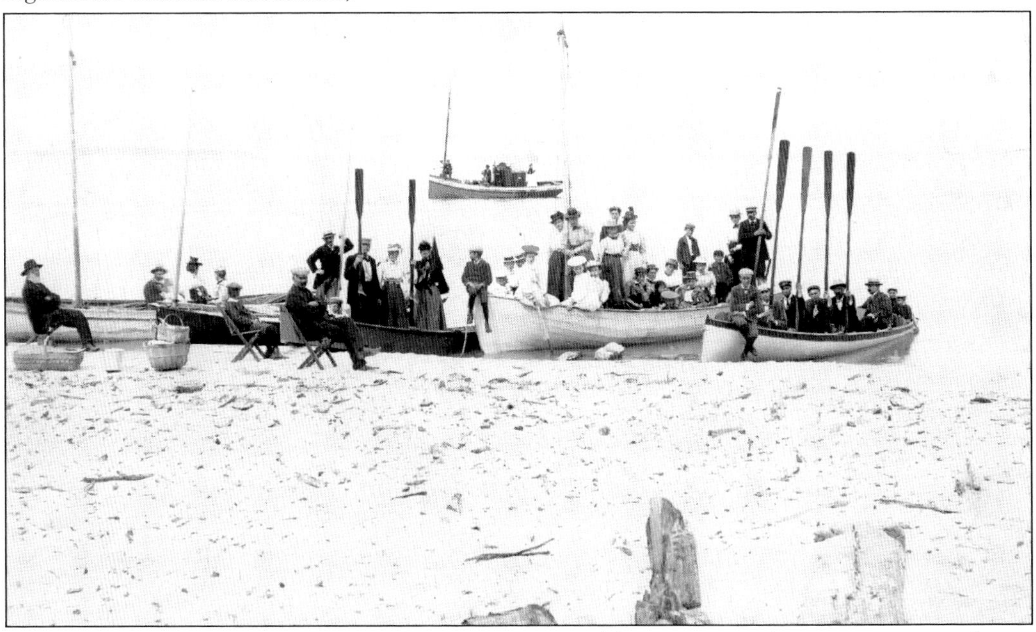

This photograph taken by Dame shows a picnic celebration. Northport was not only an important shipping port, but it also was a wonderful place for its residents and visitors to enjoy the water. Over time, the passenger service boats have disappeared and the small boats, as shown here, have been replaced by sailboats and motor craft. (Courtesy Grand Traverse Lighthouse Museum Collection.)

Today the Grand Traverse Lighthouse still stands majestically at the cape of Grand Traverse Bay and the entrance into the Manitou Passage. It continues to guide sailors and their vessels safely around the treacherous rocks and shoals. The lighthouse has been completely restored, and it turned 150 years old in 2008. (Courtesy Mark Westmaas.)

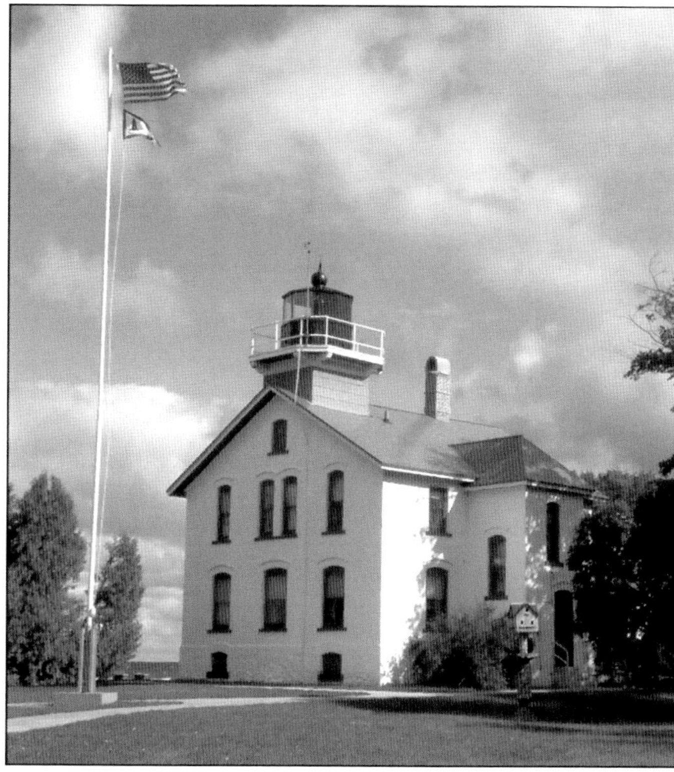

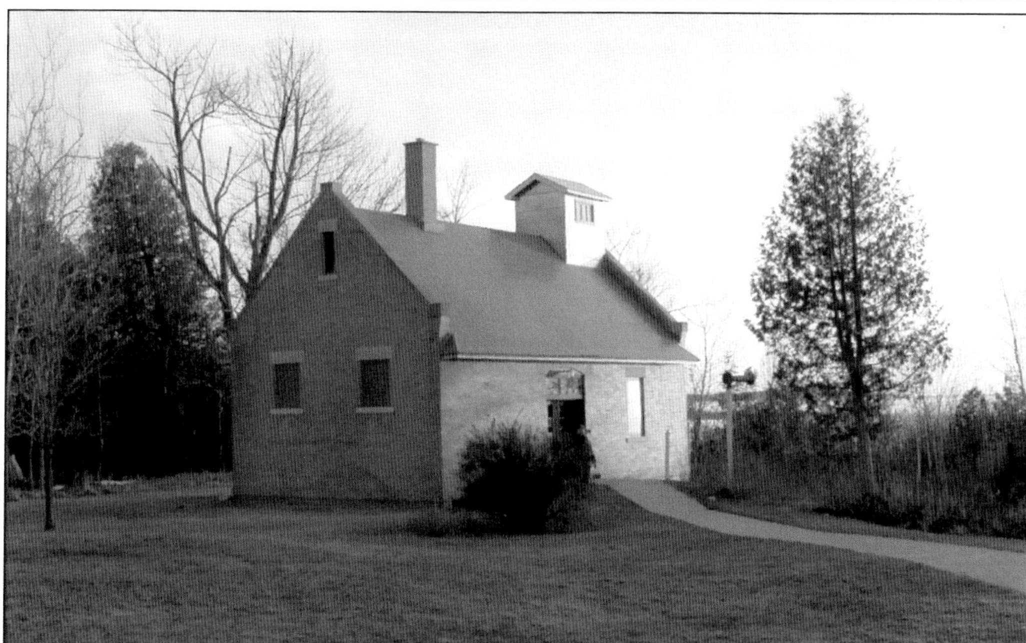

The Fog Signal Building has also been restored with a new working fog signal installed to run on compressed air, just like in the early years. During the summer months, the horn is blown every Saturday at noon as a demonstration and honor to all the lighthouse keepers and U.S. Coast Guard personnel who kept the light. (Courtesy Mark Westmaas.)

Consistent with our mission to preserve history on a local level, this book was printed in South Carolina on American-made paper and manufactured entirely in the United States. Products carrying the accredited Forest Stewardship Council (FSC) label are printed on 100 percent FSC-certified paper.

MADE IN THE USA